War of the Ages

A Complete Scriptural Guide

To

Confronting and Defeating Satan's Kingdom

Gregory R. Reid

Copyright © 2014 Gregory R Reid

All rights reserved.

ISBN: **1502370239**
ISBN-13: 978-1502370235

He Teaches My Hands To War.
- Psalm 18:34

CONTENTS

	Dedication	i
	Introduction	5
1	First Things	11
2	The Basics of Our Warfare	23
3	The Whole Armor	45
4	Battle for the Mind	61
5	Origins Part 1	81
6	Origins Part 2	93
7	Satan In The Gospels	113
8	Satan from Acts to Revelation	131
9	Fallen Angels and Demons	151
10	World Rulers	169
11	Cultural Consequences, Social Breakdown and Spiritual Open Doors	185
12	Encounters and Extractions	207
13	New Testament References	219
14	Discernment	239
15	Night Terrors	247
16	Doors of Entrance – Basics	253
17	Specific Doors of Entrance Part One	261
18	Specific Doors of Entrance Part Two	295
19	Specific Doors of Entrance Part Three	305

20	Levels and Symptoms of Demonic Influence	321
21	Rules of Engagement	333
22	Housecleaning	347
23	Prayers of Renunciation and Severing of Blood Ties	359
24	Boots On The Ground	371
	Epilog	385

DEDICATION

For those heroes of the faith who were my examples of true spiritual warriors, both those who remain on the battlefield and those who have put down their sword and headed for Home.

To all those who have stood by me over the years as I sought to carry out this calling and who stood with me during the most difficult moments to make sure that I finished my course well.

No man wages war alone. I am grateful for all those who fought and labored beside me, prayed for me, gave me godly counsel and shared the sweat of battle with me over these many years. To you, I give my deepest thanks. You share the reward of all these labors in the Kingdom of Heaven.

I believe Satan to exist for two reasons: First, the Bible says so; and second, I've done business with him.

- D. L. Moody

Gregory R Reid

INTRODUCTION

We are at war.

You may not know it. Many don't believe it. Few are prepared to fight it. But war it is, like it or not. The church is under assault, and the world lies in the hand of the Wicked One - the one who dares any believer to challenge his rule over it and welcomes all comers.

Satan is arrogant, malicious and clever. He is well-practiced, brilliant – and quite insane.

And like Hitler –quite insane and quite brilliant as well – the closer he comes to losing, the more desperate he becomes, the harder he fights and the more destruction he brings. One would do well to study the last days of the war against Nazi Germany to understand this final battle we are facing with the enemy.

He is damned, and doomed.

And, he is determined to take everyone he can to hell with him.

We ignore him – and his army – at our own peril.

I believe we are in the final hour. And I believe we are witnessing Revelation 12:12-13: "Therefore rejoice, O heavens, and you who dwell in them! Woe to the inhabitants of the earth and the sea! For the devil has come down to you, having great wrath, because he knows that he has a short time."

Most of us are too young to remember World War Two. The veterans are passing away, and with them, their memories, their experience, their courage and their lessons. They remember the days of rationing, Rosie the Riveter, scrap metal drives, green stamps and all of the things that made up their "new normal" during World War Two. They remember the horror of battlefield combat. They remember the military term, "Situation Normal Suspended: Wartime Conditions Prevail."

We have entered the spiritual equivalent of those times. And if we as the church are going to succeed as an army in leading souls out of darkness, setting captives free and becoming battle-tested warriors of Jesus that fight - not with human weapons, but with spiritual weapons far greater than those of human crafting – then we need to understand that wartime conditions for believers is prevailing, and our "normal Christian life" must be suspended to accommodate those conditions and these times.

Much has been written and taught on spiritual warfare. The range of information has gone from the profound and helpful to the speculative and inaccurate, and even to the dangerous and uninformed.

In the 1980s, spiritual warfare was something widely taught in the church. It was almost standard training for new believers, especially for youth.

Now, more than two decades later, you hardly hear anyone speak or preach on spiritual warfare, and if they do, it is likely to be followed by laughter and jokes about old church plays about demons and angels with Star Wars swords.

It has been said that Satan is equally served when we ignore him as when we are obsessed with him. If previous decades found us with an overabundance of interest in the demonic, today's church is nearly devoid of any real understanding of it. Nearly two generations of youth have been raised in the church with *no* understanding of spiritual warfare. The result: The discernment gene has nearly been programmed out of believers. What followed this void has been deception, bondage, division, confusion, and spiritual ineffectiveness.

Granted, there were some excesses in some previous deliverance ministries and the deliverance movement. That does not eliminate the need for the real thing.

That is precisely why I have endeavored to do this work. There has never been a time when spiritual darkness has been more prevalent, nor the battle to hold it back so weak. Believers cannot fight if they do not know there is even a war. Once they know there is a war, they must then be equipped to fight.

Why is a Book About the Devil Necessary?

Asking this question is a bit like a soldier asking, "Why do we need to learn about war and battles and what our enemy is like?" Because you are a soldier. And without knowing your enemy, your weapons and your rank and place in battle, you are useless, and you endanger yourself and your fellow soldiers.

In the church, asking, "Why do we need to talk about spiritual warfare and the devil?" is really a civilian's question. If you read and believe the Word of God, then you cannot escape the truth that we are at WAR with the devil. And Jesus said, "In My Name they will cast out devils." (Mark 16:17) It is not optional. It is a commission of the Gospel work.

Personally, I hope you never have to encounter the kinds of ugly, vicious demonic battles for people that I have encountered.

But if you should, (and the way the present world is deteriorating spiritually right now, you likely will) then God wants you to face it equipped, confident, and unafraid. For no blood-bought believer should fear Satan at all.

In answer to the question, "Why do we need to talk about the devil?" the scriptures say, "Lest Satan should take advantage of us; for we are not ignorant of his devices."(2 Cor.2:11) And right now, the church seems to be operating in almost complete spiritual ignorance concerning these matters. We must speak of these things because the scriptures tell us, "Have no fellowship with the unfruitful works of darkness but rather reprove them." (Eph. 5:11) That means we must expose them.

This book is written to expose the works of darkness, and help us destroy the works of the devil, just like Jesus did. Is it ugly? Yes. Is it unpleasant? Certainly. Is it a little scary? It can be, of course.

But is it necessary? Absolutely.

As Hitler marched through Europe grinding his murderous thug boots into the blood of millions of people, only a selfish, self-protecting person interested in their own welfare would have asked, "Is it necessary to stop Hitler?" Some in Europe did until the boots trampled their own land.

Like Hitler, Satan takes territory that is unguarded and undefended.

He is right now taking moral, social and political territory like a ravenous beast in our world.

And now, he intends to come for a weakened, sleeping and almost completely unprotected church world.

Is it necessary to fight this war?

The enemy is at our gates. The answer is clear, is it not?

Of all the books I have written, this one has been the most difficult and the most contested. Perhaps the very nature of a book like this is the very reason it has been fought. Satan is real. Demons are real. The last thing they want is an exposé on their nature, tricks, and tactics.

I am not an expert. I am in fact very skeptical of anyone who would call themselves one, and you should be, too. I am just a veteran of spiritual warfare. I carry to this task only the one weapon I know, the Word of God, and the experience of a lifetime in battling in the trenches against the powers of darkness.

No writings but the Holy Scriptures are perfect, but I have worked diligently to ensure that this book is thoroughly grounded in the Word of God.

This book is not light reading. It is a spiritual textbook, and it is a challenge to read in a day and age when we are used to spiritual snacks and Biblical tidbits of truth digested on a Sunday morning. This book requires discipline, prayer, and serious study. Read it with a notebook and a highlighter. Write down everything that speaks to you and take it to prayer, asking God to make it a part of your armory. I would also encourage you to keep a second notebook and make a note of every scripture contained in this book, that they may help to arm you for war.

My prayer is that this book will be simple, practical, helpful and encouraging. As you read it with prayer, may God raise you up to be the true warriors in Christ He is calling for in this treacherous hour. He did not give us armor as decoration. In the words of Mario Murillo, "The Christian life is not like a war. It IS a war." And it is to this war we have been called.

We speak of the enemy in this book only to identify, expose, and finally to defeat him. We mention his name to call him out, corner him, and then plunder him so he can no longer hide in our midst, our families, our churches and our lives.

Above all, we shout the Name above all Names, the Lord Jesus Christ, who came to destroy the works of the enemy. May all glory go to Him alone.

"For this purpose the Son of God was manifested, that He might destroy the works of the devil." (1 John 3:9) We are His hands and feet in this world. Let us put our hands to the war and battle well for the sake of Jesus and the ones He died to set free.

"Let God arise, and His enemies be scattered!" (Psalm 68:1)

Gregory R Reid

Gregory R Reid

CHAPTER 1

FIRST THINGS

In order to conduct solid spiritual warfare, it is necessary to get a foundation laid that is practical, understandable and biblical. So let's start with the basics.

1. Satan is real.

My guess is if you didn't believe that, you probably wouldn't be reading this book. But modern theologians, seminarians, and higher criticism scholars will say he does not exist. Satan loves that. I once heard a minister interviewed about the occult on Halloween say, "We don't believe there is a real devil, but it's a story." Satan probably said, "Perfect. I can take her and her church captive without a fight!"

From Genesis to Ezekiel, from Job to Jesus, from Acts to Revelation – Satan is clearly portrayed, not as a cute story, but a devastating evil being. Deny that, and you become his prey.

2. Demons are real.

You cannot read and believe the New Testament without knowing with certainty that demons are real and that we must contend with them. Jesus said, "In My Name you will cast out devils." (Mark 16:17) And again, "Heal the sick, cleanse the lepers, raise the dead, cast out devils. Freely you have received, freely give." (Matthew 10:8) It's not optional. It's a command, and a commission.

I'm stunned by the number of Christians who say they believe in Jesus, but ignore the reality of demons, Satan, and the supernatural. Do they think it was made up? Do they think that Jesus did not confront them? Or maybe He did, but they went away? I know one well- known theologian who teaches that they did go away after Jesus' resurrection.

But if you believe that the Scriptures are the true Word of God, then you must believe every word. That means you must accept that demons are real. If you want to be a warrior, you need to settle this. If you are walking with Jesus, you will more than likely confront demons in one form or another at some time. It's crucial to be prepared.

3. There are God's angels, and fallen angels.

There was a war in heaven. (Revelation 12:7-9) One-third of the angels fell with Lucifer. (Revelation 12:3-4) Two-thirds stayed with God. Later, we'll talk about the losing side.

4. Angels are messengers: for example, Gabriel and Michael.

5. Angels are not fat little babies with wings.

They are in fact terrifying. Both Daniel and John trembled in fear at their presence and John fell down on his face like a dead man when he saw the angel that spoke to him. (Revelation 22:8-9) I hear people say, "I want to see an angel!" No, you don't. You really don't. Scriptures seem to infer that they have to "dim down" to approach us, just so we won't be completely paralyzed with fear. Or worse.

6. We are not to seek angels or seek to talk to them.

Paul seemed to confront a similar issue in his day, as he spoke of "angel worship." (Col. 2:18) If you seek after one, you'll likely get a demonic counterfeit.

And if one shows up, you better ask for credentials! And if it is truly an angel of God, they won't be at all offended. They would expect you to!

They always come with a purpose, a mission, and a message. They don't come to entertain us, or move things randomly, or cast angel feathers about. (One such "manifestation" turned out to be colored chicken feathers.)

Most "angel" stories I have investigated have turned out to be imaginations, creative embellishment, plain trickery, or demonic deception. That does not mean they do not happen. They do. But we must discern and try the spirits: "Beloved, do not believe every spirit, but test the spirits, whether they are of God; because many false prophets have gone out into the world." (1 John 4:1)

7. We do have guardian angels.

"Take heed that ye despise not one of these little ones; for I say unto you, That in heaven their angels do always behold the face of my Father which is in heaven." (Matthew 18:10) Isn't that good to know?

8. There is no scriptural evidence of female angels. Why is that important? Because there *are* groups where female angels are prominent, loved and listened to – new age and occult groups.

A modern "evangelist" frequently spoke of his "angel," who showed up with bags of money telling him he'd be receiving big money in all of his meetings. Emma was "her" name (which also happens to be the name of a Japanese demon: Emma-O.)

Another couple spoke of an angel delivering precious gems to them. At the time, I was praying for the truth behind the gem phenomenon. I didn't disbelieve right away because I have learned not to "limit the Holy one of Israel." (Psalm 78:41) But when the couple said "she" gave them the gems, I recognized the red flag separating truth from error.

I am not saying absolutely, 100%, there are no female angels, but there is no *scriptural* evidence. And scripture is our basis of truth. So, we must be very careful when there is no precedence in the scriptures for something we witness or experience. Again – try the spirits!

And never, *ever* seek after angels.

9. There is no reason or room for fear concerning Satan and demons.

If you are a believer and you belong to Jesus, then you are surrendered to his Lordship, and there is no reason for fear of demons or Satan. None. If you know who Jesus is and if you know who you are in Him – if you know His authority rests on you and is in you – then you have *nothing* to fear. It is Satan and his angels and demons who fear Jesus Christ in you.

But remember, they don't fear *you*. In fact, without Jesus, Satan could crush you in a second. But when you walk in Jesus' power and authority you have nothing to be afraid of. It is *He* that they fear in *you*!

We are victims of too many Hollywood movies like *The Exorcist*. And although I have seen a few very startling manifestations in the midst of demon extractions, they were manageable because Jesus is always in control.

I know our first human response is fear concerning supernatural manifestations of evil. But in real-world conflict with the enemy, fear is his first tactic, and once he realizes it's not working, he's on the defensive from that moment on. Do not give in to fear!

Having said that, if you are not a believer in Jesus, and you are not His, you have good reason to be afraid. You have no protection. You are open game. By default, he already owns you. Only complete surrender to the Lord Jesus Christ can deliver you from the grip of darkness.

One other caution – never be arrogant about your "fearlessness." Always remember who it is that Satan fears – Jesus, not you. He just sees you as a potential threat that needs to be targeted and eliminated. To be arrogant is to lose your protection, for God resists the proud. (James 4:6) Stay humble in every battle. Do not fall into the trap of pride.

    10. Satan is not "toothless."

"Be sober, be vigilant; because your adversary the devil walks about like a roaring lion, seeking whom he may devour." (1 Peter 5:8)

I once heard a preacher say, "Satan may be a roaring lion, but he's toothless. Jesus defanged him."

If that were so, this Scripture would not warn us about him. He is vicious, relentless, and still quite determined. Do not underestimate him. Devour means to swallow up, to destroy. He's not a pretend lion. The scriptures say he is looking for someone to devour, not gum to death. This is a real war. And so we must continue to fight this real threat because he seeks every day to devour, and we are called by the Spirit of God to stop him in battle.

    11. Satan is limited.

One of the first things I learned in theology class at Bible school is that God is omnipotent (all-powerful), omniscient (all-knowing) and omnipresent (everywhere at all times).

Satan is none of these things! Not only is he not all-powerful, but his power is also quite limited and very specific. Satan is a creature on God's leash. God has said to him, "Thus far, and no farther." Granted, he can do a lot of damage under those restrictions. But it's important to know he is a limited foe. This is not Star Wars, and God and Satan are not the light and dark sides of the Force. (That is a Buddhist and Luciferian concept.) There *is* no contest of power – God has *all* the power in heaven and on earth.

God owns this planet. For now, though, Satan holds the lease. We gave it over to him in the garden through sin. Satan runs the planet, but as believers, we are here to evict him everywhere we go and bring souls into Jesus' Kingdom.

Satan is not all knowing. He's very limited. He can't "read your mind," nor can his demons. They can, however, read your feelings and fears. (Much like dogs can sense fear in people.) They note your habits, actions and weaknesses. Based on those things, they can develop a blueprint, a strategy and a plan of action to take you down. But Satan doesn't know everything. He depends on a communications center of demonic networking. He is a psychoanalyst, a war strategist and an attack coordinator. But he doesn't know even a fragment of all that God knows. In fact, we have the advantage that we are in personal communication with the One who *does* know everything, and we can count on Him to give the insight and strategy that we need to thwart the enemy's plans and attacks.

Finally, Satan is not omnipresent.

There was a cartoon of Satan outside of a church, crying. Someone asked him why. He said, "Because they're always blaming me for all these things I didn't do!" The truth is, Satan can only be one place at a time. So when we have a bad headache and say, "Satan is really attacking me," well, probably not. He's more likely busy creating wars, devising big schemes or sitting in on Congressional sessions and church committee meetings.

What he generally does is *dispatch*. He sends his generals and soldiers to do the dirty work of spiritual war against the saints. Again, Satan is just one created, limited being with limited capabilities and permissions. We will discuss what those things are in another chapter.

What You Will Learn

Throughout this book, you will learn the following:

— Who our enemy is

— What he can and cannot do

— Where he came from

— What demons are and where they come from

— Biblical facts and references concerning Satan, demons, angels and spiritual warfare

– How to protect yourself from invasion in your life and family

– How to destroy the works of the enemy

– How to understand the strategies of the enemy and how to ruin them

– How to root out darkness from the hiding places in our lives and the lives of others

– How to get free and stay free

– Understanding true deliverance – what it is and what it is not

One of the common objections to a book of this nature is that it "glorifies the devil." There will be none of that here.

This book is based on the command in Ephesians 5:11: "And have no fellowship with the unfruitful works of darkness, but rather reprove them."

That, by God's grace, is what we will do.

I've heard people say that people pay too much attention to the devil. In fact, most believers pay too *little* attention to him, or none at all. Jesus mentioned him numerous times and drove out devils, as did all early believers. Jesus was tempted by the devil, and Paul was buffeted by him and blocked by him.

This is a real war, which demands serious and biblical engagement.

In the preface to *The Screwtape Letters*, CS Lewis said, "There are two equal and opposite errors into which our race can fall about the devils. One is to disbelieve in their existence. The other is to believe, and to feel an excessive and unhealthy interest in them. They themselves are equally pleased by both errors, and hail a materialist or a magician with the same delight."

In the 1980s, there was a great emphasis in the church on spiritual warfare, deliverance and understanding the enemy. Some of it was good and quite necessary. A great deal of it was excessive, in error or just plain scripturally off. For two decades, the pendulum has swung in the opposite direction, and we are now in danger of denying the battle altogether.

At the risk of swinging the pendulum too far back the other direction, I am offering my prayerful best effort to train this generation in a battle that is ongoing, vicious and necessary. And by His grace, victorious.

Let's proceed in exposing the darkness, and armoring up warriors in Jesus for this crucial battle.

Gregory R Reid

FROM THE FRONTLINES: ON THE STREETS OF SAN FRANCISCO

I had just finished preaching at Peninsula Christian Center in Redwood City, California, and I was spending the next day in San Francisco with a friend from the church.

We were casually strolling up Geary Street, enjoying the partly cloudy, nearly perfect weather day. As we walked up the inclined street, I glanced casually across the other side of the road where the street was lined with shops. I glanced briefly at a sign that said, "Psychic Readings" and saw a woman outside sitting at a card table reading what I assumed to be Tarot cards.

Suddenly, I saw the table upended and the cards flew everywhere, strewn all over the sidewalk and street, and the woman ran across the street at breakneck speed – directly at me. She came within inches of my face, pointing her finger at me, face full of demonic rage. "You don't think I'm a Christian, do you? Well, let me tell you something, (voice changed to a demonic tenor) I've got the BLOOD OF JESUS running through my veins!!!" I had never met her, nor she, me. But something in her recognized Jesus in me, and the reaction was quick and furious. My friend was shocked and not a little bit scared.

I did not give her a response but simply kept going.

From this I learned two things: One, just because something manifests, does not mean you are supposed to engage it. Only do so if God gives you the go-ahead. If I had felt any compunction from the Spirit of God to engage, I would have done so. But when you allow the enemy to decide where and when the battle will be waged, you are already at a heavy disadvantage.

Two, when you are walking in the Spirit, spiritual warfare is the reality that unfolds when something in another person recognizes the Someone named Jesus in you.

When you know that, you are neither surprised nor unprepared when such things occur.

The one concern of the devil is to keep Christians from praying. He fears nothing from prayerless studies, prayerless work, and prayerless religion. He laughs at our toil, mocks at our wisdom, but trembles when we pray.

- Samuel Chadwick

CHAPTER TWO

THE BASICS OF OUR WARFARE

In any war, it is vital to understand the necessity of the campaign, the enemy we are fighting, and the call to arms.

Ephesians 6:10-13 gives us all three:

"Finally, my brethren, be strong in the Lord, and in the power of his might. Put on the whole armor of God, that ye may be able to stand against the wiles of the devil. For we wrestle not against flesh and blood, but against principalities, against powers, against the rulers of the darkness of this world, against spiritual wickedness in high places. Wherefore take unto you the whole armor of God, that ye may be able to withstand in the evil day, and having done all, to stand."

Let's break these verses down and extract their essence.

"Finally, my brethren, be strong in the Lord, and in the power of his might."

His might.

There are two fatal mistakes in combat. One is to not know how to use your weapons. The other is to be arrogant and careless with your weapons.

It is the same in spiritual warfare. You are not effective if you do not use your weapons of warfare. But if you are arrogant and careless about your weapons, as if you are the one with the power and not merely wielding it, you're a prime target.

It is His might, not ours. They are His weapons. We merely use them, and the power comes from Him, not us.

"Put on the whole armor, that you may be able to stand against the wiles of the devil."

Wiles: The Greek word is methodeia. It means method, trickery, lying in wait.

You should know and understand clearly that our adversary is determined to see your downfall. The minute you came to Jesus and gave your life to him, you were put on a "list." Satan will turn his trickery on you. He will get your blueprint, your schematic, and begin to devise a way to take you down. What is your weakness? Pride? Pornography? Paranoia?

Or is it fear? Rage? Insecurity? Lust? Greed? Gossip? Lying? Addictions?

Whatever your weaknesses are, the enemy will draw up a battle plan to exploit those weaknesses. He will use circumstances, thoughts, people.

Wherever Jesus went, Satan was lying in wait, like the snake that he is, looking for an opportunity to strike. Failing to defeat Jesus in the wilderness, "he departed for a little while." He slunk away. But not far. He moved people to try and kill him. He used religious people to try and trip him up. He used Herod to try and kill him before he was grown up! Then he tried to use Peter to talk Jesus out of going to the cross. Jesus rebuked him. "Get behind me, Satan!" Satan didn't know why Jesus was so determined to go to the cross, but he knew that if the Son of God were so determined, it would be very, very bad for him, whatever it was about!

Because Jesus defeated the enemy in every way at every turn, so can we. Jesus never let His guard down. He knew His enemy well; He could never give him an inch of territory.

Paul's words to us from Ephesians give us the very battle gear and strategy we need to prevent loss of territory as well. It's an entire soldier's gear and weaponry given to us to ensure that we stand against the enemy's schemes.

Before Paul describes our weapons, he describes the enemy we will use them against. Again, Satan may originate the attack plan, but it is the under-generals and demonic soldiers we must deal with.

The armor gives us a tool and a weapon for each conceivable attack. And we are to stand against it all. Spiritual warfare is a test of endurance. In fact, Daniel speaks of this demonic war by saying, "And he shall speak great words against the most High, and shall wear out the saints of the most High." (Daniel 7:25a) The word there means, "especially in the mental sense." The enemy seeks to wear us out. Someone once said that the rock that the hammer won't break, time and tide will wear away, so we must guard against being worn down in battle, especially mentally. We will deal more with the battle for the mind in chapter four.

Stand Against

We must be determined to outlast the enemy and his attacks and stand no matter what. Giving up under the attacks is never an option.

Against The Wiles

What are Satan's "wiles"? The word here is *"methodeia."* He has a *method* of attack. He has a blueprint, a war plan specifically designed for you. He's mapped your weaknesses. He knows if you are vulnerable to substance abuse, sexual sins, fears, certain insecurities. Does criticism cripple you? He knows it and will move people to criticize you unfairly. Do you feel inadequate in ministry? He knows that, and whispers thoughts of failure in your ear to get you to quit, or move you to carry out plans that are not God's in order for you to look "successful." Or he will just help you seethe in resentment and covet other ministers who have larger congregations, or other families that have bigger houses, nicer cars, better jobs, etc. You get the idea.

Methodeia also infers that the enemy lies in wait. Like in Eden, waiting to corner and trap Eve, he waits, observes, readies his spiritual poison. The serpent now crawls underfoot, in the spiritual grass of our lives, hiding and looking for a vulnerable moment when we are not on guard.

When should we be on guard against him? 24/7. How? By constant prayer and constant Word. We don't hunt for him; we simply assume he is always lurking and always wishes our defeat, and take all the security measures necessary to deny him entrance.

There are three areas that are vital to take care of if we do not want to fall: arrogance, pride, and an unexamined heart.

Arrogance deceives us into thinking, "I am a believer saved by grace; therefore, Satan can't touch me." Your very arrogance and presumption give him the open door to touch you.

Pride does not allow you to recognize your vulnerabilities. Thus they remain unprotected.

An unexamined heart allows pockets of sin, pride, evil thoughts, lust, greed, fear, hatred, resentment, unforgiveness, self-pity and a nest of other nasty vipers to remain hidden, but they eventually give birth:
"But every man is tempted, when he is drawn away of his own lust, and

enticed. Then when lust hath conceived, it bringeth forth sin: and sin, when it is finished, bringeth forth death." (James 1:14-15)

True warriors must first of all be humble before their God. They acknowledge that all they have is because of Jesus.

True warriors know that it is only by grace that they stand, and without His power and cleansing blood, they would fall back into every sin they ever did.

True warriors live in brokenness and humility. Psalm 139 is their creed: "Search me, O God, and know my heart: try me, and know my thoughts; And see if there be any wicked way in me, and lead me in the way everlasting." (Psalm 139:23-24)

"God resists the proud and gives grace to the humble." (1 Peter 5:5) Humility hides you in God's grace and makes you almost undetectable to the enemy. Daily ask for cleansing. Ask Him to expose any hidden attitude, sin, or motive. Stay cleansed. "Create in me a clean heart O God, and renew a right spirit within me." (Psalm 51:10)

One of the consistent features of fallen ministers has been spiritual arrogance and sense of privilege and invulnerability.

I must include this for those in ministry, for it was one of the clearest words God has given me in my lifetime. As a young minister, I saw time after time as men of God that I knew who were living in sexual or financial sin would preach and the anointing of God was poured out through them. "Why, God?" I asked Him. "This is so contradictory!" I found my answer in Romans 11:29. "For the gifts and the calling of God are irrevocable." (NKJV)

Irrevocable.

This is truly one of the most sobering verses in the Bible. I heard God tell me, "Do not ever make the mistake of assuming that because my anointing is on your ministry that you are walking rightly before me." I have never forgotten that, and I have prayed God will take me out of ministry before that would happen. I would rather be in right standing with Jesus in my personal life than be the most anointed preacher on the planet and be living a double life and bring reproach on His name. "Therefore let him who thinks he stands take heed lest he fall." (1 Cor. 10:12) Make your relationship with Jesus your first priority, always. Better to be sure you are walking with him than to be the most anointed minister on the face of the earth and to be deceived into thinking that the anointing was "proof" that God approved of your personal life.

Be thankful if God has brought exposure to those things, even if for a while you are removed from the ministry to get those things right with God. And God can and *will* restore those who humble themselves before Him and allow that necessary work of breaking and restoration.

But those who are restored from falling are also a special target for the enemy, for they are living examples of God's mercy and grace. "And some of those of understanding shall fall, to refine them, purify them, and make them white, until the time of the end; because it is still for the appointed time." (Daniel 11:35-36) Let he who has ears let him hear.

Not Flesh and Blood

This battle is a wrestling match. The picture given by Strong's Concordance is this: "A contest between two in which each endeavors to throw the other, and which is decided when the victor is able to hold his opponent down with his hand upon his neck."

This makes it clear that this is a ground war, or more accurately, hand-to-hand combat.

Politicians and sometimes career military desk jockeys run wars by public opinion, committees, or a map with war pieces. But it's the soldiers with boots on the ground that have the real sense of battle. They are up close and personal with a living breathing enemy that wants them dead.

In the much talk and desk jockey instruction on spiritual warfare, remember this is not a game or an exercise. Those that do spiritual warfare understand Paul's meaning here. We are not lobbing missiles from afar. We are not observing and negotiating. We are in the enemy's face, raw contact, fighting an enemy that wants our death and destruction. Our assignment is to, by prayer, fasting, Word warfare and aggressive taking of spiritual territory, pin down the enemy's neck and keep him under subjection to the authority of the Lord Jesus Christ.

But against who do we fight? Not flesh and blood. Not abortionists, not pornographers, evil politicians, greedy corporations, not New Agers, witches, Satanists, gays or any other person or group. That is flesh and blood. Rather, we fight against those who rule them and move them to sin and do evil, those who pull the puppet strings on those who are slaves to Satan – those of flesh and blood who are without Jesus.

That does not mean we do not address these issues, and occasionally confront people. Paul did, and Peter did. Peter confronted Simon the sorcerer (Acts 8:18-24), and Paul confronted Elymas, the sorcerer. (Acts 13:6-12) But in confronting the people (only under the direction of the Spirit), he was, in fact, wrestling with the spirit that opposed the gospel. And whenever Paul engaged in politics, it was only to seek furtherance of the gospel message.

In all our political and social dealings, let us never forget that our job is not to attack sinners but to bring people to Christ. We wrestle with their demonic controllers to demand the release of their captives.

Who Do We Fight? A Closer Look

Paul now goes into some ranking order. Every army has a rank and file. Human armies do, angelic armies do, and Satan's armies do. There are Commanders in Chief. (Jesus for the angels, Satan for the fallen angels and demons). There is little understanding in modern Evangelical teaching of the difference between them. Fallen angels and demons are not the same things. (More on that in chapter 9.) Many have been involved in what appeared to be a "simple" deliverance, and were not prepared when a demon called on its direct upward authority – sometimes a stronger rank of demon – sometimes a principality. Things can get very ugly should that happen.

Against Principalities

The word *principalities* here is the Greek word *arche*. It means chiefs, beginnings, starters, leaders, originators, first placers – rulers.

This seems to indicate that at the highest level, we fight the originators under Satan's command – perhaps the one-third of the angels that fell with him from heaven. (Revelation 12:4a, 7-8)

There is a body of Jewish work that indicates that these "fallen ones" taught humans much of their evil – war, sexual perversion, bestiality, the occult, etc. Genesis seems to reflect that Cain's ancestral lineage and progeny produced human chaos, godlessness, and evil that led to the flood, aided by the fallen ones that Genesis refers to as the sons of God who, as a result of their intermingling with human women created a race of giants. (This is a very controversial subject and I will deal with it more in chapter 9.)

But that these fallen ones are the principalities that we do warfare with is pretty much biblically indisputable. I believe that these principalities or "originators" rule this sinful earth through those who follow their own lusts, and these principalities have organized themselves over cities, nations, and regions. (See references concerning the book of Daniel later.) Those in the kingdom of God who seek to inundate a city, or a country, or a people group to bring people to Christ must understand this.

Not long ago, I took a team of our youth from church to New Mexico to minister to the Navajo Nation.

The Navajo people are some of the noblest and precious people I have ever known. And, they are one of the most spiritually oppressed.

The night before our mission, we arrived in Gallup and stayed at a motel. In the middle of the night, I was viciously attacked in my waking/dream state by a wolf demon that was seeking to tear out my throat.

I called on Jesus and battled it until its grip was broken and I was able to come fully awake. What could it mean? Having been exposed as a child to an occult circle whose "totem" was a wolf, I dismissed it as a memory backwash.

The next morning, we drove to our mission outreach. We turned left onto a small back road to the church, marked by a sign that said, "Lobo Valley."

Lobo means Wolf. We were driving into Wolf Valley.

My attack was not coincidental. There was a principality who wore a wolf's face guarding the very territory we sought to impact with the gospel.

Ask God for specific understanding and revelation of who and what you are challenging in the heavenlies as you prepare to fight for the people of that territory to hear the Gospel and come to Christ.

Against Powers

The word *powers* is the Greek word *exousia*. It means authorities, rulers, a thing subject to authority.

There is so little correct teaching on authority in the modern church that it has crippled our war.

The errors run along two lines: One, that authority is dominant, absolute and controlling, wielded by pastors and ministers at their whim, and we must obey utterly without question. Two, the belief that I am my own authority, I have no need to be under anyone's authority, I only obey God.

Both are in error. The first, because it is extreme and unbiblical. There are parameters to spiritual authority. If an authority tells you to sin or violates your God-given sovereignty (i.e., who to marry, where to live) - *run*. Pastors are servants, not overlords.

The second is in error because it leads to rebellion, sinful autonomy, and self-godhood. There is another book to be written about spiritual authority (for now I recommend Gene Edwards' *A Tale of Three Kings.*) You must understand that all kingdoms function through authority. If you do not understand that, spiritual warfare will be very dangerous for you.

We wrestle against powers – authorities. They are creatures subject to authority – Satanic authority, and Jesus's ultimate authority. Just as in an earthly army, generals will command troops, colonels outrank lieutenants, sergeants will order PFC's. There are ranks, greater and lesser, stronger and weaker, supervisors and grunts, but all respond to command-and-control, authority and orders. Angels are under Archangels - the generals like Michael and Gabriel – and it is logical to assume the rank flows down from there, all under the authority of the Commander-In-Chief Jesus Christ.

They said of Jesus that He taught as one who had authority, not like the Scribes. (Matthew 7:29) Jewish rabbinical authority or semikhah was transmitted through the laying-on-of-hands commissioning of a Rabbi who in so doing passed that authority on to another. Jesus' authority came from His Father at His baptism.

A soldier came to Him and recognized His authority to just command, and it would be done:

"The centurion answered and said, 'Lord, I am not worthy that You should come under my roof. But only speak a word, and my servant will be healed. For I also am a man under authority, having soldiers under me. And I say to this one, "Go," and he goes; and to another, "Come," and he comes; and to my servant, "Do this," and he does it.'" (Matthew 8:5-9 NKJV)
He recognized authority, and he knew that Jesus had the authority to command healing from afar with just a word. "All power (exousia) is given

to me in heaven and in earth." (Matthew 28:18)

The astonishing thing is that He gave *us* that authority. "Then he called his twelve disciples together and gave them power and authority over all devils, and to cure all diseases." (Luke 9:1)

There you have it. That is our commission. We have both the forceful power and the legal right – the power of attorney, so to speak, given by Jesus to act as His representative to make sure that His will is carried out - to do warfare and defeat demons wherever we may find them.

The demonic realm operates with Satan at command, giving orders to fallen angels, then they order demons, and demons are the foot soldiers. There is one extra component – the inhabited human, who then becomes a vehicle and a vessel to do evil, create chaos, destroy lives and hurt the kingdom of God wherever possible.

Jesus is our commander, who commands God's general angels, who in turn dispatch the rank and file angel army to do war and assist us. "Are they not all ministering spirits sent forth to minister for those who will inherit salvation?" (Hebrews 1:14)

But unlike the demonic realm, angels don't inhabit us. Our direct authority, power, commissioning and equipping (battle readiness) come from Jesus – the sending of the Holy Spirit to live in us and act through us in Jesus's name. The Holy Spirit is the ultimate weapon of mass destruction to the kingdom of darkness. Jesus came to destroy the works of the devil. "For this purpose the Son of God was manifested, that He might destroy the works of the devil." (1 John 3:8b) He has given us the power of attorney spiritually to go and make sure that command is carried out.

Satan wages war with limited information, tattered communication lines and chaotic soldiers. By the Holy Spirit, we wage war with all access to all battle information needed at all times because the one who is all-knowing is in us! He knows Satan's plans before we do, and will tell us exactly what we need to know to defeat those plans.

Understanding authority is important on many levels. First, it helps you understand the parameters of authority. Satan is bound, as are his forces, by rules and must obey God's authority in Christ.

Second, if the demon is present in a place, situation, family or person, it is because it was given a legal right to be there through someone's sin or disobedience or some other circumstance that allows the enemy to get a foothold. Knowing that will help us discern what allowed it, and revoke its authority, overruling it in the name of Jesus.

Do not confuse this understanding with the Scripture about the man who was born blind. It was asked, "Who sinned, this man or his parents that he was born blind?" Jesus answered, "Neither, but that the works of God should be made manifest in him." (John 9:2-3) But in the case of demon influence, someone always opened the door somewhere.

The enemy does not want you to grasp Jesus' authority.

I remember hearing a story of American World War II prisoners who were on an island in a prison camp. They were brutally humiliated, mistreated and beaten every day. Each morning, the soldiers were forced to stand and be mocked and brutalized for hours at the commandant's whim.

Somehow the soldiers managed to cobble together parts to make a shortwave radio from which they learned that America had won the war – three weeks before!

The men lined up, as usual, the next morning, but when the commandant started his verbal attack, the American commander shouted, "Stand down! *I'm* in command now!" And the commandant and the soldiers knew the charade was over – the Americans knew they had won the war!

Satan and his forces are just like that. They will attack, humiliate, torment and ravage any child of God who doesn't understand their authority, but when they finally understand that Jesus Christ crushed the head of the enemy and defeated him at the cross, then Satan knows his charade is over. When you then take that authority over him, he loses all his power over you!

We fight with authorities who have varying degrees of power and legal right. The most important thing you can understand is that all of those authorities of the demonic, regardless of their place and strength, will bow to the only true authority there is – the Lord Jesus Christ.

We Are Wrestling with the Rulers of Darkness of This World

These rulers – *kosmokrators* - are princes of the age, princes of darkness. These are the "powers behind the thrones of men." They are the controllers of the Stalins, the Assads, the bin Ladens, the Hitlers, the abortionists, pornographers, the gay lobbies and the drug cartels, using people as pawns, organizing them into mass spiritual destructiveness.

The Greek word also indicates they are princes of ignorance, blindness, and shadiness. It is a shadow kingdom, a shadow government, keeping the very people they use, and have insulated from the truth, completely blind and ignorant of their presence and power.

We are not fighting the human princes of the earth, but rather the princes of this age that control them.

We Wrestle with Spiritual Wickedness in High Places

I love the King James version. It paints such a clear and startling picture of what we fight. We battle wickedness. We battle wicked things and wicked creatures. They are nasty, filthy *wickednesses*.

The word is *poneria*: depravity. Malice. Evil purposes and desires.

They are not Darth Vader, a creature evil and malevolent until the mask comes off at the end and he is redeemed. No – they are evil to the core. There is no good in them. They cannot be saved.

Satan cannot be saved. He doesn't want to be.

The problem with sin is, what begins as ugly and repulsive to us - once it gains a foothold in our life – then becomes just uncomfortable, then as we indulge it repeatedly it becomes comfortable, then numbing, then needful, and finally, it is systemically ingrained. It begins to obliterate our personality and our identity. We can become our sin.

I have often heard people that counsel a family member who was abused and verbally humiliated by a drunk family member say, "remember, that's the alcohol talking." True, although it began through a sinful choice. Alcohol was given permission to alter their personality and identity. Eventually, the alcohol becomes dominant over everything in their lives, and without salvation and deliverance, in the end, the person would rather die from it then live without it. The sin eventually blots out the identity of the person God made in His image. It is our mission to restore them in Jesus to that identity. Thank God none of us have to get to that place. There is true deliverance from any life-enslaving addiction and sin through the power of the Lord Jesus Christ.

I had a relative who was about as serious a drinker as you can be. Eventually, doctors removed two-thirds of his stomach and told him if he took another drink, he would die. He did – and he did. Nothing – not family, kids or friends were more important than his alcohol. He became his addiction. He was blotted out by the sin. Terrifying! *Poneria*. Depravity. Deprived of life. Deprived of hope. Deprived of God.

The book of Romans speaks of those who indulge same-sex activity as those who "received in themselves the penalty for their error (wandering, dilution, led astray from the right way, mental straying.) "Likewise also the men, leaving the natural use of the woman, burned in their lust for one another, men with men committing what is shameful, and receiving in themselves the penalty of their error which was due." (Romans 1:27, NKJV) *In* themselves. Sin alters who we are. It molds our entire character.

These evil creatures we battle are depraved. Their goal is to take us to where they are, both spiritually, and eventually in hell. It's the ultimate example of "misery loves company."

There are many kinds of sins. Each has its own unique signature, potency, and penalty. I used to tell people, "sin is sin." No, not really. Murder is as forgivable as stealing, but the *consequences* are far different. And Jesus' warning against injuring children and its dire consequences seem to indicate God himself doesn't see all sins as the same. Everyone is redeemable, and certainly, the pride that makes me think your sin is worse than mine makes mine worse! However, consequentially, sins carry different weights and measures of destructiveness. But all unchecked and undealt with sin results in enslavement to the powers of darkness.

Socially, some sins and industries certainly demand addressing – pornography, abortion, slavery, child abuse. But let us remember – those who practice and promote such things are slaves to sin (as we once were). When we fight these institutions, remember, we are fighting the *poneiros* and the depraved evil creatures that are feeding off both victims *and* sinners, like vampires from hell.

In High Places

We wrestle with depraved creatures who shuttle from Earth to the heavenlies – the high places. Perhaps that is our stratosphere, but it is more. These high places are in a place that we cannot see with our natural eyes. But as we enter the throne room of God in intercessory prayer as Daniel, we will lock horns (pardon the phrase) with these malignant powers. As we intercede for the lost, we must confront the enemy and bring them into submission to Jesus, demanding that they release their prey.

I also believe one of the reasons Christian media is fought so viciously is because the battle is in the "high places" – against the "prince of the power of the air."

We Stand

Take on the whole armor – *panoplia* - all the weapons in our armory - in order to withstand. The Greek word is *antihistemi*, meaning to know your place, be intact, stand unharmed, stand immovable, stand ready and prepared – one who does not hesitate. One who does not waver.

We are made to "sit together in heavenly places in Christ Jesus," (Ephesians 2:6) from where we get and keep the right perspective. We "walk as children of light" (Ephesians 5:8) and we stand against the enemy.

Standing is one of the most crucial war positions we must take. I have long understood that as believers, we are given "territory." When you gave your life to Jesus, Jesus took back enemy territory, set you on it, and commissioned you to defend it, stand firm, stand fast, and to be "unmovable, always abounding in the work of the Lord." (1 Corinthians 15:58)

I also understood from the beginning that the enemy would come at you with a barrage of attacks and a battering ram of evil to try to get you to either fall or to move. One of my favorite stories in the Bible is about one of David's "mighty men," Shammah, who stood in the field of common lentils to defend it against the attacking Philistines:

"And after him was Shammah the son of Agee the Hararite. And the Philistines were gathered together into a troop, where was a piece of ground full of lentils: and the people fled from the Philistines. But he stood in the midst of the ground, and defended it, and slew the Philistines: and the Lord wrought a great victory." (2 Samuel 23:11-12)

It is a perfect picture of our commission to stand. "But," someone might protest, "Why me? Why is Satan always attacking me? I don't have a big ministry. I'm no real threat to Satan. Why the attack?"

It's not about what you *do*. It's that you belong to Jesus, and the land you stand on now is Jesus' property. Satan wants it back.

Satan wants you to fall, or move from your place in God. He wants to get you to give up, walk away.

Don't do any of those things. Stand and keep standing, no matter how fierce the attacks. You may feel battered, bruised and weak. Just. Stand. God is able to make you stand. (Romans 14:4)

We Stand in the Evil Day

Surely, there have been evil days in other areas, in other countries everywhere. Reading *Foxe's Book of Martyrs,* an account of early church martyrs and the hideous torture of those who chose to follow Jesus to the death, made me realize how easy most of us have it in the Western church.

Having said that, I also remember a message my pastor friend Rick Howard gave on running the race. He said, concerning *our* fight in comparison with the first church's battles, "Our lions may be different, our arenas may not be the same, but they are no less real." Lions – and the roaring lion, Satan - come in many forms.

In some ways, unpersecuted believers have a trickier battle. Satan thrives in the grays of the moral uncertainties and easy temptations of our sin, sex, and sorcery-drenched society. Those under persecution know their enemy. Ours hides in seductive clothes and beautiful baubles, shiny things and toys.

This is all the more reason our standing must be determined and our vision eagle-sharp.

Our evil day, I believe, is unprecedented in history, because it is building for the final age of complete lawlessness.

The evil day – *poneros* – means the hurtful day, the harassed day, the laborious day, perilous, painful and diseased day.

Don't these descriptions pretty much sum up the hour we live in?

The evil day also means the Satanic day. The corrupt day. Many of the things Jesus used to describe the last days are very sobering. (Matthew 24) We would have tribulation, He said, such as the world had never seen or ever would again. I believe we are in that very hour.

I believe our time is uniquely evil, uniquely poisoned, Satanic and corrupt, uniquely treacherous and dangerous for those who will stand committed to Jesus to the end. But "where sin abounded, grace did much more abound." (Romans 5:20) He will give us all we need to stand in the evil day!

The post-Christian world is about to turn on real believers in a frightening, unprecedented way. Those who stand for truth, and thus by default against idolatry, against drugs, against the occult, against homosexuality, against gay marriage, and against false religions will be vilified, hated, selected and eventually persecuted and eliminated.

The US lost the war in Vietnam, in part, because of the uncertainty of why we were fighting. Without a clear goal and objective, any nation or army will lose the will to fight – and the will to win.

We defeated Germany because we had a clear face of the enemy – Hitler – and we did whatever was necessary to take him out.

Our clear face of the enemy is Satan – the destroyer. Never forget how evil and destructive he is, and that we must fight with resolve and determination to stand and be victorious in Jesus at all costs.

Gregory R Reid

FROM THE FRONTLINES: A LESSON IN WOLVES

Bryce came to our youth outreach, invited by another youth who had met him at the mall and was impressed by his loving nature and knowledge of the Bible.

It was a "way too busy" time in my life in which, unfortunately, the bulk of the work and ministry was done by the head of our youth outreach because I traveled frequently, coming home for every Monday night and Friday night Bible study and event I could.

One Monday night, Bryce came to Bible study at my house. He offered to open in prayer. To my shock, his prayer covered nearly every single point in my message that I had yet to preach that night!

I was *so* impressed. I was impressed enough to allow this college-age young man to come to our studies and activities. We were always looking for godly volunteers.

A short while after, Bryce asked to be released to work with the youth at our sister church who acted as our spiritual covering, which was about 35 miles away. I said of course; I recommended him to the pastors. And then I left town for several days.

I was greeted by a message on my answering machine from the pastors a few days later when I returned home. I called them immediately. I was devastated to learn that this "trusted" young man – the young man that I had recommended to them – had molested a 17-year-old boy from their youth group that weekend while I was out of town.

There was no apology that was ever going to make this right. I wouldn't have blamed them for never having anything to do with me again. I had missed God in a horrendous way and unwittingly sent a wolf in sheep's clothing to them. I know the pastors and the boy have forgiven me, but that horrible error I made cost someone their innocence and damaged good and godly relationships nearly beyond repair. It hurts still.

Within the next two days, I learned that Bryce had hit on several of our other young teen boys! Thankfully, he did not succeed in molesting them.

I called Bryce to my house, and we sat at my table. "You've got one shot to repent and make this right," I told him plainly. And he smirked. He refused to even answer me. I slammed my fist on the table. "Do you think this is funny?" I yelled. "You ruined a young man's life! You have ONE CHANCE to confess this and make it right!" The smirk and the stonewalling continued. I finally ordered him to leave and never return to our youth outreach again.

That Friday I arrived late to our youth center to see him sitting halfway in the back of the 20 rows of folding chairs in the middle of the kids during worship. It was packed that night. I sat in the back row, praying and steaming mad.

In the middle of a worship song, he raised his hands, arms swaying in worship as if nothing at all had happened and he was perfect with God and with us. I quickly and quietly extended my hand in his direction and whispered, "You foul spirit, I rebuke you in the Name of Jesus!" Instantly, his hands contorted and curled into twisted claws without him even hearing my prayer.

So, I thought, that is what is behind this…

What followed later was a failed deliverance. He refused to repent. And so the demon stayed in him, and *he* left.

Months later, I learned that he had gained another pastor's trust, and he was scheduled to babysit their young teen boys alone for an entire weekend!

A call to the pastor, unfortunately, found resistance and denial, and the pastor put his own children in the hands of a demonized pedophile.

Lessons from the battle:

1. Paul said, "Know those who labor among you." (1 Thess. 5:12) Don't be fooled by gifts, prophecies, niceness, Bible knowledge or "words from God." Satan comes as an angel of light and his servants as ministers of righteousness.

2. "Lay hands suddenly on no man." (1 Tim. 5:22) Take time to verify, get background checks, do whatever you have to do to know the people around you before you put them into a leadership role of any kind.
3. Don't get so busy that the flock you are called to tend is ever unguarded. Satan and his demons are always seeking sheep to devour.

Never think that you are beyond being fooled. Stay in prayer and keep your sword of discernment sharp and ready. More is at stake in this hour than you can know.

Gregory R Reid

The best way to keep the devil off our territory is to keep him busy on his own, defending his kingdom from our bold attacks....

- A.B. Simpson

Gregory R Reid

CHAPTER THREE
THE WHOLE ARMOR – READY FOR WAR

"Stand therefore, having girded your waist with truth, having put on the breastplate of righteousness, and having shod your feet with the preparation of the gospel of peace; above all, taking the shield of faith with which you will be able to quench all the fiery darts of the wicked one. And take the helmet of salvation, and the sword of the Spirit, which is the word of God; praying always with all prayer and supplication in the Spirit, being watchful to this end with all perseverance and supplication for all the saints." (Ephesians 6:14-18)

There are eight parts to the armor God gives us. Six are for war and for battle. Two are for strategy.

Paul was a Roman, and it is very likely he drew his battle pictures from Roman armory and soldiers. A glimpse into actual Roman armor may give us some understanding of the Spirit's intent.

Notice that there is no armor, and no protection, for your backside. That means there is no retreat in this life. To retreat is to perish. To retreat is to leave yourself vulnerable to all of the enemies' weaponry.

I heard a story that spoke to me deeply about the necessity of a no-retreat stance.

In 1883, the island of Krakatoa exploded. It was so loud that the explosion was literally heard around the world. It created a tsunami that rapidly moved away from the explosion, building strength and height and headed for all ships in the way.

A ship with a complement of over 50 passengers was right in its path. The captain learned of the impending tsunami and had to make a fateful decision: either turn the boat away from Krakatoa and ride it out, hoping to outrun the death wave, or turn toward the tsunami and take their chances.

The Captain put everyone below, turned the ship toward the wave, then had his men strap him to the captain's wheel so he could not leave his post, no matter the danger, fear or outcome.

They rode over the tsunami. All survived.

Tie yourself to the wheel of this battle so that escape, running or quitting is not an option.

Having Your Loins Girt with Truth

The Roman soldier's "belt" was called a cingulum, and it was not a belt as we think of it, but rather a carrying band for money, a sword, writing instruments and other necessities. The cingulum also had a set of bells that hung down the front.

This belt had two purposes: To protect the groin and to intimidate the enemy. Imagine the sound of thousands of bells clanging together and approaching!

The belt also kept the armor in place and supported the sword.

For us, the belt of truth is what keeps everything in place. Truth keeps everything in perspective and gives us clarity in battle.

We have never been in an age where truth is so disregarded and discarded. Satan has created a fog of war in which there are no absolutes, truth is relative, and the boundaries are blurred to the point of nonexistence.

One only needs to look around to realize that the belt of truth is nearly completely gone from the church in our day. Truth has become a sloppy, relativistic "felt needs" mixture of half-doctrine and experiential-but-Biblically-untested religion – more like a loose sash full of holes and undone threads rather than a belt that can actually hold everything together.

The truth of God's Word that we carry in our lives binds everything together. Without it, we are unprotected, vulnerable and a target for every arrow and blow.

Truth – moral certainty from God and about God – holds everything together.

In the fog of war, the belt of truth keeps all our armor right where it should be. God's truth gives us certainty, clarity, and deliberateness as we march into battle. I often think of the expression, "It has a ring of truth to it," and our Belt of Truth sends forth the ringing bells that announce that God's truth is on the ground, and is approaching the enemy to do battle.

Soldiering is not an individual endeavor. Without a "band of brothers," we will find ourselves alone in battle and easy prey. When the soldier next to me has bells ringing as well, it reminds me that I am not alone and that their life depends as much on me as mine depends on them. We must "speak the truth in love" to each other. The scriptures we speak, the principles and truths we put forth, are like these bells that speak not only to our own hearts but must be spoken to those around us who we fight beside to brace and strengthen them as well.

Satan and his demons don't fear those who carry no certainty of truth. The church has grown weak and ineffective in battle because the foundations of truth have been torn up and torn down. Much of the Western church is weak on divorce, weak on speaking against the occult and false religions, weakened by excess and half-commitment, weak on preaching the Blood, the Cross and the return of Jesus. The enemy fears them not.

Maybe the reason we can't wear the belt of truth is that we have become fat from gorging on spiritual junk food, touchy-feely Christianity, filthy entertainment, and pitiful theology laced with compromise.

God needs soldiers in this hour who have been fed on the lean, mean diet of the truth of God's Word and have no moral uncertainty as to who our enemy is, and what they need to do to engage and defeat him.

"Great is the laxity of falsehood. Truth binds the man," said Hugo Grotius.

An army that is settled and clear on the absolute truth of God's Word is the only army that will make the enemy tremble.

Paul no doubt had this verse in mind when he wrote of this belt of truth: "Righteousness shall be the belt of his loins, and faithfulness the belt of his waist." (Isaiah 11:5) Righteousness is God's truth understood in our hearts and lived out in our lives. Faithfulness is the certainty that God will give us victory in battle.

So what is the "truth" of this belt of truth? It is what is true in any matter under consideration. The truth of God's Word speaks to any and all situations, people, difficulties, and needs, sins and dilemmas. There is nothing in this life that God's truth does not address, directly and implicitly.

The disarming of the church in the last few decades has come from those who read God's plain and simple truth, find that it conflicts with their sins or personal feelings and thoughts, their weaknesses or the world's social changes, and decide, "Well, maybe that's not what it really means." Then they proceed to change, twist or distort God's Word to match their own desires or perceptions.

"Gravity," pondered the man on the roof. "What goes up, must come down. But maybe they got it wrong. Maybe that's not what it really means," he said, jumping to his death at the end of his foolish attempt to get around the law of gravity. He tested the truth to his own demise.

In God's world, God's Word and God's truth are neither vague nor uncertain nor unknowable. He said what He meant, and means what He said. Toying with truth and doing the "Did God really say?" trick was the devil's game. It worked in the garden. It works still.

Soldiers are prepared with truth. They've been given the battle plan of God's Word, and they do not question the Commander's orders. The orders are clear; they carry them out.

In spiritual warfare, that kind of clarity cuts through all the delusions, fog and confusion and gets to the heart of the matter. It's a clarity that scares Satan to the core. This truth and certainty, like the belt that keeps all the armor in place, leaves us unencumbered for action. We're not distracted.
We run straight into battle with a single heart knowing "truth is our shield and buckler." (Psalm 91:4)

A Crucial Issue

I need to be very blunt with you here. I believe there are a very specific applications and very specific reasons that this belt of truth is placed over the groin area.

There has never been a time in history where human sexuality has been more exploited, distorted and perverted. We are reaching a level not seen since the goat orgies of the Pan worshippers and the attempted rape of angels in Sodom and Gomorrah. The advent of the internet, widespread pornography and the degrading of humans – women, men and children - visible to anyone with a computer or smartphone, has torn our spiritual fabric in a way that has given free rein to sexual perversion spirits that are infecting the media, culture, music, families and even churches. Evangelist David Wilkerson was shown this coming "baptism of filth" in 1973 in a vision, and it is here.

The sexuality of every man, woman, and child is being attacked. Warping, twisting and corrupting our sexuality is Satan's #1 weapon in this hour, and no one is exempt – not pastors, not children. With our welcoming the internet, and with the vast (and largely unmonitored) world of cartoons, music, movies, video games and television, our souls have become sieves that allow darkness in without editing, blocking or refusing.

As believers in this age, many people have already been saturated in this filth and delusion before they came to Christ, so God must go about the hard work of reconstructing them mentally, emotionally and spiritually to be fitted to truth. Church-raised believers fight a battle from children's church to college and beyond to keep out the ugliness and constant visual and sound assault of spiritual wickedness designed to defile them. In an age where we have gone from debating whether Christians should see movies at all, to accepting gay marriage just within a few decades, it seems we are in a triage mode right now to preserve the holiness of sex, marriage, and moral sanctity.

We have no choice. We must put on this armor and guard with everything we have the sacred gift of our sexuality – guard our hearts – our minds – our bodies. Having our loins girt with truth protects us from the most vulnerable assaults of all.

Having Your Feet Shod With the Preparation of the Gospel of Peace

These shoes or sandals are meant for running, for marching, and for climbing. It is an action part of our armor. I always think of the military phrase "boots on the ground" when I read this. For Roman soldiers, they wore sandals. For us, boots.

It's about being prepared to do battle. But it is also about being ready to preach Jesus to the lost. Our feet carry us daily in our walk with Jesus. These "Good News Shoes" make us able to traverse rough territories and not be seriously injured. "How beautiful on the mountains are the feet of him who brings good news, who proclaims peace, who brings glad tidings of good things, who proclaims salvation, who says to Zion, 'Your God reigns!'" (Isaiah 52:7 NKJV) Our shoes are part of an offensive campaign to bring good news – the war is won; the captives can now go free!

The Breastplate of Righteousness

The breastplate covers us from navel to neck. It protects our vital organs – specifically, the heart. Our heart can be a tremendous gift in God's hands or a terribly wicked thing in the flesh or in the hands of Satan. We've grown up hearing the phrase, "Trust your heart," or "Trust your feelings." That's a bad idea. That's the worst thing you can do. "The heart is deceitful above all things and desperately wicked; who can know it?" (Jeremiah 17:9) What does this tell us? In themselves, our hearts are not good, kind and trustable according to scriptures. The unredeemed heart is wicked! Without Jesus, our heart's capacity for deception, self-justification, blame shifting and incredible evil is limitless. That's startling, isn't it? But it's the truth. I was reminded yesterday that Hitler would cry over an injured dog but shed not one tear over the slaughter of millions of innocent people, including children. Doesn't that say something about the unredeemed heart's capacity for deception?

The story is told of a pilot caught in a fog in a plane without working instruments. He felt for sure that he was flying straight and true. But he plunged directly and fatally into a mountain – upside down. His inner-ear mechanism, his "feeling" that he was flying right, deceived him to death.

Our "feelings" can do the same thing. God didn't say *not* to feel, but that all our heart's thoughts and feelings must be subject to the Word of God and truth.

Some Jewish Rabbis refer to gentiles as "those who follow their noses." I think that's a pretty painfully good description of our hearts when they follow the instincts of the flesh, like an animal following the scent of sin and wrong desires, passions and lusts. Don't follow your nose! Listen, follow and obey the Spirit and the Word in all things.

The breastplate of righteousness is not only a guardian to protect our hearts and lead us toward godly thoughts, godly feelings, and godly actions, but it also means the "breastplate of justice." "He has shown thee, o man, what is good, and what does the Lord require of thee, but to do justly and to love mercy and to walk humbly with thy God?" (Micah 6:8) Do *justice*.

The Gospel message is also about doing justice. I'm not talking about the new Gospel-less emergent socialism. I'm talking about real, facts-on-the-ground being willing to do something when people are hurt, poor, betrayed, abused. Anyone can write a check and attend a cause concert. That's all good. But many of the same folks wouldn't lift a finger to do something themselves. "If a brother or sister is naked and destitute of daily food, and one of you says to them, 'Depart in peace, be warmed and filled,' but you do not give them the things which are needed for the body, what does it profit?" (James 2:15-16 NKJV)

Our war is a *now* war. It's boots on the ground, shields up. "We're coming to bring justice." We take a homeless man out to eat. We visit an AIDS ward. We become a CASA volunteer to be Jesus' arms to an abused child. We speak out against abuse and lies. Remember? This is hand-to-hand combat! Enough talk. The breastplate of justice isn't a badge of honor. It's a protection so our hearts can carry out justice every day whenever we can, with a "full heart."

Two stories reflect this for me. One is from the great missionary writer Amy Carmichael, who spent her entire life in Dunhavur, India, taking in orphaned and abandoned children. At some point, she was horrified to learn that little girls were being used in temple prostitution. She realized that they must do anything they could to rescue these children. "Surely the Gospel includes this," she wrote.

The second is a story I heard the late David Wilkerson tell about walking the mean streets of New York and seeing an older group of young men beating up a little boy. David was suddenly seized with spiritual anger at this injustice. He picked up a baseball bat and ran swinging and screaming like a crazy man. The terrified older boys fled, and the boy was saved.

Please don't debate the theology of this with me here. The boy was saved.

The breastplate of justice – get a lion's heart from it!

What is this righteousness, this right-standing with God that guards our hearts? One of the first of a warrior's lessons is when you stand up to fight, the first thing the enemy does is lob a sky-full of fiery missiles at you.

You know, don't you?

"You really messed up this morning."

"Still looking at pornography, eh?"

"Hypocrite."

"You're stupid. You can't even read the Bible."

"You're fat. You're ugly. You're a wimp. You're a failure. You're a loser."

Satan uses anything to hurt your heart, grab your attention, get you to lose your focus, and make you fall. These attacks on our vulnerabilities and failures are very effective in debilitating us from our identity in Jesus and our purpose in Him.

So you put on the breastplate of righteousness. *His* righteousness. We have none in ourselves. Satan knows it, so he takes out his laundry list of all our sins and failures and starts hurling them at us. Unprotected, we whimper, bleed and run off to lick our wounds and bemoan our unworthiness.

Get up! You *are* unworthy in yourself. Only He is worthy! You are unrighteous in yourself. But you have the righteousness of Christ! "For He has made Him to be sin for us, who knew no sin; that we might be made the righteousness of God in Him." (2 Cor. 5:21) The breastplate is His righteousness. Satan can't get behind that shield unless you lay it down.
Don't try to fight his accusations. Just say, "That's right. I've done all those things. I do have those sins and failures. But Jesus saved me and has forgiven me and is using me, so get out of my way!"

Use this breastplate. Put it on daily, and expect the attacks on your faith, your integrity, and your purity. Fight to keep your heart right. "Keep your heart with all diligence, for out of it are the issues of life." (Proverbs 4:23) A clear, clean heart standing under Jesus' grace and righteousness will give you a clear vision for the things that make for good warfare with good results. And if you fall – just get up. Get cleansed. Wartime is no time to mourn your failures. GET MOVING!

Above All, The Shield of Faith

This does not mean "above all" as a matter of importance, but positionally, "above you" – above your head, your body, your heart, your whole being. Use it to shield everything.

The shield Paul was probably referencing was not a little round Hollywood thing. It was a full body shield, able to cover the head, feet, sides, and four corners.

This shield was often coated with oil to make the arrows slip off rather than penetrate. The oil, of course, symbolizes the Holy Spirit and His anointing. We – and that shield – need to be daily anointed and covered with the power of the Holy Spirit.

Fiery Darts

What are the fiery darts? The *falarica* was a stick or cane covered in combustible material and set afire. They were made to stick to the shield and burn it, and the intent was to (1) fasten to and burn the body if it got through the shield, or (2) burn the shield, causing the soldier to cast it down and thus become completely vulnerable.

Now listen. Spiritual warfare is not a joke. If you mean business, then the minute you get into the battle, the darts will come in fast and furious. Don't be shocked. Just get your shield up. You'll feel like you're "on fire" with attacks. DO NOT PUT THE SHIELD DOWN. Hold it up! It won't burn through. If you abandon it in a panic, you're an instant target. "I didn't think that being a Christian would be so hard!" It's a war, not a sport or a video game. Press forward! He promised the overwhelming victory would be ours.

The Fiery Darts of the Wicked One

The Wicked One – Satan. The Greek word for wicked is *poneros*. It means malicious, depraved. Satan is the depraved one. He is the one with nothing but evil purposes and desires and no boundaries.

Let's take this battle right to his throne room!

The Helmet of Salvation

The helmet of salvation provided deliverance from the harassment of enemies. It protects from the clamor and clash of war. "Shell shock" was once one of the primary afflictions of returning war veterans. The constant explosions, the shouting, the screams, and the fear were traumatic, and their effects were experienced long after the war.

When you engage in spiritual warfare, you will be faced with spiritual noise and confusion. You will hear the enemy's voices, accusations, and ungodly suggestions. The helmet of salvation protects your ears, to dampen the noise and clamor and allow focus. It protects your eyes, so you will not be distracted or blinded by the enemy's confusion, distraction, and lies. It protects your mouth – keeping you from uttering things that cause you to fall into the enemy's traps in the midst of battle.

It is a helmet of salvation – the assurance that your eternal salvation is *already accomplished*. The battle you fight is not to determine your salvation but the eternal destiny of others.

The helmet protects what you see, what you hear and what you think and say. It protects your mind. The battle for the mind is so important that it will take another entire chapter to cover it in chapter 4.

The Sword of the Spirit Which is the Word of God

We love the long swords, the Lord of the Rings-type sword battles. It's dramatic, a choreographed dance to the finish.

Well, that's not *this* sword.

It's a dagger. It's SHORT.

Why? It's up close and personal hand-to-hand combat. Spiritual warfare isn't a spectator sport; it isn't lobbing rocks from behind safe walls. If you want to be effective, you have to get the enemy by the neck and put the dagger of truth straight into his heart.

This is the "Sword of the Spirit" – the Spirit of God. He is the power behind the sword. And by the way, the Spirit is not an "it." He's not the light side of the force. He is a person. And He brings power (dunamis – dynamite) to the battle.

And what is the sword we wield under His power? The Word of God.

This is where we need help to understand word meanings. There are two main words in the New Testament for "word." One is *logos* – the written word. The other is *rhema* – the living word. *Rhema* is the word used in this passage.

The Scriptures, the written Word – is God's Word, through and through, infallible and perfect, containing all we need for life and godliness. Read it. Memorize it! Make it your lifeblood and your food and drink. May it be said of us like was said of John Bunyan: "Prick him, and he bleeds scripture."

But the word must be proclaimed in the power of the Holy Spirit to hurt the enemy. It's not enough just to quote a few lines. I daresay thousands of unsaved ministers read a few scriptures from the pulpit every week and they believe it not, and it does not affect the hearts of unbelieving hearers. They do not have the authority given by the anointing and empowering of the Holy Spirit.

Why did the people turn from the Scribes and Pharisees and follow Jesus? They, after all, read and knew the scriptures. But of Jesus they said, "He taught them as one having authority, and not as the scribes." (Matthew 7:29) Authority: Jurisdiction, power.

Jurisdiction and power are things the enemy understands. He knows if you have it. And he certainly knows if you don't.

When Jesus spoke, things happened. Why? "How God anointed Jesus of Nazareth with the Holy Ghost and with power; who went about doing good, and healing all those who were oppressed of the devil; for God was with Him." (Acts 10:38)

He spoke *rhema*. He *was* the Word, speaking the written word – the scriptures. And the Holy Spirit exploded into our physical world with the Living Word. (*Rhema*.)

How does that relate to our battle?

You can have a great battle plan, but if you hand it to the enemy and say, "You're in trouble, look at this!" then they will simply laugh and wipe you out tomorrow.

Why? You had a great plan. But a plan won't execute itself. You have to carry it out – you have to bring it down on the enemy's head with force, swiftness, and determination – with jurisdiction and power!

We have the battle plan – the written Word (*logos*.) It has all we need! But if you just say, "Well, Satan's lost. It says here…" what good is that? You have to press the matter. The Word must go from being an affirmation to a proclamation. A war cry!

Whispered threats away from the battle are useless. You must take the Word *to* the battle and proclaim Jesus' authority, power and jurisdiction over the enemy's forces. The devil will know when you carry the anointing to do so. Then you will see corresponding results and the standing down of the enemy.

The written Word of God is food and instruction, truth and light and life. But haven't you had the experience of reading the same verse 20 times, and on the 21st time the words just jump off of the page, light up like a brilliant light and become real to you? That's *rhema*. That is God breathing on the written word and bringing it to powerful life.

But you must *wield* the written Word as a *rhema* word, bringing it to bear in the authority of God's power to deliver. We first yield to the *logos*; then we will wield the *rhema*!

"For the Word of God is living and powerful, and sharper than any two-edged sword, piercing even to the division of soul and spirit, and of joints and marrow, and is a discerner of the thoughts and intents of the heart." (Hebrews 4:12)

The Word-dagger, in combat, cuts through all the bluster and bluffing and threatening and lies of the enemy and gets to the heart – forcing truth to be spoken, lies to be exposed and discernment to work in order to dislodge the enemy at every level.

Praying and Watching…With All Perseverance

Soldiers never let their guard down. Soldiers are vigilant and watchful. Spiritual warriors are prayer warriors, praying without ceasing, watchmen on the walls of God's house, watching for the encroaching enemy and ready to go to war at a moment's notice.

Ready to sign up?

FROM THE FRONTLINES: IT'S NO JOKE

God had given us a group of kids – hardcore, street kids, some were abused, some were trying to quit drugs, some trying to get out of the occult, stop drinking, and everything in-between. God brought them to us to teach the Word, pray with, and disciple. It was tough. The world had a firm grip on them. Satan didn't give up easily.

Behind the scenes, I worked with law enforcement exposing criminal occult groups. I knew these groups had a prime interest in recruiting kids – for drugs, for crime, for sacrifice. We warned our youth. Mostly, they didn't listen or didn't believe they were in danger.

My doorbell rang at 3:00 a.m. – a rather frequent, but always unnerving, experience. I went downstairs and opened the door to see Shannon and another youth group friend. "Shannon's really wasted. He wanted me to bring him here." I called his mom, who was already aware of his struggles and party friends. We were doing everything we could to hang onto him. I put him on the phone with her. "Mom, I'm gonna crash here. I'll come home in the morning, that ok?" He asked me if it was ok with me. "Sure." I talked to her and assured her he'd be ok.

Shannon had decided to go way off the reservation that night. He'd taken some hard drugs at the home of some very well-to-do drug dealers, where a massive party was in full swing.

Shannon was nearly beside himself recounting the noise, the chaos, the drugs flowing like a river, and then the distinct cloud of evil that suddenly permeated the entire house. He walked from room to room and finally sat down in the living room. He looked over and saw the dealers cutting cocaine on top of an elaborate glass coffee table, etched with a huge pentagram that was white with cocaine. All the blood drained from his face and he quietly got up and left the room, grabbed one of our other wayward kids and said, "Get me out of here! Take me to Greg's NOW!"

That's how I ended up with my 3:00 a.m. visitor.

"I didn't believe you guys!" Shannon told me, shaking with fear. "None of us really did. We thought all this devil worship stuff wasn't real. Now I know it's real. I'm really scared!"

There was a reason to be scared. I knew of many kids who ended up in jail, a mental hospital or even dead because they ended up at these adult parties designed to recruit and use kids for their evil purposes.

I spent a couple of hours calming Shannon down, praying for him, going through prayers of renunciation and repentance with him, until he finally was able to rest. I threw a blanket over him on the couch and stayed with him until he was asleep, returning to my room, listening, standing watch in case it all hit him again.

It was a scenario to be repeated many times over the years. Warnings given, warnings ignored, wake-up calls and prices paid.

The devil is real. Youth are his favorite target. And he's open 24/7 at Parties-R-Us. Accept his invitation at your own risk!

Temptations at first are like Elijah's cloud, no bigger than a man's hand, but if we give way to them they will soon overspread the whole soul. Satan nestles himself when we dwell upon the thoughts of sin; we cannot prevent the sudden risings of sin, but by grace we may keep them down, and they should never long remain without opposition.

- Richard Sibbes

Gregory R Reid

4 BATTLE FOR THE MIND

Of all the many battlefields of spiritual warfare, one of the most critical, contested and difficult is the battle for the mind. An entire book could be written on this, and others better equipped than this writer have done so.

Nevertheless, the basics need to be covered. Let's start by having a primary understanding of what we are made of. In our most simple state, we are:

- Body
- Soul (which includes our mind, will, emotions, etc.)
- Spirit

For unbelievers, the body is simply a vessel, a container. For the believer, we are a specific container – we become the temple of the Holy Spirit. It's sad to hear the media trying to advertise gyms, diet plans or some other health product while misquoting the scriptures, flippantly saying, "Your body is a temple!" The scriptures – meant for believers – say, in some pretty sobering words:

"What? Don't you know that your body is the temple of the Holy Spirit which is in you, which you have of God, and you are not your own? If any man defile the temple of God, him shall God destroy; for the temple of God is holy, which temple ye are." (1 Corinthians 6:19)

So, our bodies as believers are God's house, His temple. I believe this reference was meant to point to the Old Testament temple as well, which was three main parts: The outer court, the inner court, and the Holy of Holies.

I believe our spirit – the real essence of who we are – is where Jesus lives by His Spirit in us, and nothing unclean or evil can dwell there. Our spirit becomes His dwelling place -the Holy of Holies.

The question often comes up, "Can a Christian have a demon?" (I once heard a preacher say, "Why would you want one?") It is a huge question and a huge debate. I will deal with this more in depth later, but as one who was once 100% convinced that a believer could *not* have a demon, a number of radical and startling encounters convinced me otherwise. I can't answer all the arguments people give as to why a Christian can't have a demon. But I can give a bit of a picture here for you. First of all, this argument always is presented as, "Christians can't be possessed," which brings up pictures of Linda Blair in *The Exorcist*. That's full possession. And that, in my experience, is rare. But there are an extensive range of influences that can affect someone demonically that don't approach that level of violent takeover.

In fact, the word "possession" is "demonized" in the original New Testament language. Rarely is it the level where a person has no control whatsoever. New Testament references, as we will see, showed everything from that violent level, as in the man in the tombs, to the boy with a deaf and mute spirit, to a woman with a spirit of divination.

That brings me to another matter before I proceed. Those who argue the nuances of demons and their influences - either those who believe they can have *no* influence over a believer, or those who think believers are completely infested with them - are both off the mark. The fact is, the matter of demon influence, deliverance - or as I've come to call it, demon extraction - is never cut and dry, one size fits all. There are those who have been excessive in "deliverance" who believe there's a demon in and attached to everything, and have created a great deal of confusion and false information in their sincere desire to "get a handle on it." And my conservative friends are adamant and often unyielding in their attempt to prove that a Christian can't have any kind of demon influence. (A position that at the root may be more often motivated by fear of demons, the unknown and the supernatural rather than a strictly theological concern.)

I understand the desire to deny any possibility that demons can touch a believer. Frankly, a lot of that reaction for me personally was a knee-jerk response to the off-base excesses of many "deliverance" books and ministries.

But a careful scriptural reading and understanding, as well as numerous drastic encounters in the course of demon extractions - even with believers - brought me to a different conclusion and a very uncomfortable one. And while it is possible to find a few scripture prooftexts to "prove" that Christians can't have demons at all, there is, in fact, no definitive verse that says that they cannot. What the scriptures do tell us is that Satan walks as a roaring lion seeking whom he may devour, and the vast majority of scriptures concerning demons and spiritual warfare are for believers.

The reality is, all of this scares most believers. And that is understandable. Nevertheless, we must war, because God commanded it in Christ. So we must get over the fear and deal with "facts on the ground." Our first priority is getting rid of the thing. But many times, I find that people we prayed for *had* received Jesus at some point. Someone may say, "Well, then they must not be saved." If that's your hard and fast position, I'm not going to argue you away from that. But when you're involved in the situation – when you are in battle against these evil things -you just *do*. You don't discuss or debate.

I did receive what I believe to be a pivotal understanding of how demonization can take place even for a believer. We are like the Old Testament temple which is made up of the Outer Court, the Inner Court and the Holy of Holies. The outer court could be attended by Gentiles as well as Jews. Our outer courts – our bodies, mind, emotions – can indeed be touched by darkness. In fact – and here's the key – if we open the doors to the forbidden or unclean, they have a legal right to afflict us. We, in fact, have seceded territory to the enemy when we open certain doors to sin.

I do not believe evil can enter our "holy of holies." But the "outer court"? Absolutely. Again, doubters will say, "Well, demons can oppress us, but not possess us." This is more of a semantics issue, but I concede that "possession" is rare. But what is "oppression?" What are the limits? Satan can lie to you, make you ill, give you a headache? Sure. Then why is it so hard to understand that he is not limited by a tiny bit of skull bone which prevents infiltration in mind, into emotions? You can call it oppression, call it influence, whatever you must, but be sure of this: if we open the wrong doors, demons can have any number of levels of influence on us. If a thief breaks into your property, it doesn't matter if they just get inside the gate or get right into the house, it is still a violation of our sovereign property. In the same way, if a demon has access to our "property," either just inside the gate or right into our living rooms, the wording doesn't matter. A violation of our God-given temple is still a violation.

Our bodies can, in fact, feel both the presence of the Holy Spirit (Holy Spirit goosebumps, we used to call them) and also feel ungodly, sensual lusts, correct? Our minds also can be containers of the Word of God, or retainers of media filth and perversion, lies and deceptions.

Though, as I said, I believe Satan cannot enter the Holy of Holies of our spirit where Jesus dwells, demon influence can most definitely breach the outer courts of our mind, soul, and body. And again, if we open the doors, they have the legal right to do so.

I trust that will partially answer the question of whether a believer can be demon influenced before I continue with the understanding of the battle for the mind. This book is not written primarily to convince people who believe otherwise – although it would be wonderful if that was one of the results of this effort - rather it was written to equip people for real warfare to extract the demonic, whether the person we are praying for claims to be saved or not.

We must guard all the gates of body, mind, and soul against the enemy.

The battle for the mind is one of the most critical battles we wage as believers. Our active participation, awareness, and vigilance in securing and keeping our minds in Christ are essential.

Sanity

Deliverance from demons brings freedom, healing, joy, and so many other things. But one of the chief things it brings is sanity. It brings spiritual sanity, emotional sanity and mental freedom from torment. Only those who have experienced such excruciating bondage and been set free can fully understand what a great healing this is.

When Jesus delivered the man who had become a tomb-dwelling animal that nothing and no one could tame, a great miracle occurred: "Then they went out to see what had happened, and came to Jesus, and found the man from whom the demons had departed, sitting at the feet of Jesus, clothed **and in his right mind** [emphasis mine.] And they were afraid." (Luke 8:35)

Demons are chaotic, evil, sinful, full of rages and lust and destructive impulses. They are filthy minded, God-hating, blasphemous mockers and corrupters of innocence. They are insane.

When demons attach to, infiltrate and start to take over a human vessel, it is like pouring garbage and decaying filth into drinking water. It poisons everything in them and around them.

When a sinister demon mind begins to infiltrate our mind, the result is confusion and mental chaos. The mind is one of the easiest gateways to our entire lives, and we must guard our thought life diligently.

When a demon is beginning to infect a human mind, a number of things may occur: disorganized thinking, wicked impulses, raging headaches, grotesque or sexually perverted imagery, lies, mocking voices.

We were not created to be inhabited by evil. It is no wonder that most people who have been demonized and then set free describe the horrors of feeling like they were losing their minds. They were. Another mind was taking it over and imposing its will, wickedness and insanity on them.

What a relief to be set free! You can imagine the sense of gratefulness and peace that overcame the man of the tombs!

We all as believers fight this battle to one degree or another. It is a lifelong battle, but God has given us every tool we need to overcome the enemy's attacks.

A Transformed Mind

"And be not conformed to this world but be transformed by the renewing of your mind." (Romans 12:2)

A transformed mind is a safeguard against demonic intrusion.

The word "conformed" here means "molded to." Remember Silly Putty? It's like that; the soft substance molds to and mirrors and copies the object it surrounds or is pressed into.

Our minds are the silly putty, the soft substance, but more like clay.

Paul said, "See the world? Don't mold yourself to it. Don't look like it, act like it, or feel like it." And remember, clay can take on a form, but then it hardens. Don't let things get molded into your mind and then hardened to be like the world's image.

"But be transformed." The Greek word is *metamorphoo*. It's where we get the word metamorphosis. Like a butterfly, let the cocoon of the old life die and be "morphed" into a new creature in Christ.

I just recently saw a movie called *Metamorphosis* by Illustra Media which was a stunning scientific examination of the transformation from caterpillar to butterfly. This little creature enters the chrysalis and literally becomes soup – and from that soup, an altogether different DNA develops to form and create a butterfly. It was illustrated like a model T car putting a garage over itself, closing the doors, and then emerging as a helicopter. It's really more dramatic than that, but you get the picture.

That's what God wants to do with our mind. We come to Jesus filled with worldly ideas, human logic, fleshly ways of thinking, acting and feeling.

God's intention is to not let us be molded even more to the world, but to enter His chrysalis and become completely morphed into His altogether different species, a "new creation in Christ." (2 Cor. 5:17)

As different as a caterpillar is from a butterfly, so you need to be transformed to be different – utterly other – than the world.

The key to defeating satanic and demonic assaults in our minds is to stop conforming to the world and let God start transforming our minds by His Word and His Spirit. (Note: I am aware that the New Age and New Spirituality movements make frequent use of the words "transform" and "transformation." Let's not be afraid to use it in its Biblical context, since it is God that established it in His Word - not as some cosmic mind trick where we "transform" into "divine oneness," but transformation of our minds as a literal new creation miracle - and *only* to be had by surrendering to Jesus Christ as Lord, and through the power of His Word.)

So how do we accommodate this transformation, how do we nurture it, let it work? By daily prayer and fellowship with Jesus, by strength-building and challenging relationships with other believers, but most importantly, by the Word of God. "The entrance of thy words giveth light; it giveth understanding to the simple." (Psalm 119:130)

The power of the Word of God is the power that transforms our minds. It teaches us to think like God thinks, act like Jesus acts, and walk like He walks.

Satan hates truth. He is the father of lies. He warps our minds through the world, the media, social settings, ungodly activities and surroundings.
God has to repair us. You are transformed "by the renewing of your mind." The word "renew" is literally "renovate." It is the ultimate extreme home makeover in the house of our mind. Through the Word of God, Jesus comes in, throws out the spiritual trash, knocks down the useless and hurtful walls of rebellion and resistance, scrubs the rooms clean, then fills it with Himself and His Word.

There is a portion of scripture in Nehemiah that I think is very important here. Nehemiah had spent a long time rebuilding Jerusalem and restoring the Temple of the Lord. He had succeeded in running the enemy out and unifying the city. Then he returned back to Babylon to his regular job as the King's cupbearer. After a while, he returned to Jerusalem to find that Tobiah, one of his chief opponents to rebuilding, had convinced Eliashib to let him move his stuff into one of the rooms in the Temple of God. He was furious. "And it grieved me sore; therefore I cast forth all the household stuff of Tobiah out of the chamber." (Nehemiah 13:8)

We can be saved, Spirit-filled and on our way to Glory, but the enemy, like Tobiah, is just waiting for the opportunity to sneak all his junk back into our minds. We cannot let our guard down even for an instant. Eternal vigilance, as someone said, is the cost of freedom.

Before we come to Jesus we are blind:

"In whom the god of this world hath blinded the minds of them which believe not, lest the light of the glorious gospel of Christ, who is the image of God, should shine unto them." (2 Corinthians 4:4)

Satan is the "god of this world." But we are called to overthrow his authority over the prisoners that he has blinded, by bringing them out of captivity into the Kingdom of God. Our call as believers is to set the captives free. Until Jesus returns, we will be on the battlefield to claim souls for His Kingdom.

Without Christ, people's minds are blinded. Many people forget this very important element when they are evangelizing. Yes, know your Word – yes, strategize and get the right things ready - but you have to remember that when you are talking to someone about Jesus, they have been blinded by Satan. It takes prayer and the power of the Holy Spirit to lift that blindness so they can hear the truth and see Jesus.

Lately, the Evangelical church has become wrapped up in methods. We try to be "seeker friendly," we try to be careful not to offend, or we feel we have to "serve the world" to show them Jesus, or we want to "speak to the culture." We are so afraid of offending people or being called "haters" that we have turned ourselves into pretzels trying to figure out how to reach people. Jesus didn't preach any of that. He just said, "Go, preach the Good News, make disciples." We need less method and more prayer because Paul makes it clear that leading people to Jesus is a spiritual battle. Satan has blinded them, and he will resist any attempt to remove that veil from their eyes. It's not about clever methods or presentations. It's about giving the most clear, simple proclamation of Jesus' crucifixion, resurrection and need for repentance leading to eternal life that we possibly can. The blindness must first be removed.

Ungodly, unsaved minds think in corrupt, ungodly ways. "Because that, when they knew God, they glorified him not as God, neither were thankful;

but became futile in their thoughts, and their foolish heart was darkened." (Romans 1:21 NKJV) They become covered in darkness. Their minds are filled with darkness.

When it says that they became "futile in their thoughts", it means, "vain in their imaginations." Vain – profitless, passively empty. That is why Yoga and Eastern meditation are so dangerous – they teach you to empty your mind. Satan seeks a mind that is "passively empty." We are never to empty our minds as believers. We are to fill our minds with the Word of God and prayer.

"Vain in their imaginations" – the word imaginations or thoughts here is *"dialogismos"* from which we get the word dialogue – in other words, they became empty in their self-debates, hesitating, doubting. And so they became not only blind but covered in darkness.

"And even as they did not like to retain God in their knowledge, God gave them over to a reprobate mind, to do those things which are not convenient...." (Romans 1:28)

As unbelievers, our minds are surrendered to vain and profitless thoughts and become "reprobate." That word is "adokimos." It means useless. Disapproved. Castaway. Our minds become useless, simply following our base and sinful instincts. When we come to Jesus, we have a lot of work that needs to be done in changing all of that! That is called sanctification, and renewing or renovating our mind is what sanctification does. We start to think like Jesus and begin to put away those old ways of ungodly, worldly thinking and reasoning. When we begin to walk with Jesus and read His Word, we become aware that we've been thinking wrong. One short jaunt through the book of Proverbs will make you realize that your former ways of thinking and acting were completely wrong. Now we have to let His Word renovate us, tear down the old way of thinking and acting, and begin to do things His way.

This was clearly illustrated to me by the Holy Spirit when I was in Bible School. I loved to argue. I loved to debate. In fact, we would stay up half the night debating issues such as when the rapture would occur, whether you had to speak in tongues to be filled with the Holy Spirit, etc.

One night we were in the middle of a particularly ugly debate, and I was, in my prideful thinking, *winning*. It was almost a complete mouth-shutting victory, and I felt spiritually justified because I believed I was *right*.

Suddenly, the Word I had hidden in my heart came blazing into my mind: "Only by pride comes contention." (Proverbs 13:10a) My mouth dropped open, I began to stutter, and I just stopped and ended the debate. The Word of God had come roaring into the house of my mind and faced me with the plain truth that it was my pride that motivated me to argue, not God's Spirit! *That's* renovation. I had to let that Word cast down that ungodly way of thinking.

"Casting down imaginations, and every high thing that exalteth itself against the knowledge of God, and bringing into captivity every thought to the obedience of Christ." (2 Cor. 10:5)

The word "imaginations" is "arguments" and comes from the root word "*logismos*" – logic. Human logic. In other words, human ungodly logic is rooted in pride which exalts itself against God's truth. Ungodly human logic has to go. As believers, we must reject the ungodly logic and thinking that we learned in the world and learn to think according to the truth of God's Word.

That isn't easy, because our minds are used to thinking in ungodly ways. It doesn't change automatically. It happens by renovation, and also, according to this verse, by bringing our thoughts into captivity to obey Christ. In one translation, it says we must spear our thoughts and take them as prisoners of war to obey Jesus. We have to spear them. We have to recognize ungodly thoughts and ungodly logic and force them to surrender to the truth of God's Word.

We had an ungodly mind before we came to Christ, but as believers, we still wrestle with a carnal mind. It is the post-Christ un-transformed mind that is used to thinking in flesh ways, sinful ways. It is the reason so many of us are capable of such acts of love and worship on a Sunday and act like the world and the devil the rest of the week – they are still carnally minded. "Because the carnal mind is enmity against God: for it is not subject to the law of God, neither indeed can be." (Romans 8:7) Our flesh-driven thoughts are hostile to God. Those thoughts have to go and make way for thinking *His* way.

One of the ways the enemy tries to trip us up is by complicating our faith. Be careful of "deeper life club" type Christian movements, with complicated doctrines, hoops you have to jump through to have the right kind of faith or be healed, and numerous other complex teachings. Paul said, "But I fear, lest by any means, as the serpent beguiled Eve, so your minds should be corrupted from the simplicity that is in Christ." (2

Corinthians 11:3). The Gospel is simple. Don't let Satan make it complicated for you.

"And be renewed in the spirit of your mind." (Eph. 4:23) The word used here is also "renovated." God wants to do a top to bottom renovation. It is so important that we understand the radical difference between our pre-Jesus mind and our new birth mind. We are molded by everyone and everything around us into thinking certain ways. The world fills us with lies: Look out for #1; as long as it feels good and it doesn't hurt anybody, do it; all paths lead to God; all religions are the same, etc. These things are created and propagated from generation to generation by the father of lies – Satan - with the express purpose of keeping people separated from God.

Once we come to Jesus, we are confronted for the first time with the truth of God's Word vs. the lies of Satan and the world. And it can be very jarring.

When I first came to Christ, I believed, and told others, that all paths led to God. Our house Bible study leader sat me down and made me read what the Bible said on the subject: "I am the way, the truth and the life; no one comes to the Father except by me." (John 14:6) "Neither is there salvation in any other: for there is none other name under heaven given among men, whereby we must be saved." (Acts 4:12) I was shocked and angry.

I had to decide to either believe what Jesus and the Word of God said and throw away the lies I had believed all my life, or hang on to the lies and throw away the Word of God. I could feel the anger of rebellion welling up in my heart as I pondered this decision. When I decided to believe God's Word, it took the biggest chunk out of my occult-riddled worldview, and the dominos began to fall one by one. I replaced each of the lies I had been fed with the truth. And through His Word, God renovated my mind from an occult-addled, confused and fragile demonized mess into a mind that thought clearly for the first time in my life. It was nothing short of a miracle.

When I came to Jesus, one of the first things I had to face was my addiction to the occult. Although I had gotten rid of all the occult tools I used, I still had an "occult personality." My "occult powers" (which were in fact just demons that used me) had given me a sense of power, specialness, and importance. I could do things no one else could do. It was a powerful drug. I could not only use those "powers" to impress people, but scare them as well.

But when I surrendered my life to Jesus, I no longer had those "powers." I wasn't special anymore and I had nothing with which to command fear, respect, or even attention from others. I was a "nobody." I felt the emptiness in my mind and emotions, which were now void of the false sense of importance that the occult lies had given me. Now I just felt pain. I had no defense against it. But as I began to feed on the Word of God, He gave me comfort and a new identity. I was no longer someone who did the occult – I was a child of God. I no longer needed the occult power – I had the power of the Holy Spirit. In time, I would learn that I didn't need to "do" things to get people to love me or respect me. I made friends who just loved me because I was their brother in Jesus.

Layer by layer, Jesus began to renovate my mind and emotions. Some things were so deeply engraved in my personality that it took a great deal of renovation to change them. Forgive these personal examples, but having walked through these things, I think they may help you understand how it works.

When I was in my second semester of Bible School, God brought me under the care of a very discerning and caring Spirit filled Episcopal priest and his wife. He had watched me for several weeks before approaching me about teaching him guitar. (I was a part-time guitar instructor at the school.) But halfway through the first lesson, he told me the real reason he wanted to meet with me was that God had shown him how injured I was, and he wanted to pray for some healing to come into my life. I said yes. What followed were several excruciating weeks of facing the truth about myself.

My friend started by telling me to make a list of everything I had to be thankful for. My immediate reaction was, "Well, that won't take long." That's when I first became aware of how bitter and despondent I had become. And I began to wonder if that reaction in itself wasn't really me. It was a bitter response the enemy had been feeding me for some time.

I sat down to write that day, fully expecting to be done in a short minute or two. I just began with basics. 'Thank You I'm alive." (A cynical voice in my mind said, "As if I want to be.") "Thank you that I have friends." ("Even though they just tolerate me," the voice added.) "Thank you for my family. Thank you for my health. Thank you for Jesus." I just kept writing, and as I did, the cynical voice receded, and I found I had more and more things to thank God for. I ended up with several pages of things I was thankful for – and I was broken. "I am so sorry, Jesus," I prayed. "I've been so ungrateful." Suddenly, a lie was broken…the lie that I had nothing to be thankful for.

A lifetime of hurt, fear, and self-hatred had opened my mind and emotions to the ugly words of the enemy. I had just received them and became cynical and bitter. I just repeated the lies that Satan poured into my mind and heart. Soon they hardened like cement. Jesus, through His Word, broke through that hardness of heart, and through His love, set me free.

This spiritual exercise illustrates what the verse means about taking your thoughts captive. I had to spear these lies with the truth and take them prisoner and make them acknowledge the truth of God's goodness. Soon the big lies began to fall, and in time, so did all the little ones attached to them.

The battle for the mind includes many things. Jesus has to tear down pride, fear, doubt, rationalizing our sins, human logic that resists truth, self-hatred, unforgiveness, the many dark hiding places of lust, the cycle of depression fed by despair. It takes a deliberate choice to let the Word of Christ dwell in us richly, plant His Word into our minds and hearts, and allow it to grow the fruit of the Spirit in us – love, joy, peace, longsuffering, temperance, goodness, gentleness, meekness, faith. Yes, it will take time!

"But why can't God just snap His fingers and change how we think?" Well, we aren't computers. He can't just wipe our memories and download a new program. We are humans with hurts, sins, feelings, and histories. "Line upon line, precept upon precept" seems to be the way we learn – one thing at a time.

Secondly, our minds become hardened with ungodly thoughts and lies, and it takes time to un-harden us. I once heard an illustration that helped me to understand how this works. Imagine a hill on which rain falls for a long period of time. Eventually, rivulets form and run the water down the hill. The water continues to erode the soil, and the rivulets become rivers. The rains stop, the riverbeds dry, but the minute the rain falls again, it will flow right down that riverbed, because it's been dug into a channel that water will flow down.

That's how our minds work. When you receive the same words, thoughts, or lies over and over - even though you may at first resist them - eventually they will wear a "rut" in your thoughts. For example: If you grew up being told you are a loser, you may at first be hurt and reject it. But if it gets repeated over and over, eventually you will receive that lie and believe it to be true. It will run a rut right into your whole way of life, controlling your actions, relationships, and view of God. And even though it is a lie, all Satan has to do is whisper the lie in your ear and you will accept it, because you are used to it.

We have to recognize the lies that have molded our thinking, and that is why we must let Jesus "renovate" our minds by His Word. Simply, it is the battle of truth vs. lies, the lies we have received from the enemy vs. the truth of the Word of God.

I was challenged – and I challenge you – to begin this very simple practice that can be a mighty tool in God's hands to renovate your mind and deliver you from lies, false accusations and impressions, and many other flesh traps in your mind. Get a notebook. Spend some time with Jesus and His Word. On one side of the notebook paper, write down all the lies. Write down everything God brings to mind, whether they are attacks on your character, your sense of failure, thoughts of condemnation or fear. Write out the thoughts clearly, such as, "I have failed God. I can't be forgiven." On the other side, search and find the truth antidote to the lie. For example, "If we confess our sins, He is faithful and just to forgive us our sins and to cleanse us from all unrighteousness." (1 John 1:9) Then speak out that truth and renounce the lie in prayer. Do that for each and every lie you have written down.

Continue to speak the truth against the lies, until the truth goes way down into your heart and fills the cracks and ravines of lies in your mind and emotions. In time, you will be speaking only truth. The scriptures will defeat the lies, and you will begin to grow the fruit of the Spirit in your character and life. Everyone's lies and everyone's mental struggles with this are different. Take your time. Take as long as it takes. God is transforming you into His image and likeness. It will be well worth the battle.

It is important to know that we have a real enemy who has a large army of unclean spirits whose job it is to try to tear down the faith of believers and bring them to ruin. It is crucial that we discern our thoughts. The enemy and his forces can most definitely whisper all manner of thoughts into our ears. He can flash vile images in front of us, bring up past sins, whisper lies and say the most horrible things to hurt our faith, attempting to get us to own those thoughts. It is so important you understand this: **Just because a thought comes to you, doesn't mean it is yours or originated with you.**

It is a common experience that when someone sets their face to seek after God and His Word, their minds are suddenly barraged with all manner of evil thoughts, unclean thoughts, thoughts of hatred, rage, self-pity, you name it. Don't own the thoughts. They are not necessarily yours! When

Jesus was in the wilderness, Satan was right there to tempt him every way he could. Jesus answered each temptation with the truth of the Word of God. You must too.

We will fight this battle whether we want to or not. So get ready to fight. And remember, as someone once said, you can't keep the birds from flying over your head, but you can keep them from making a nest in your hair. Know that the thoughts will come. Just don't leave spiritual trash around for those demonic thoughts to feed on.

"For to be carnally minded is death, but to be spiritually minded is life and peace." (Romans 8:6) Keep your mind on the things of the Spirit. Feed on the Word of God, prayer, and fellowship. With them come life and peace. But if you feed the flesh, the result will be spiritual decay and death.

"Thou wilt keep Him in perfect peace whose mind is stayed on thee, because He trusteth in thee." (Isaiah 26:3)

FROM THE FRONTLINES: HOME AT LAST

"I always had two bullets with me," Johnny told me. "One for you, and one for Tim," referring to the leader of our at-risk youth ministry. He said he was always looking for an opportunity to "take a shot."

He was intimidated into coming to our Bible study. One of the high school girls who was recently saved and went to school with him invited him. "No way!" Johnny told her in front of everyone on a hiking trip. "I'm not going to some stupid Bible study!" "What's the matter?" she taunted. "Afraid of a little Bible study?" It was just enough to make him go!

Johnny was 17 and had already lived a lifetime of hell. Unwanted, given up to the foster system, he suffered inhumane treatment, was finally adopted, moved with his family to Germany where drugs, Satan worship, and the death of a friend scarred his heart almost beyond repair.

Johnny was deeply involved in the occult. And he was completely demonized.

He went with us on nearly every outing and event we had. But it was risky. Every time he went with us, things happened. Car problems. Flat tires. A freak wind that brought my car hood down on my head when I was checking the radiator.

Only much later did Johnny tell us that he had been working curses on us and enjoyed watching the chaos.

We took him with us to a Christian concert at our sister church. He growled at some people he was introduced to.

Later there was a failed deliverance in which one of the elders was rewarded with a ripped dress coat for his efforts to help!

Everything came to a head one Monday night. I was teaching the 15 or 20 kids in the living room, and Johnny was sitting on the floor right in front of me. While I was teaching, Johnny put both of his hands together in a "devil's horn" fashion. I let it go on for a while; then I couldn't take the disruption anymore. "Johnny, KNOCK IT OFF!" I told him, and he looked like I had pulled him out of a trance. "What?" Johnny said, genuinely confused. "I didn't do anything!"

I realized it wasn't him doing it.

After the meeting, I was busy talking to the kids, when one of our adult leaders grabbed me. "Johnny wants to receive Jesus!" "That's great," I said, a little skeptical. "But he wants YOU to pray for him!"

I felt terribly convicted because I realized he probably asked *me* to pray for him because he really didn't think that I cared about him. I was just always yelling at him. "Forgive me, Jesus," I prayed and went out to the big van where Johnny, the youth leader and two others were waiting.

There were no seats in the back of the van. So we just sat on the floor in a circle, and I began to explain to Johnny how to receive Jesus. He was ready, he said.

"Jesus, I know you died for me," I led.

"Jesus, I know you died for me," he repeated with great difficulty.

"Jesus, I know I'm a sinner," I continued.

"Jesus, I know I'm NOT A SINNER!" the demon growled through him, and Johnny was completely taken over.

He suddenly began to slither around the van like a snake. We tried to restrain him. He bit through the leather glove of one of our leaders.

We prayed and bound the demon until we could get Johnny to speak again.

"Jesus come into my heart," I continued to try to lead him.

"Je-Je-Je-NOOOOOOO!" it screamed, and it went on and on.

"What am I missing, Father?" I prayed. It suddenly came to me.

"Johnny, renounce the blood oath you made to Satan," I told him.

"NOOOOO!!!!" the demon screamed, and I knew this was it.

With great difficulty, Johnny renounced his blood oath. The demon wrenched his body, growled, screamed, tried to get Johnny to physically escape us…and then Johnny went completely limp. We waited for a moment, praying that it was done. It was. We stood back in awe as he prayed and asked Jesus into his heart to be his Lord and Savior.

My partner was holding him from behind. Johnny began to cry quietly. "I just want a home. I just want to belong." Gone was the sense of evil, the demonic torment, the wrenching, screaming, and horrific battle. It was done. God returned to us a child of God who was free to experience all God had ahead for him without the bondage of darkness he had known all his short life.

After more prayer and words of encouragement, we all exited the van. Johnny was SHINING. Every one of the kids who knew him just looked at him, and they *knew* Jesus had set him free.

It was not an easy road. He had much healing to endure and many challenges to face.

But I am thankful to report that he still loves Jesus with all his heart and has been blessed with a family, children and all the good things of life God wanted for him.

He finally found a home in Jesus. He finally found a place to belong.

'There is no neutral ground in the universe; every square inch, every split second, is claimed by God and counter-claimed by Satan.

- C.S. Lewis

5 ORIGINS PART 1

Where did Satan come from? Where did demons come from?

These are very serious and in a way inscrutable questions. God did not come right out and say specifically in His Word in the way that other events are told – the birth of Moses, the missionary journeys of Paul, for example. But we know two things by scripture – there is a real Satan, an adversary, and both Old Testament and New Testament are full of references to him, as well as demons. In the church, his existence is mainly questioned by apostate seminary professors who excel in tearing down the Word of God, and by the fearful that believe if they just whistle in the dark and pretend he's not real and that the scriptures about him are just stories, they have nothing to be afraid of.

But the ultimate proof of his existence is that (1) the scriptures reference him and his activities in many, many places, and (2) his ongoing activities are very plain to see in our world if one is brave enough to look for the truth.

There are also two very crucial passages in the Word that give what I believe to be clear references to, and indications of the nature of, the one we call Satan, the Adversary. As with many portions of scripture, these passages point to something or someone beyond their initial reference. The Psalms are full of such references, where David speaks in the first person or about personal events, but then the verse points to a coming event in the life of the Messiah to come.

In the same way, these two passages we will look at will start at one level then project outside of that parameter.

To expand on this a little, there are four levels of studying scripture according to Jewish teaching. (1) Peshat – the plain meaning of the passage. (2) Remez – hints, deeper meaning, allegoric or symbolic (3) Derash – as in, a sermon taken from the passage – and (4) Sod – the secret meaning.

It is my thought that these two scriptures contain all of these elements, and with that understanding, we can get the "big picture" of who our enemy is and where he comes from.

The Ezekiel Picture

"Son of man, take up a lamentation upon the king of Tyrus, and say unto him, Thus saith the Lord God; Thou sealest up the sum, full of wisdom, and perfect in beauty. Thou hast been in Eden the garden of God; every precious stone was thy covering, the sardius, topaz, and the diamond, the beryl, the onyx, and the jasper, the sapphire, the emerald, and the carbuncle, and gold: the workmanship of thy tabrets and of thy pipes was prepared in thee in the day that thou wast created. Thou art the anointed cherub that covereth; and I have set thee so: thou wast upon the holy mountain of God; thou hast walked up and down in the midst of the stones of fire. Thou wast perfect in thy ways from the day that thou wast created, till iniquity was found in thee. By the multitude of thy merchandise they have filled the midst of thee with violence, and thou hast sinned: therefore I will cast thee as profane out of the mountain of God: and I will destroy thee, O covering cherub, from the midst of the stones of fire. Thine heart was lifted up because of thy beauty, thou hast corrupted thy wisdom by reason of thy brightness: I will cast thee to the ground, I will lay thee before kings, that they may behold thee. Thou hast defiled thy sanctuaries by the multitude of thine iniquities, by the iniquity of thy traffick; therefore will I bring forth a fire from the midst of thee, it shall devour thee, and I will bring thee to ashes upon the earth in the sight of all them that behold thee. All they that know thee among the people shall be astonished at thee: thou shalt be a terror, and never shalt thou be any more."(Ezekiel 28:12-19)

What began apparently as a judgment on the King of Tyre (or perhaps speaking of the real "king" ruling Tyre, or both) seems to lift our eyes higher to another judgment - the first one - the one on the Adversary. There are several things we can glean from these verses about our enemy:

- He was originally full of wisdom and beautiful.
- He was in Eden (as the serpent).
- He was covered with precious gems.
- It appears that his body was fashioned for worship and music. Some have speculated that he actually led worship in heaven. This is possible. One thing is sure: He knows music well enough to have used it to turn people away from God, and his creativity is seemingly unending in this department. I have always lamented the inability of Christians to tap into God's unlimited creativity in this regard, being satisfied to be derivative rather than supernaturally creative with music: "They sound just like (fill in secular band name)" rather than being unlike anything that's EVER been done.
- He was a covering cherub. Cherubim were in the presence of God,

and they were guardians. Our Adversary once guarded the precious things of God, including possibly music.
- Iniquity was found in him. He became enamored of his own beauty; he fell in love with himself, apparently.

The Isaiah Picture

"How art thou fallen from heaven, O Lucifer, son of the morning! how art thou cut down to the ground, which didst weaken the nations! For thou hast said in thine heart, I will ascend into heaven, I will exalt my throne above the stars of God: I will sit also upon the mount of the congregation, in the sides of the north: I will ascend above the heights of the clouds; I will be like the most High. Yet thou shalt be brought down to hell, to the sides of the pit." (Isaiah 14:12-15)

This is the one scriptural reference to the Adversary by his "given name" – Lucifer – light-bearer. From these verses, we learn that:

- He is a destroyer of nations.
- He wanted to be higher than God.

This passage also gives us a reference to the first sin ever committed. It wasn't Adam and Eve eating the forbidden fruit. It was Lucifer, and the first sin was pride. This should give us serious pause about our tendency to categorize sins into "greater and lesser" with the most obvious – or personally distasteful – sins getting top billing. Pride appears to be the one that is above most others. In Obadiah 6, we read, "The pride of thine heart hath deceived thee." Pride makes us blind to our own sinfulness and depravity.

"I will…" Self-will is the genesis of all sin. It destroyed all Lucifer was, and it will do the same to us if we do not crucify self-will. What a contrast to Jesus, the Son of Adam, who cried, "Nevertheless, not *my* will but *thine* be done."

"I will," Lucifer defiantly cried, and lost it all. A number of years ago, I was heavily involved in extracting young people out of the occult. One of the biggest stumbling blocks we encountered was the Church of Satan, a group that built everything they did on antichristian ideals. Anton Lavey, the founder, wrote a book called *The Satanic Bible* that had as its founding principle a declaration by this last century's most notorious black magick practitioner, Aleister Crowley: "Do what thou wilt shall be the whole of the law." In other words, being a true follower of Satan is simply a matter of rebelling against everything God's law forbids and living a totally selfish, self-centered lifestyle free of God's rules.

It sounds pretty extreme, doesn't it? But one night we were doing a teaching for a church on occultism and the Bible, and my co-teacher brought up the "do as you will" principle of the church of Satan. Then he shocked the entire church by telling them if they lived their life by their own will, rather than complete submission to the will of God, they were no better than Satanists, since they were living by the law of "do what you will." It was hard to argue with that! It made everyone re-examine how they were living their lives, realizing that "I will" in defiance of or in disregard to GOD'S will, plants us right in the center of the Adversary's will. Our life must always reflect Jesus' "Thy will, not mine" of the garden of Gethsemane to defeat the "my will, not Thine" of our flesh.

Satan may still think he's Lucifer. Sin will completely deceive you like that. And there are hundreds of thousands of his followers worldwide who also believe he is the light-bearer and the rightful ruler of the universe. Many of them are in extremely powerful political and financial positions. Their agenda is to completely demolish the Christian worldview, and establish a secular one in which all religions are "tolerated" (except for Jews and Christians) and Lucifer is secretly worshipped as the ruler of this world.

As we know, in the end, he will be destroyed. But for now, he's still at work, and that is why we must be prepared and trained to engage him.

Next, we need to look at our Adversary's appearance in the book of Genesis.

The Eden Picture

In the first pages of Genesis, we find the first lie and the second sin:

"Now the serpent was more cunning than any beast of the field which the Lord God had made. And he said to the woman, 'Has God indeed said, "You shall not eat of every tree of the garden"?'" (Genesis 3:1)

Genesis 3:1 is really the key to understanding all of Satan's lies. "Did God really say?" He didn't outright call God a liar; she wouldn't fall for that. No, this was far more subtle. He was saying, "Eve, is that what God really said? Really?" He was planting the idea that maybe she had misunderstood God's command forbidding her to eat the fruit from the tree of knowledge of good and evil.

This is crucial to understanding almost everything about deception, especially spiritual deception in the church in this hour. Almost every departure from sound doctrine, Biblical faith, and solid truth has come from those who approached scriptures that they objected to or that did not make sense to their human mind, and rather than just accepting it as God's Word and living accordingly, they began to seek "alternate interpretations and explanations." In the process, they ended up distorting the truth to fit their human, sin-twisted perceptions. Over the years, I have heard and seen every kind of distortion of the Word of God, from making God into a woman, to God approving of gay relationships, to rewriting God's promises to Israel to make them now exclusively meant for the church, to finding "scriptural permission" to talk to the dead, to justifying premarital sex, to reinterpreting the clear scriptures concerning the return of Jesus and the events of the last days. All of these evil distortions were built on the original lie: "Is that what God really said? Maybe you just misinterpreted it…"

But there is a deeper level to this original lie, as you can see when you read further: "And the woman said to the serpent, 'We may eat the fruit of the trees of the garden; but of the fruit of the tree which is in the midst of the garden, God has said, 'You shall not eat it, nor shall you touch it, lest you die.'" (Genesis 3:2-3 NKJV)

What happened here? Eve gave her interpretation: God said they couldn't eat it or touch it. But there is no record that God said they could not touch it. *She* added that. Something in her heart was already at work, distorting God's Word to them. That is how subtle a lie can be. It begins to distort your perception of God and His Word. All it takes is just a little shading, a little twist.

Big lies and deceptions in the church didn't start as big lies. They started just the way that I described above. Something in our sinful nature refuses and rebels against God's clear Word. So we decide to change it, just a little. For example, "Be ye not unequally yoked together with unbelievers: for what fellowship hath righteousness with unrighteousness? and what communion hath light with darkness?" (2 Cor. 6:14) This is a real challenge for young people who are believers. It means – plainly - that you should not seek a life partner who is an unbeliever. How much clearer can this be? And yet, a few years ago, I found a "seasoned" Christian telling young people that this really referred to business relationships. I was dumbfounded. He had actually deceived himself into thinking God cared more that we are not unequally joined with a business partner, than that we are not spiritually joined with a spouse who doesn't know Jesus. But the desire of many Christians to justify rushing out and marrying an unbeliever has often caused them to twist the scriptures to say that it doesn't apply the way it plainly states. **It's very easy to make the scriptures say what you want them to say if you are determined to justify what you want to do.**

Apparently, there was a similar problem in the days of Peter, as he wrote:

"And account that the longsuffering of our Lord is salvation; even as our beloved brother Paul also according to the wisdom given unto him hath written unto you; As also in all his epistles, speaking in them of these things; in which are some things hard to be understood, which they that are unlearned and unstable wrest, **as they do also the other scriptures**, (emphasis mine) unto their own destruction." (2 Peter 3:15-16)

Even then, people were twisting (wresting) the scriptures they thought too hard to understand and brought destruction down on their heads.

There was an old expression that is true and wise to this day – **God said it; I believe it; that settles it.** Live by that, and deception won't have a chance to twist your view of the Word of God.

The serpent saw a soft spot of vulnerability in Eve and he went for it. "And the serpent said unto the woman, Ye shall not surely die: For God doth know that in the day ye eat thereof, then your eyes shall be opened, and ye shall be as gods, knowing good and evil."

Satan's mask finally comes off. First, he planted the seed of doubt. Then, Eve made up her own version of God's will, and now he outright accuses God of lying:

This is where Eve – and then Adam – and then all of us – fell. With this simple method, he succeeded with them – as he does with us – in getting them to:

- Doubt God's love
- Doubt God's goodness
- Doubt God's wisdom
- Trust their own wisdom and knowledge

Eve ate; Adam ate. Sin entered, and we died.

Then came the beginning of all blame-shifting in history:

"Then the man said, 'The woman whom You gave to be with me, she gave me of the tree, and I ate.' And the Lord God said to the woman, 'What is this you have done?' The woman said, 'The serpent deceived me, and I ate.'" (Genesis 3:12-13)

Blame shifting is another fruit of sin and deception. Immediately after this act of disobedience by Adam and Eve, they sought someone else to blame to avoid the truth. Later in scripture, we will read of King Saul doing this when He disobeyed God:

"Then Samuel went to Saul, and Saul said to him, 'Blessed are you of the Lord! I have performed the commandment of the Lord.' But Samuel said, 'What then is this bleating of the sheep in my ears, and the lowing of the oxen which I hear?' And Saul said, 'They have brought them from the Amalekites; for the people spared the best of the sheep and the oxen, to sacrifice to the Lord your God; and the rest we have utterly destroyed.'" (1 Samuel 15:13-15)

But the command was to destroy *everything*. He said, in essence, "The people made me do it." His disobedience cost him the Kingdom.

God's way is never to blame someone else. David said, "Against You and You alone have I sinned and done this evil in Your sight: That You may be found just when You speak, and blameless when You judge."(Psalm 51:4) The man crying out for mercy in the temple said, "God be merciful to me, a sinner." (Luke 18:13) Blaming others leads to self-pity and will cripple our walk. But when you take responsibility for your own heart and say, "God be merciful to me, a sinner," then that brings God's mercy and forgiveness. Jesus said of the man in the temple that he went back home justified rather than the Pharisee that just came to brag about how much better he was than everyone else.

This secondary fruit of sin - blaming others - can be seen in every level of society. Children blame their parents; spouses blame the other spouse; people blame the government, law enforcement, schools, movies, and so forth. People are saying that people kill because of too many guns, because of society, movies, bad parents, Twinkies, drugs, you name it. And yes, things do contribute to acts of violence. But what is really behind it? Sin. Without Christ, people are controlled by their sin nature, and they will do horrendous things: Murder, rape, abuse, steal, lie, cheat on their spouse, hit their kids, molest innocent children, become proud, arrogant religious people, all the above. Ultimately, I cannot point the finger at anyone and say, "You made me do this." I am ultimately the one that must account for what I do.

What does this have to do with Satan and spiritual warfare? Simple. He loves the blame game. He has created a whole cottage industry around it. No one is really to blame for anything; we are merely a product of our environment and upbringing. Many psychologists and sociologists believe if you change the behavior, you can change the person. But the fact is, you can modify behavior and never change the heart at all.

When I was training criminal justice classes on child sexual abuse, I pointed out the absurdity of giving a pedophile a reduced sentence for good behavior because "the person had not exhibited pedophile behavior" in prison. That's because there are no children in prison to act out on. The good behavior was due to lack of accessibility, not lack of desire. Most of the time, the minute they were returned to society, the heart of sin kicked back in and they returned to their old behavior.

Yes, people are sinned against, and that often creates damage that makes it easier for that person to act out and do horrendous things. God takes all that into account. But until we stop blaming others for how we turned out and why we act out, then we will never get delivered. Satan will gladly keep you bound your entire life blaming others for why you are what and who you are, and why you do what you do. Jesus wants to stop that madness, shine the light of truth into your own heart, and get you to pray, "I have done this. I'm the one responsible." Full confession, full forgiveness. May God give us the grace to deny the sinful desire to blame others - which only reinforces the sin nature in us - and come broken to the cross and let Him set us free from our sins.

There is a great deal of mystery concerning the serpent that spoke to Eve. Some liberal scholars have deemed this allegory, but it is literal, though not in the sense that we understand what every part means. Eden was in a place unlike any we can understand. There were no barriers in Adam and Eve's relationship with God. The creatures had not yet fallen under a curse.

And although there are things we don't understand, we *can* ascertain some certainties. The serpent was, or was inhabited by, Satan. The root word for serpent here – nachash – is a word often tied to divination, observation, knowledge through experience (in this case, the tree of knowledge of good and evil that the serpent wanted them to eat of.) In the Arabic root khanasa, it means someone or something that "draws away" or seduces. From that root word also comes the Arabic word for "devil."

We know that Eve was neither surprised by nor afraid of the serpent. It was apparently something she was familiar with. When the scriptures speak of the "fiery serpents" that poisoned the Israelites in the wilderness, the word is "seraph nachash" – the word seraph is a beautiful flying serpent. This is where the word seraphim comes from, an angelic creature that serves God. Thus, it is not a stretch to suppose the serpent was something Eve was familiar with, had no reason to mistrust, and was beautiful and persuasive.

We don't know for sure, but what we do know is that he was the first manifestation of Lucifer/Satan in the scriptures. From that point on after the fall, one of the most prevalent false gods and idols that were worshipped was the serpent. The dragon is also a classic pagan god, and the book of Revelation is the bookend of this mysterious etiology of the devil, as it speaks of him: "So the great dragon was cast out, that serpent of old, called the Devil and Satan, who deceives the whole world; he was cast to the earth, and his angels were cast out with him." (Revelation 12:9)

Someone wrote, "He started as a serpent in Eden, and ended as a dragon in Revelation. Someone's been feeding that thing!"

Dragon means "a fabulous, fascinating kind of serpent." It also is an alternate form of "to look." In other words, this was an angelic evil creature that had sharp vision, could fascinate and seduce people, and was a great serpent or seraphim, but still nothing but a snake down here. From his fall to the end, his goal was to "deceive the whole world." Deception is his worldwide goal, and only One could conquer him.

The promise after the curse of sin is that, "I will put enmity between you and the woman, and between your seed and her Seed; He shall bruise your head, and you shall bruise His heel." (Genesis 3:15) Satan's seed – those who were cast out of heaven with him, and perhaps those that serve him on earth – would be defeated by Eve's bloodline – her seed – the Seed that became Jesus the Messiah, who, although Satan bruised his heel by crucifying him, crushed his head when He rose from the dead in paying for our redemption.

And he's been furious about it ever since. Thus, the mockery of Jesus, the scholars determined to say he wasn't real or wasn't God's Son, thus the blasphemy and the determination to remove Him and His followers from the world square so he can proclaim himself to be god at the very last. (He's not. His "reign" will be quite short.)

I really don't think Satan wanted Jesus to go to the cross. I don't think he had the insight or foresight, with all his Seraph "sharp vision" to know where all this was going. I believe one of the reasons that the prophecies concerning Messiah, especially in Isaiah concerning his suffering, were so inscrutable even to the best Jewish Rabbis, is because God kept the master plan veiled until it was accomplished. Only after the Resurrection could all those scriptures make perfect sense in the light of Jesus' fulfillment of them. I do not think it was in Satan's plan to crucify Jesus. In fact, his plan was to get him to serve him. We will read more about that later. I don't think he knew exactly what Jesus was up to. But when the Son of God made determined moves to go, not away from suffering, but toward it, and when He announced His intention to actually go to the cross, Satan couldn't have understood what it all meant. But he knew if Jesus was determined to go to the cross, it was going to be bad for the kingdom of darkness. I think that Jesus' words to Peter, "Get thee behind me Satan!"(Matthew 6:23) was Jesus' recognizing that the devil was trying to keep him from the Cross.

When the suffering of Jesus finally commenced, I am sure that Satan in his mad rage reveled in making him suffer and be humiliated. He couldn't help himself. But he couldn't have known that His death and resurrection meant his complete undoing. And that is what it meant.

The Seed finally bruised the serpent's head. And the call since then is for every believer to grasp and take hold of that victory and authority, and never again allow the enemy to bruise our heels!

The nearer we come to God, the thicker the hosts of darkness in heavenly places. The safe place lies in obedience to God's Word, singleness of heart and holy vigilance. When Christians speak of standing in a place where they do not need to watch, they are in great danger.

- A.B. Simpson

6 ORIGINS PART 2

The Job Mention

Next, we want to look at Job and his encounter with evil. Job has been thought to be perhaps the oldest book in the Bible. This story is a crucial and clear glimpse into the sinister nature of our enemy and how he works to destroy the people of God. You can clearly see his hatred, his mockery of God and his desire to see man suffer.

"Now there was a day when the sons of God came to present themselves before the LORD, and Satan also came among them. And the LORD said to Satan, 'From where do you come?' So Satan answered the Lord and said, 'From going to and fro on the earth, and from walking back and forth on it.' Then the Lord said to Satan, 'Have you considered My servant Job, that there is none like him on the earth, a blameless and upright man, one who fears God and shuns evil?' So Satan answered the Lord and said, 'Does Job fear God for nothing? Have You not made a hedge around him, around his household, and around all that he has on every side? You have blessed the work of his hands, and his possessions have increased in the land. But now, stretch out Your hand and touch all that he has, and he will surely curse You to Your face!' And the Lord said to Satan, 'Behold, all that he has is in your power; only do not lay a hand on his person.' So Satan went out from the presence of the Lord." (Job 1:6-12)

It would take another whole book to go through all the implications of this account. Satan goes on to destroy all of Job's property and take all of his family, except for his wife. Then he afflicts his body in suffering that was excruciating.

But let's look at the malignant being that was the instigator of his suffering. Some very key things can be learned here.

1. The "sons of God" (The Old Testament spoke almost exclusively of angels when using this term) presented themselves before God. "And Satan also," indicating that he too had to account to God, but he was not the same as them – likely an indication that he was a ruler among them, not just one of them.

2. You can see his ugly heart and bitter spirit when he essentially says, "Nobody serves you for nothing. Job is only serving you because you have

made his life so easy. Take all that away; then you'll see the real Job!" He's like a lot of bitter people I know who are cynical about everything. They trust no one. Their words are sarcastic and poisonous. The more our words are filled with these characteristics, the more we are like Satan and not Jesus. It's an important test I think. Jesus said, "Assuredly, I say to you, whoever does not receive the kingdom of God as a little child will by no means enter it." (Luke 18:17) Children are innocent, trusting, wide-eyed in faith and free of bitter sarcasm and cynicism. We must strive to have that child heart in the Father's Kingdom.

3. God permitted this test. But He did not cause the loss, or the sickness or death. This is important because I know a lot of Christians that, when something horrible happens like a death or a terrible illness, say, "It must be God's will." But God is not the author of death or disease. He is the healer. God allowed Satan to do what was in his twisted heart to do – what he always does – kill, steal and destroy. (John 10:10)

Remember that Satan is on a leash. He cannot indiscriminately do what he wants. He too accounts to God. He is limited.

Then why does he have such a powerful presence and influence on this earth? Why are destruction and death everywhere? When Adam sinned in the garden, he essentially signed over this planet's rulership to Satan for the duration. It is all about free will. When man, by his sin, disobeys and disinvites God out of his world, then the enemy has legal right to come in and take what he wants. But even that is limited. Part of that limitation, and the very crucial part of our work is that he is restrained, limited and bound by the prayers of the saints and by their active presence in this world, and around those who are in darkness. We are God's agents to retake the spiritual territory that the enemy has taken for himself.

Also, remember that no matter how much leeway Satan was allowed in Job's life, the end of Job's life was blessing, and God was vindicated. Job is the ultimate proof of Romans 8:28: God is at work in *all* things to produce good! He is not the author of evil, or sickness, or death, but He *is* the redeemer of all things for the believer. And that makes Satan furious.

No matter what your trial, remember that if you keep your eyes fixed on Jesus and trust in His love and faithfulness, He will see you through, make you strong, and turn your trials into gold. He promised He would!

The Daniel Verses

There are two very crucial passages in the book of Daniel that address spiritual warfare and the reality of the invisible battle that we face. The first is in Daniel 8:15-17:

"Then it happened, when I, Daniel, had seen the vision and was seeking the meaning, that suddenly there stood before me one having the appearance of a man. And I heard a man's voice between the banks of the Ulai, who called, and said, 'Gabriel, make this man understand the vision.' So he came near where I stood, and when he came I was afraid and fell on my face; but he said to me, 'Understand, son of man, that the vision refers to the time of the end.'"

This is the first glimpse into the work of what we have come to refer to as an archangel. Different from other kinds of angels, they are apparently the Generals in God's army. Jewish belief is that Michael stands on one side of God, and Gabriel on the other. What we do know is that Gabriel is mentioned twice in the book of Daniel, and twice in the book of Luke, when he spoke to Mary and then to Zechariah. He was a messenger of God. He had the appearance of a man. Angels either look much like humans or can take on their appearance. Certainly, they do not *all* look like us. Note the frightening depiction of an angel in Ezekiel:

"Now as I looked at the living creatures, behold, a wheel was on the earth beside each living creature with its four faces. The appearance of the wheels and their workings was like the color of beryl, and all four had the same likeness. The appearance of their workings was, as it were, a wheel in the middle of a wheel." (Ezekiel 1:15-16)

As I said before, one should be careful telling God that you want to see an angel. You may get to and regret that you asked!

As we look at the next glimpses into spiritual conflict and revelation in Daniel, we're going to understand something about engaging in spiritual warfare:

"On the twenty-fourth day of the first month, as I was standing on the bank of the great river, the Tigris, I looked up and there before me was a man dressed in linen, with a belt of fine gold from Uphaz around his waist. His body was like topaz, his face like lightning, his eyes like flaming torches, his arms and legs like the gleam of burnished bronze, and his voice like the sound of a multitude. I, Daniel, was the only one who saw the vision; those who were with me did not see it, but such terror overwhelmed them that they fled and hid themselves. So I was left alone, gazing at this great vision; I had no strength left, my face turned deathly pale and I was helpless. Then I heard him speaking, and as I listened to him, I fell into a deep sleep, my face to the ground. (Daniel 10:4-9)

Notice that:

1. Even though Daniel was the only one who saw the vision, everyone else was affected by what was happening. Spiritual warfare is not a game, and when you are truly in the middle of a spiritual battle, it will affect you. These men felt a great terror because even though they did not know what was happening, the presence of heavenly warriors was affecting the very atmosphere they were in. In almost every instance of encounters with angels in the scriptures, the reaction is not like we see in many circles, where people are jumping, screaming, manifesting weird things such as barking like dogs, roaring or slithering like snakes. (That shows me that God's angels are not being manifested, but some other spirit is.)

No, when God's angels show up, the reaction is almost universally the same – the fear of God – falling on their faces – a sense of terror – wanting to hide their faces.

Now, some may say, "Well, that's the Old Testament. We're under grace." Yes. But God does not change. He is still holy beyond our ability to grasp, and His presence is awesome and awe-full. When Peter, James, and John saw Jesus transfigured and speaking with Moses and Elijah, Peter was so unnerved and afraid that he just blurted out, "It's great to be here! Do you want me to make tents for you?" They had been praying, and it says they were "heavy with sleep" – very similar to what Daniel experienced in his encounter.

"Then it happened, as they were parting from Him, that Peter said to Jesus, 'Master, it is good for us to be here; and let us make three tabernacles: one for You, one for Moses, and one for Elijah'—not knowing what he said."

After Peter blurted out this suggestion, "a cloud came and overshadowed them; **and they were fearful** as they entered the cloud." (Luke 9:33-34) [emphasis mine].

Now *that* sounds like a true spiritual encounter, not like much of the circus-like atmosphere some claim is the Holy Spirit.

Even when John - the disciple closest to Jesus - saw the glorified Jesus, he said, "I fell at his feet as dead." (Revelation 1:17) The experience was just that overwhelming.

2. Daniel's encounter with this raw spiritual world affected him to the degree that he had no physical strength left. "My vigor was turned to frailty in me." "I retained no strength." Entering the true arena of the raw spiritual world can be by nature draining and cause one to tremble.

Just the presence of the Holy Spirit, by and large, does not do this; but when God truly begins to *pour out* His Holy Spirit in a gathering or in a church, things like this can occur. Every true Holy Spirit revival over the centuries came with a sense of fear and awe so powerful that people often spent entire nights till dawn on their faces before our Holy God, trembling and weeping.

The debate about "falling out" under the power of God has been largely muddied by the excesses and the professional "pushers" and "catchers" of the last few decades in Spirit-filled circles. I myself have been shoved over on many occasions until I finally decided not to allow either emotional persuasion or forceful hands to cause me to fall. But I have also experienced the real thing. There have been times I have been in prayer meetings that the power of the Holy Spirit literally short-circuited me to where I either fell or just sat in a corner, unable to get up without assistance. What else would you expect from being in the presence of such a Mighty God?

We have unfortunately made a "thing" of falling, and now many people are *expected* to fall when they are prayed for. We must be very careful not to "fall prey" to emotional experiences. The real thing is enough. If one researches revivals throughout history, they will find two things: One, falling out was common. Two, bizarre, ungodly manifestations always crept into every true revival. So we must be careful not to deny God's Spirit, and at the same time, be bold enough to stop and root out the demonic weirdness that Satan tries to manifest to attempt to discredit the true work of God.

I am aware, as you should be, that there is a demonic counterpart and counterfeit to the "laying on of hands" or "impartation" in the Hindu world called "Shaktipat." It is the "conferring of spiritual energy upon one person by another through a word, a look, or a touch." And the reactions of those under that demonic influence look *identical* to much of the extreme Charismatic manifestations such as uncontrolled laughter, barking, convulsing, etc. We need to be discerning and careful. There *is* a counterfeit.

But there is also a legitimate laying on of hands in scripture – to heal, to commission, to anoint with the Spirit of God. Be careful not to throw out the real just because there is a false.

I understand why God only showed Moses part of Himself. The scriptures say, "Our God is a consuming fire." (Hebrews 12:29) Jesus had to redeem us with His blood before we could ever be capable of standing in His presence.

"Come boldly before His throne of grace." Yes, absolutely, but also come with reverent fear. Come with the understanding that without His blood, we could not come at all.

Why the need to point out these effects of real angelic encounters, the presence of the Spirit of God and the raw spiritual world Daniel, Peter and John witnessed? Because when you engage in true spiritual warfare, *it takes a toll*. Just being in the presence of God or the angelic has a physical effect; that much is scripturally clear. But when you take up spiritual weapons alongside God's warriors and engage in the warfare Paul speaks of, it is not bloodless, it is not fun, and it is not without cost. It will *cost* you to do real spiritual warfare. That is why I sincerely question some who treat it like it was a sport, or a game, or something fun to do. It can be treacherous and dangerous.

I remember in the 1980s at the height of the popularity of the spiritual warfare teaching that Christian bookstores sold little plastic David and Goliath armor sets. I am afraid far too many Christians think of spiritual warfare like that – safe, bloodless, and without difficulty. Not so. We are not given the armor for decoration. It is for war. It is not a fake or pretend war. It is not a war if there is no genuine conflict and cost. I don't mean to scare you, but I'd rather scare you out of taking on spiritual warfare foolishly than be responsible for your downfall because you missed this part of the class!

"But the Bible says we have the victory!" Absolutely. If we are in Christ, we are guaranteed heaven, and all the promises of the Word of God are ours. But we are to take that victory that we have into the arena where darkness rules, and if you think it will yield without a battle, you don't know thing one about true warfare. So as you prepare to armor up, please understand this: *This is a real war.* You cannot let down your armor.

The second section of Daniel is where one of my favorite creations of God comes in - Michael, one of God's Chief Generals in battle:

"And, behold, a hand touched me, which set me upon my knees and upon the palms of my hands. And he said unto me, O Daniel, a man greatly beloved, understand the words that I speak unto thee, and stand upright: for unto thee am I now sent. And when he had spoken this word unto me, I stood trembling. Then said he unto me, Fear not, Daniel: for from the first day that thou didst set thine heart to understand, and to chasten thyself before thy God, thy words were heard, and I am come for thy words. But the prince of the kingdom of Persia withstood me one and twenty days: but, lo, Michael, one of the chief princes, came to help me; and I remained there with the kings of Persia. Now I am come to make thee understand what shall befall thy people in the latter days: for yet the vision is for many days." (Daniel 10:10-14).

We are not told who is speaking to Daniel here: It might have been Gabriel, we simply do not know. But they explain clearly that there was a battle to get Daniel's prayer answer to him. The messenger of the Lord was being fought to keep that answer away from Daniel caused by another "Prince" what Paul referred to as a principality. That prince's assignment was over Persia. Michael came to help the unidentified messenger break through to get the message to Daniel.

I think we can make far too much of "Well, that was the Old Testament" without understanding that though Jesus came to destroy the works of the devil, that work is ongoing, and when you step into the world of spiritual warfare and battle between the heavenly warriors both godly and hellish, the battle still rages. I am greatly encouraged by the fact that prayer is a battle to wrest territory from Satan and his servants, and often, the lack of immediate results or answers may have nothing to do with my praying wrongly, or God not caring. I am encouraged to know my prayer was heard the moment I prayed. But the answers may have to be brought through a battle in the heavenlies. Press on and press in! God's warriors are on your side!

Here is the next mention of Michael:

"Then he said, 'Do you know why I have come to you? And now I must return to fight with the prince of Persia; and when I have gone forth, indeed the prince of Greece will come. But I will tell you what is noted in the Scripture of Truth. (No one upholds me against these, except Michael your prince.)'" (Daniel 10:20-21)

Again, it is a picture of Michael at war. He is clearly a warrior angel.

The New Testament makes mention of him twice as well: Once in Jude, in this rather mysterious passage:

"Yet Michael the archangel, in contending with the devil, when he disputed about the body of Moses, dared not bring against him a reviling accusation, but said, 'The Lord rebuke you!'" (Jude 1:9)

We are told nothing about this fight, but the writer assumes his Jewish readers knew, so whatever it was about, it is lost to our modern understanding. What we do know is that this archangel was fighting with Satan about Moses' body. Some thought it had to do with the burial of Moses. Moses left the Israelites to go to the mountain and die alone. Some Jewish writers speculated that the battle was to keep his burial place a secret so that the Jews would not make it into a shrine for idolatrous worship. No one knows for sure. But it is clear it was a spiritual battle, and again, Michael was at the forefront of the battle.

The other portion in scripture where Michael is mentioned is in Revelation, concerning the great battle in the heavenlies where Satan is cast down. We will speak more about that later.

The Daniel portions clearly outline that there is a war in the heavenlies. There are principalities that rule over countries; Daniel mentions Greece and Persia. We can surmise that this is so for every country, and perhaps for every city. Princes or principalities rule over the world under Satan's dominion. True spiritual warfare, especially for those who are to be engaged in intercessory prayer for the lost to be saved in cities and nations, must include this understanding of prayer strategy.

Much has been written about "mapping" areas for prayer, much which has been helpful, and some which is not. I remember some years ago I was asked to speak at a very critical intercessor's conference and brief them on the very serious crisis with child abductions, child trading, child pornography, and occult crimes.

My briefing was difficult for the audience to listen to. I did my best to balance the painful facts I had to present with a Biblically based plan for intercession. One of the things I made plain is that if we are to take spiritual warfare seriously, we need to understand that it is not a game, and there can be *live casualties*. (Christians in Muslim, communist and other Christian-hostile countries understand this.)

I think that after the briefing, they had a clearer understanding that (1) mapping and warfare are important, and (2) we are not shadow-boxing with pretend forces. They are real, and when they get ahold of human vessels such as the kinds of people who would sacrifice children or use them as sex slaves, there is no greater evil and no more dangerous evil.

It is worth noting that one pastor did not attend, signaling that he was not going to be part of a class that "glorified the devil." Yet days later, he released a long e-mail about what he "saw in the Spirit" regarding a local river in their region. He explained elaborately how to know if the demon principality in the river was a python strangling spirit or a poison snake spirit. Please forgive me, but when you engage raw evil such as we did, confronting pedophiles, child murderers and human traffickers, this kind of spiritual speculation and imagination are not just dangerous, but a hindrance to the TRUE work of rescuing the lost.

The Daniel picture makes it plain that there are Princes over areas that need to be fought with, as Paul confirmed and as we learned in chapter 2. We must contend with them in Jesus if we are to take souls for Jesus. Mapping is part of this strategizing. Get the history of the land. Understand who has been in power and why. Is the area known for violence, drugs, child abuse? Read the local news to find out how these demons are manifesting: Meth labs? Psychic conferences? Adult bookstores? All of that is part of the warfare.

Again, like a physical war, the armies have rank and file. Under the principalities, or princes will be their sergeants, lieutenants, captains, foot soldiers. Find their activities, and you can learn what their command and control system over an area is, and pray accordingly.

For example, I live on the El Paso, Texas/Juarez, Mexico border. We are known for massive drug activity across the border and cartel bloodshed in the extreme. We are also known as a center for occult activity nationally, and unfortunately, we are known for division within churches and lack of working together for the Gospel. In addition, the ruling families and power players in our city have almost all been very high in the Masonic order. So we have occult spirits, a spirit of division, and a principality that feeds on bloodshed.

It was no surprise that as we mapped the history of our area, we learned that when the Catholic church drove the Aztec human sacrifice cult out of Southern Mexico, they largely settled in Chihuahua, the state that surrounds Juarez, Mexico. I believe that the reason for all the bloodshed from the cartels is it is the same principality that ruled over the Aztecs, now manifesting through the cartels in Juarez, which are among the bloodiest in history.

In the same way, there are ruling principalities that create massive human sacrifices: The Holocaust. The Inquisition. 9/11. And now, the worldwide wave of Islamic Jihadism and bloodshed. Same evil Prince, just manifesting in different times, and different places.

So in our mapping and learning warfare, stay sober and sane as you do, get the facts on the ground and learn the history of the place and proceed from there. Don't get goofy, please. This is not some psychic guessing game. We need to have a true understanding of what we are fighting and how. Avoid "divine imagination" visioning of the "spirit world" which is a new age practice, not a work of God.

And please count the cost. Be prepared for real war. A few years ago, we had a border prayer meeting that was supposed to face the devil down. A lot of people showed up singing, praying, yelling, and "taking authority," which I know God loved and appreciated. However, a sudden thunderstorm came up and everyone scattered to the four winds. End of prayer meeting. We have to get a little braver than that to fight in this very real war. When the fun's over, the war begins.

Satan and King David

"Now Satan stood up against Israel, and moved David to number Israel." (1 Chronicles 21:1)

This is a brief passage, with little explanation, dealing with Satan and King David. He managed to get David to do a head count. It seemed to be important to Satan, probably because it caused David to stop trusting God, and start looking at his human resources. It was a bad idea. It should make those who do constant head counts at church to see how many attended pause and reconsider. "Some trust in chariots, and some in horses, but we will remember the Name of the Lord our God." (Psalm 20:7) Satan will take any opportunity he can to get us to take our eyes off of our Source, our Provider, our Father who knows all our needs – and try to get us to rely on our bank accounts, our human gifting, the number of people in our congregation. Whenever we take our eyes off of Jesus and put them on our own strength, we have stepped into the enemy's trap.

The Zechariah Mention

The final mention of Satan in the Old Testament contains one of the most encouraging revelations in all of scripture – and is a crucial look into how God sees the battle, and how we must see it – especially in times of difficulty and failure.

"Then he showed me Joshua the high priest standing before the Angel of the Lord, and Satan standing at his right hand to oppose him. And the Lord said to Satan, 'The Lord rebuke you, Satan! The Lord who has chosen Jerusalem rebuke you! Is this not a brand plucked from the fire?' Now Joshua was clothed with filthy garments, and was standing before the Angel. Then He answered and spoke to those who stood before Him, saying, 'Take away the filthy garments from him.' And to him He said, 'See, I have removed your iniquity from you, and I will clothe you with rich robes.' And I said, 'Let them put a clean turban on his head.' So they put a clean turban on his head, and they put the clothes on him. And the Angel of the Lord stood by." (Zechariah 3:1-5 NKJV)

Others, such as author and Pastor Rick Howard have written more extensive and insightful works which detail the rich blessings concerning this chapter. (I highly recommend the book *Restoring Restorers* by Rick C. Howard.) But for our understanding in spiritual battle, I will outline a few extremely important insights.

Joshua was one of the priests who was commissioned to be part of the return of Israel to their land after their exile in Babylon. We do not know much about him, but this passage, combined with others, seems to indicate that the rebuilding was a difficult, painful, and sometimes stunted process. Some have said that Joshua was mired in a sense of failure because of these things. All we know from this passage is that his calling was being contended by none other than Satan himself. Joshua was standing next to the Angel of the Lord; alongside stood Satan to oppose him.

The Lord *Himself* stepped in, and rebuked Satan on Joshua's behalf, reminding Satan that He had chosen him – chosen Jerusalem – and in an accurate reading, "I *perpetually* choose them." It was a complete rejection of Satan's accusations against Joshua, and the Lord wanted Joshua to hear it. He was chosen. God would not un choose him!

The scriptures say Joshua stood there in "filthy garments." The words translate as 'excrement bespattered" garments. The Bible doesn't hold back for polite company. Imagine – for whatever reason – the shame and embarrassment Joshua must have felt, knowing that his garments were splattered in feces, garments that should have been pure and white and holy.

We do not know what caused this staining, or what Joshua did to incur it, if indeed he did; or if he simply represented the people as High Priest in their stained condition. But we do know that as a servant of God, his calling and standing had been defiled, and was now attacked.

Rather than reject him and allow Satan to attack him, God stepped in and had Joshua's filthy clothes removed and had him clothed in spotless, pure clothes and a clean turban.

This story is remarkable for any believer. It is a powerful illustration of where God really stands with them and feels about them! In our walk, any number of things will happen, accusations will be made, and we may find ourselves ensnared in sins and missteps that temporarily defile and dirty our walk. We feel the shame of it, the embarrassment of it, the humiliation of it. And Satan is always right there to make sure he rubs our noses in it. But God steps in and washes us and gives us clean clothes! "If we confess our sins, He is faithful and just to forgive us our sins and to cleanse us from all unrighteousness." (1 John 1:9). Isn't that astonishing, wonderful, freeing, healing? As one friend once said, "God is not against you in your sin. He is with you *against* your sin!" Amen!

One of Satan's primary names is The Accuser. The minute you come to Christ, Satan is already scanning your weaknesses and former sins and current temptation vulnerabilities, and he will trip you up right off the starting line, right out of the gate if he can. That is when he throws it all on you: "Failure! You're a terrible Christian! Do you think God is going to forgive you after you went back to the very sin he saved you from? You're not Christian material…" You can fill in your own condemnations which have undoubtedly been thrown at you.

That is when we need to understand this picture from Zechariah and realize as quickly as we sinned, Satan is as quick to condemn and accuse; and just as quickly, God is ready to cleanse, forgive and wash and clothe you in spotless new garments.

Nothing infuriates Satan more than his accusations being met by God's rebuke and Jesus setting us back on our feet!

Remember: Satan stood to oppose Joshua. Why? Because he had a commission and a job to do for God's Kingdom, and Satan wanted it stopped.

Each of you has a job to do for the Kingdom of God. God has called you, chosen you, and given you a ministry uniquely your own. Satan knows that and will start immediately to try to undermine it. He doesn't care how. He will use discouragement, doubt, depression, trials, failure or shame. He will use anything and everything to make sure you are stopped before you even begin to walk in your calling.

And, he never stops. I have known so, so many Christians who had promising callings and incredible gifting but were tripped up – especially by moral failure – and just quit. That is exactly what Satan was after. But God is a restorer, and if you let Him, He will pick you up, cleanse and forgive you, heal you and deliver you, and set you back on the road of that calling He had given you.

The only failure is to quit. The only thing that matters is that when you fall, fall toward the Cross! Get cleansed, get up and get going!

I heard someone say, "I can't help that person, because I failed in that same area they are struggling with, a few years back." My reply was that a drowning person does not care if you failed a swimming test once or twice. All they care about is *can you save them?* Never let your past - or your past failures - be used by the enemy to disqualify you from helping *now*.

My spiritual mother once told me of a hymn they had sung in church that spoke of a little bird who was disobedient, and flew where it shouldn't. Its wing was broken, and it never again flew as high as it could before. She sat down and lovingly wrote the author of the hymn, and convinced him to alter it. Now the hymn speaks of a broken wing, the Master who comes and heals the wing, and now the little bird can fly higher than it ever did before. That's my God!

Let this story of Joshua encourage you to lay down all the sins, baggage and shame, be refitted in robes of righteousness, and regain your calling in Him!

Gregory R Reid

FROM THE FRONTLINES: LEARNING CURVE

I am going to share a very personal story here. I was fifteen, I was a brand-new believer, and I was about as hurting and fragmented as a young boy could be. A lifetime of occult practicing, drinking and a host of other soul-searing sins had left me at the King's door a walking disaster.

I was like a huge ball of yarn that some satanic kitty had gotten hold of and had me so tangled, strangled and knotted that you couldn't even find the thread to start to unravel the mess. Worse, I had built a moat around my rickety castle of a heart so that people wouldn't even get close. Most Sunday nights, I sat out in a car outside church smoking and feeling completely alone in the world. I was a 15-year-old wounded mess.

I was finally desperate enough to take one of the adults in our church aside and tell him my problems. He said, "I know who you need to talk to." He brought me to another adult who heard me out, nodded patiently and said, "I know who you can talk to," and passed me on to the next person.

I wasn't mad. I was just grateful to get punted down the field a bit in my desperate attempt to get healed. It was the most love and attention I had gotten in a long time. They were wise enough to know that, although they did care, they couldn't handle the deep issues I had.

Finally, they introduced me to one of the godliest, caring, Jesus-loving people you could ever know. And nothing that I will share here diminishes this wonderful person one bit. In retrospect, he was like so many in the beginning days of the Jesus movement that knew demonic warfare was real and wanted to help. There were no manuals then. There was just "do your best," and I honor him for at least trying to help someone as hopeless as I was. In retrospect, there *were* demonic issues – bad ones – but he was not equipped, and I was not ready.

I followed him to his home at 10 PM where he sat me in a chair and attempted to perform a deliverance on me.

He really wanted to see me set free.

I desperately wanted to be free.

He began to attempt to cast out demons. Nothing. He called them out, commanded them to speak. Silence. I wasn't sure what I was supposed to do, but all I felt was scared, cornered and on the spot.

By nearly seven in the morning, he was exhausted and completely baffled and frustrated. I was getting confused and desperate.

Finally, perhaps out of exhaustion and frustration at the lack of response, he just told me to name all the sins and struggles I had one by one. And I did. Fear. Loneliness. Rejection. Smoking. Drinking. Lust. Hate. The list was long and thorough.

He then proceeded to cast out each of my sins and problems. "Spirit of anger, come out! Spirit of loneliness, come out! Spirit of fear, come out!" He encouraged – and expected, because that was what was expected back then – for me to react, manifest somehow – a cough, vomiting, something. But there was nothing, so he said a closing prayer. And he warned me that the demons would return much stronger if I returned to my sins.

As the sun rose, I went home and got ready for school. I was completely exhausted.

I really, really wanted it to work. I needed a miracle. I would have stayed as long as it took.

But by the next day, every single problem, sin, and struggle remained entrenched and unchanged.

I will always thank God for the effort and time this man of God extended to me. And I know he helped many, many people. I was, in the end, simply beyond the reach of a simple set of prayers. My wounding was too deep, and the real demonic stronghold required a much more serious prayer struggle. Thankfully, God did all of that…in His time.

God bless you, friend, wherever you are.

Initially hurt and discouraged, I can now look back without a hint of those feelings and write down a few of the lessons I learned through that experience.

1. Do not assume there are demons present just because a person is wounded, or entrenched in some particular sin. Yes, demonic influence may accompany some things as flies are attracted to decay and death. But that does not mean a demon is IN someone.
2. Don't experiment. Don't just guess or name random things hoping something will respond. On the off chance that there is something there, it will know right away that you do not know who or what it is, or how to deal with it, and it might manifest just to confuse, confound and defeat you. Don't get dragged into a session of guesswork. If you don't know by the Holy Spirit, don't try to find something.
3. If you are being prayed for, don't make something up just because you feel pressured to do something or say something or name something. I have seen far too many people make things up just because of the pressure to do something. If it's not there, don't make it up. Someone under great stress and emotional pressure that is expected to "manifest" can actually act something out that certainly looks and acts like a demon but may not be at all.
4. You can't cast out the flesh. A problem is a problem, and a sin is a sin, and a demon is a demon. If a demon has attached to a sinful behavior or a deep wound, God will reveal that. Don't expect to have flesh problems or emotional wounds cast out.
5. "Deliverance" is not a one-size-fits-all operation. Don't approach it that way. Put the how-to manual and the demon checklists away. Go in dependent only on one Book, and one Person – Jesus Christ – and God will give you the way and the discernment to ferret out the enemy and give you the victory for that person.

We all learned the hard way what to do and what not to do in those early days. My prayer is that some of the more unwise – though well-meaning – "deliverance methods" will finally be let go of in exchange for a Holy Spirit-led way of expelling the enemy wherever he may hide.

Satan thought he had won, and was smug in his victory, smiling to himself, having the last word. So he thought. Then God raised Jesus from the dead, and life and salvation became the last words.

William J Bausch

Gregory R Reid

7 SATAN IN THE GOSPELS

When Jesus was born, it is as if the entire story of history, mankind and the Creator shifted and focused on the events chronicled in the four Gospels. Where Satan has been the original sinner, the first corrupter and the behind-the-scenes Adversary in the Old Testament, now you can see the battle lines being drawn, the enemy outed, and his activities intensified.

He's worried…

God took on flesh and tabernacled with men. What did it mean? Whatever it meant – he was going to do everything he could to stop it.

He'd managed to enslave Israel under cruel and pagan Rome. (Exile had cured Israel of its addiction to foreign gods – finally.) So far, this "crush your head" thing hadn't happened. Serpent he was, and serpent he remained. Still, he knew God continued to intervene in man's history with prophets and priests…and the chatter about a coming Redeemer was reaching a fever pitch.

Satan became very proactive after the "event." He never saw *that* coming. A baby? A water trough? A dirt-poor family? What was "He" up to?

"He" (God) was doing the prophecy thing again. "Unto us a child is born, a son is given. And His Name shall be called Wonderful, Counselor, the mighty God, Father of the Eternal, the prince of peace." (Isaiah 9:6)

He was *here*.

Although Satan surely had a good idea who He was now, apparently, the attempts to get the information to Herod experienced major technical difficulties (interference from God) as Herod wasn't certain who this child was. But Herod, an evil, demonic pagan king in a Jewish land, only knew wise men had come to worship this "King." Somewhere. Unclear on who He was, Herod took no chances. He slaughtered all child and infant king-usurper possibilities.

But Herod – and Satan – were thwarted, despite their best attempts, as Jesus' parents "were warned in a dream" and fled till the danger was past. God was – as He always is – one step ahead of Satan.

I am sure Satan kept a watchful eye over Jesus' formative years. But they were, apparently, average - even mundane. He was a regular Jewish boy, learning Torah and His stepfather's trade. He merely "grew, and waxed strong in spirit, filled with wisdom: and the grace of God was upon Him." (Luke 2:40) Nothing to get nervous about here...

Then, at around age 12, the age when Jewish boys are preparing to be brought into the company of men, something happened that surely caught Satan's attention. In a surprise move, Jesus walked away from his parents in Jerusalem and ended up in the temple with the Rabbis, asking, learning, answering, and stunning them with His answers and understanding. (Luke 2:47)

When His parents confronted Him, He plainly said, "Didn't you know I must be about My Father's business?" (Luke 2:49) He'd said it! He was not Joseph's son but God's!

Jesus had done what would become a pattern for Him. He would disappear, take an unexpected turn, end up with unlikely people like the woman at the well and the prostitute and Zaccheus; then He would often melt through a crowd, or transform suddenly and be in the company of the prophets of old...

Satan knew men were predictable. Dangle a woman – adultery followed. Show them the money – greed and war resulted. Distract them with the things of this world – their hearts would turn from God to worthless baubles and lustful pleasures.

Not Jesus. "I do what I see My Father doing." That was His pattern, His modus operandi, and Satan couldn't predict it, because he could not manipulate it like he could with sinful humans! But, he was about to try.

Jesus declared His identity to His parents, then, nothing – for another 18 years!

Then came age 30 at which time a young man could become a Rabbi, and then came John, and the baptism, and the dove and voice from heaven.

Jesus knew exactly who He was. And so did Satan.

You could almost feel the foundations of the world start to tremble.

The die had been cast. The eternal plan for redemption was now unfolding.

The one who would "crush his head" had come. And Satan was going to pull out the stops to derail Him.

After His baptism, the Holy Spirit immediately led Jesus into the wilderness to be tempted for 40 days by the devil. It was like the book of Job, part two. God allowed Satan to tempt Jesus. In Job's case, Satan gloated as he afflicted Job. And, he lost.

Now, everything was at stake. The battle was engaged. All heaven held its breath.

"Then Jesus, being filled with the Holy Spirit, returned from the Jordan and was led by the Spirit into the wilderness, being tempted for forty days by the devil." (Luke 4:1-2)

Jesus went from being filled with the Spirit to being tempted by Satan. Sound familiar? How many of us have experienced a great touch of God on our lives, only to be followed by a satanic onslaught?

People think if they are believers, things should be easy, and if difficulties arise, it's "the devil." Not always. God's desire is fruit, character, and Christlikeness.

That is not imparted. That is grown and developed by His Spirit over time.

God allows wilderness time when there is no answer but His Word, no comfort but His love, and no strength but His strength.

But, Satan never misses an opportunity like a wilderness to try to make us fall.

Wildernesses are times of great weakness and vulnerabilities. Jesus was experiencing both when Satan made his next appearance.

Lust of the Flesh, Lust of the Eye, The Pride of Life

"For all that is in the world, the lust of the flesh, and the lust of the eyes, and the pride of life, is not of the Father, but is of the world." (1 John 2:15-16)

John outlined three distinct areas that ensnare us, areas that Satan uses consistently to make us fall. They are worldly, ungodly traps.

Here, we will see how Satan tried to use each of these to ensnare Jesus.

Feed Your Flesh!

"If You are the Son of God, command this stone to become bread."

Jesus was hungry. His physical flesh was weak. Wanting to eat was not a sin. But Satan used Jesus' weakness to try to tempt him – not to eat, but to solve His hunger His own way. Jesus thwarted this attempt by saying, "It is written, 'Man shall not live by bread alone, but by every word of God.'" (Luke 4:4.) Jesus thwarted Satan with the Word of God. Satan was tempting him not to trust God but to take things into His own hands. And so he does with us. Trust and obedience are precious to God. Satan tempts us to become our own little gods. I fear that a number of believers fit this picture. They're ok with going to church and paying a tithe and maybe attending a function or two, but that's as far as they want God to interfere. All the "big decisions" they do without consulting Him. But God wants to be the One we come to with our decisions. He wants to be the one we trust to take care of things when things go wrong. He wants to be the first one we turn to.

Jesus answered this temptation with the Word of God.

The second attack – the "lust of the eyes" – followed:

"Then the devil, taking Him up on a high mountain, showed Him all the kingdoms of the world in a moment of time. And the devil said to Him, 'All this authority I will give You, and their glory; for this has been delivered to me, and I give it to whomever I wish. Therefore, if You will worship before me, all will be Yours.'" (Luke 4:5-7)

Surely, Satan thought, Jesus would be snared by this – the lust of the eyes – to be given all the kingdoms, if only He would worship him!

We need to note something here: Satan made it plain that all the kingdoms of the world were free for him to give to whomever he wished! Again, when Adam and Eve obeyed Lucifer and disobeyed God, they handed over the keys of this planet to Satan. Yes, Jesus is Lord of all. He is the owner of this planet. But because of our disobedience, Satan has the lease until He returns. He is free to hand over these worldly powers to whoever He wants. If that were not so, Jesus would have immediately rebuked that lie, and he certainly would not have been tempted by the offer. But again, Jesus answered with the Word:

"And Jesus answered and said to him, 'Get behind Me, Satan! For it is written, you shall worship the Lord your God, and Him only you shall serve.'" (Luke 4:8)

He answered him with the Word of God.

That is one of two times Jesus used the phrase "get behind me, Satan." The first here, where Satan offered him all this world had to offer; the second, when Satan used Peter, trying to persuade Him not to die on the cross.

The third temptation – the "pride of life" temptation, was the final one:

"Then he brought Him to Jerusalem, set Him on the pinnacle of the temple, and said to Him, 'If You are the Son of God, throw Yourself down from here. For it is written: "He shall give His angels charge over you, To keep you," and, "In their hands they shall bear you up, Lest you dash your foot against a stone."' And Jesus answered and said to him, 'It has been said, "You shall not tempt the Lord your God."'" (Luke 4:9-12)

There was the temptation: Pride. "You are, after all, the son of God, right? Prove it!"

Not only that, but Satan just comes right out and quotes the Scriptures. Surprised? Don't be. He knows the Scriptures inside out, backward and forward, to a degree few preachers even do! Of course, he would – it's the one book that can derail him.

How many times have you been reading the scriptures when suddenly the Scriptures are thrown in your face to bring condemnation, or guilt, or fear, or defeat, or worry, or doubt, or any number of other ungodly reactions? And your reaction is fear and confusion. How many young Christians read about the "unforgivable sin," only to have that followed by a voice, and an image of their sin, and that voice saying, "You did it. You committed the unforgivable sin! That's why you feel so far from God!" or any other kind of mental and spiritual attack. If you understand that Satan also knows the Word of God and uses it consistently to attack believers, as he tried to do with Jesus, then you can arm yourself with counter-Scriptures to attack back! Don't be defeated or fooled by this very common form of demonic attack on your walk with God.

Again, Jesus simply answered with the Word of God. "It is written. It is written. It is written!" And Satan was done.

For the moment.

No matter what our situation, or temptation, or struggle, if we could just learn to respond with the Word of God instead of our own machinations and schemes and desperate attempts to figure things out, or figure a way out! The Word of God is sufficient for all things. Tempted? Bury yourself in the Gospels or the Epistles. Facing decisions? Read the Proverbs. Being tested, wounded, frightened or confused? Nestle into the Psalms.

And don't be afraid to proclaim that Word out loud. There have been many times when I am assaulted by thoughts, or fears, or even direct demonic harassment in the middle of the night. But if I can just get up, pick up the scriptures and read them out loud for a while (the book of Psalms seems especially suited for this), then in a short time, my mind is comforted, the troubles fade, and Satan and his demons do not stay around to receive a Bible reading! The Word of God is just that powerful.

If Jesus answered everything Satan threw at Him with the Word – shouldn't we?

Yet Not Quite Gone...

"Now when the devil had ended every temptation, he departed from Him until an opportune time." (Luke 4:13)

Wouldn't it be wonderful if we just had to face temptation or the enemy once or twice, and he just went away? He didn't with Jesus, nor will he with us. The wording here implies that he simply withdrew himself a little...stepped back into the shadows...until he got another opportunity. Jesus never let His guard down. Neither should we. God grants us times of rest and times of relief from warfare, but even in those times, we must not let down our guard. Satan is out of sight...but still looking for an open shot. And it is at times of ease that we can be most vulnerable. King David learned that. In all his battles, he remained strong. It was when he let his guard down and let the others fight while he stayed at home that he fell into the trap with Bathsheba and forever changed the history of Israel. **Rest in God – but always keep your hand on the hilt of your sword!**

Satan is a Word Stealer

When Jesus was teaching on the parable of the sower, He said, "And these are they by the way side, where the Word is sown; but when they have heard, Satan cometh immediately, and taketh away the word that was sown in their hearts." (Mark 4:15)

Here we can clearly see that one of Satan's chief strategies is to snatch the Word of God out of people's hearts. People will come to church, hear a message, leave, and then "Satan cometh immediately" to steal that Word from their hearts. God places such a high premium on hearing the Word and doing it, on studying it and passing it on to the next generation, that Satan does everything he can to make sure that Word is the last priority for believers. At best, he will tolerate little bite-sized devotions which are weak on the Word and strong on feel-good pop "Christian" principles. But he truly fears the Word-soaked believer.

Satan has made great strides in our modern church to minimize the value of the Word of God. He has glutted the marketplace with so many questionable translations – some which are downright unbiblical in nearly every portion – that the average believer is overwhelmed with Bible "overchoice" and usually chooses one of the "easy to understand" versions, often ones that end up being some of the most un-biblical Bibles!

In our modern PowerPoint era, most Christians don't even bring their Bible to church. Since we display the needed scriptures (if they are used at all) on the screen, in a dozen or so translations, two things happen: One, we assume we do not need to bring our own Word. Two, if we do, the version we are reading (especially if we are reading KJV or NKJV) doesn't read anything like the version on the screen! (Try this sometime, you'll see what I mean.) Young people especially get confused by this, and they often just stop bringing their Bibles. If it's not important to us, why should it be important to them? We need to set the example. Yes, I know there are phone Bibles now. It's not the same. Is it? When you bring it, carry it, cherish it, it marks you publicly. A phone can't do that.

We are so far removed from the Jews and the early church, who made the reading and teaching of the Torah and the Word of God one of the most crucial things they did to secure their spiritual strength and faith. To this day in Israel, most orthodox Jewish boys have memorized the entire Torah by the age of 12!

Because we don't put the Word of God into our hearts diligently, deliberately and consistently, when we do receive the Word in church, or on TV or in print, Satan quickly steals it. Why? The soil of our heart is not Word-prepared! It is the Word that plows, breaks up the fallow ground, and conditions the soil of our hearts to receive the good seed of the Word of God. If we haven't done our work in this, the Word will fall on unprepared ground and will quickly get snatched away. Every true soldier of the Lord must make the Word of God priority.

One of the most major obstacles we face is the glut of technology. We are so inundated by media, movies, music, social media and the internet, that the Word of God simply takes a back seat to everything else. It is a fight – but a necessary one – to cut out deliberate blocks of time to bury your heart and mind in the Word of God.

And while many in the modern church downplay the scriptures as "shared stories from our tribal ancestors," try to denigrate people who take the Bible seriously as "word worshippers" and do as little as possible to instill a sense of the holiness, gravity, and necessity of the Word of God, the truth is, if it wasn't vital, why would Satan steal it? It is because it has the power – lived and spoken through sold-out believers – to systematically tear apart his kingdom of lies. That is all the more reason we must get serious in this hour and commit to a life of Word-soaked living.

Satan Uses People

"And He began to teach them that the Son of Man must suffer many things, and be rejected by the elders and chief priests and scribes, and be killed, and after three days rise again. He spoke this word openly. Then Peter took Him aside and began to rebuke Him. But when He had turned around and looked at His disciples, He rebuked Peter, saying, 'Get behind Me, Satan! For you are not mindful of the things of God, but the things of men.'" (Mark 8:31-34)

As much as we love our brothers and sisters in Christ and our families, be aware that Satan is not beyond using them to hinder us. (Or us to hinder them!) Peter's intentions were "humanly" good – he didn't want to see Jesus harmed or the "agenda" stopped. But Jesus saw clearly through Peter's words and saw who was urging him to speak – Satan. The first time He said, "Get behind me!" was in the wilderness temptation. Now, He was rebuking Satan in one of his nearest disciples.

We must be aware that even Christians, and those close to us, can speak to discourage us, steer us wrongly, distract us, or put us in fear or doubt. They do not mean to be mouthpieces for the enemy, but sometimes they - and sometimes we - are. Guard your heart against such attacks, and stay strong in Jesus so you will not be the vessel that is used to speak for the enemy – even if you are well-intentioned.

Satan is a Binder

"Now He was teaching in one of the synagogues on the Sabbath. And behold, there was a woman who had a spirit of infirmity eighteen years, and was bent over and could in no way raise herself up. But when Jesus saw her, He called her to Him and said to her, 'Woman, you are loosed from your infirmity.' And He laid His hands on her, and immediately she was made straight, and glorified God. But the ruler of the synagogue answered with indignation because Jesus had healed on the Sabbath; and he said to the crowd, 'There are six days on which men ought to work; therefore come and be healed on them, and not on the Sabbath day.' The Lord then answered him and said, 'Hypocrite! Does not each one of you on the Sabbath loose his ox or donkey from the stall, and lead it away to water it? So ought not this woman, being a daughter of Abraham, whom Satan has bound—think of it—for eighteen years, be loosed from this bond on the Sabbath?'" (Luke 13:11-16)

This poor woman was bound with illness for eighteen years! Jesus called it a "spirit of infirmity." Though this was a demonic binding, it wasn't necessarily a demon. Jesus never laid hands on a demonized person, and in this case, there was no dramatic demonic outcry or ugly deliverance. He simply laid His hand on her, and she was healed. Sometimes just the physical healing produces the deliverance. A binding does not necessarily mean demonization.

Satan is all about binding people, making them sick, making them hurt, breaking their relationships, anything that makes them feel bound.

Satan and his demons feed off of wounding, pain, brokenness and suffering, illness and grief. After all, they are the cause of it. That is their fodder. There is a reason the Jews referred to him as "Beelzebub," a mockery of the god of Ekron, "Baal-Zebul." It means Lord of the Flies. It partially came from the idea that Satan was the fly god – and flies feed off of death and corruption. That's who Satan is. Jesus came to shatter every chain and heal our hearts. He came to deny the enemy the right to feed off of us like spiritual vampires, denying him the right to feed off of our wounds, our sins, and our failures and broken places. Satan is the one that binds us. In just a moment, the Son of God can set us free.

Satan Is A Sifter

"And the Lord said, 'Simon, Simon! Indeed, Satan has asked for you, that he may sift you as wheat. But I have prayed for you, that your faith should not fail; and when you have returned to Me, strengthen your brethren.'" (Luke 22:31-32)

Satan is a sifter. His great desire is to take us, as he did Peter, and sift us like wheat. Peter was strong, arrogant, and confident in himself that he would never desert nor deny Jesus. Satan did indeed sift him. He beat him. He cracked him. But Jesus prayed that through that test, Peter's faith would not fail, and that afterward, he would help those around him.

Yes, the enemy attacks us. But remember what I said earlier concerning Job: Satan is on a leash. He can only go so far, and no farther. It's a real test: Jesus prayed for Peter that he would pass the test. He prays for us as well that we would remain steadfast in our faith no matter what is thrown at us. And though we do not know why He allows the tests, be sure of this: When we come out the other side – and by faith, we will – it will be with a treasure storehouse of experience, grace and healing to extend to those who also are passing through the valley of the shadow of death. God wastes nothing. As Pastor Rick Howard has often pointed out, our past and our experiences are the octaves that God uses to speak into the lives of others.

Are you passing through a time of sifting, when it seems you are losing your moorings and your hope? Remember these words of Jesus. He is praying for you that you will not fail. He is on your side. And when you endure and come out the other side, you will be a valuable tool in His hands to bring the healing comfort of God to those who are fighting alone.

Total Possession?

"Now after the piece of bread, Satan entered him. Then Jesus said to him, 'What you do, do quickly.'" (John 13:27)

We use the word possession far too freely concerning demons. I have struggled for a long time as to what to call this thing Jesus does in casting out demons. The word exorcism brings up too many Hollywood images. The word deliverance is a bit too tied to what has sometimes been extreme and off base in theology and methodology. So I have settled for demon extraction. Which, I suppose, makes us the DEA – demon extraction agents!

The word "possessed" is not accurate. The word is "demonized." This makes more sense than a word that brings up images of The Exorcist, The Omen, and other Hollywood nonsense. The word demonized indicates a *range* of influences. It can simply be mild oppression, causing headaches, confusion, etc., or more severe attachment (usually through opening a door to sin) in which the person begins to lose some bodily functions, mental capacities or emotional restraints, even losing time, to the very rare case of what some call "perfect possession" in which the person's will is nearly eradicated, buried and completely dominated by a demon.

Does Satan possess people? As far as I know, that has only happened in the case of Judas when he agreed to betray Jesus, and will only happen once again when the antichrist will be his vessel.

There is a wide spectrum of demon influences from minimal to complete takeover that can occur. And we mustn't be too caught up in semantics about whether a person is "possessed," "oppressed" or any other word complication. No matter what degree, a demonized person must be set free by the power of Jesus' Name and His shed blood. And He will do it through us if we are willing and prepared.

FROM THE FRONTLINES: CONTAINMENT

It was the end of a very long night. I was tired and was ready to go home and collapse. It had been the end of an extraordinarily busy season in our church, and in my personal life.

I got a text from one of my friends as I got home: "Have you heard anything from Billy? I just feel really uneasy about him."

A few minutes later, I received texts from several of our young people saying they had received texts from Billy that were disturbing and worrisome – they were not "him." "He says he's going to make God prove himself. I don't think we can wait till this weekend to pray for him," texted John. Just moments later, John and Andy called. They were on the way to Billy's house. "We might need you," they said. "Let me know," I replied wearily – and warily. I got off the phone, sat in my office chair, and ran my hand through my hair. "This is why I didn't want to get back into this business," I said to God. "I'm just so tired."

Moments later, it's like God shook me by the shoulders with both hands and said, "Get in the car and get those boys out of there *now*!" I had been selfishly worried about how tired I felt, when suddenly I knew that these young men were in serious danger. I jumped in my car and sped down to Billy's apartment in a very bad part of town that he shared with his family.

Things had already gotten out of hand by the time I pulled in. It was a creepy, half-moon night and the entire atmosphere outside was charged with evil and menace. Billy was not Billy anymore. John and Andy had half-surrounded him, and whatever had a hold of Billy was now becoming quite dangerous. "Annnndyyyyyy!!!!!" the demonic voice growled, as Billy's hand reached for Andy. I blocked him in the most passive way I could, and I began praying in the Spirit and pleading the blood of Jesus. "Annnndyyyy!!!" it growled again. "I know youuuu!!!" I turned for a moment and spoke to Andy and John. "This is going to get kind of ugly I think," I told them. I asked for Andy's Bible, and began intermittently reading from Psalm 91 and Revelation. Billy made several semi-lunges toward Andy, and I again blocked him. It laughed, sneered, and mocked. It spoke in ungodly tongues. It did demonic rap. What was most stunning is that Billy's face had completely transformed. His eyes were as black as midnight, yet they were literally glowing. They were slits of evil, radiating venom and malice.

After a few moments, John went inside with Billy's family, and I told Andy to go ahead and go home. I did not want him injured. He was the youngest of our team, and this demon was determined to injure him in some way. He left, and I found myself facing Billy and this ugly menace alone. Not something I had planned on, nor something I ever recommend. Avoiding such a situation was part of my training on spiritual warfare. But here I was, facing down the unknown factor alone.

It was obvious that Billy had done copious amounts of drinking. That already put this in a bad situation. He had voluntarily, deliberately opened the door, and it had given this thing permission to take full control.

In addition, Billy was gone. In absentia. Not present, not one little shred of his will to enlist in the fight against this thing. At best, this was going to be a draw. It is never advisable to attempt a demon extraction when the person is under the influence of substances. In most instances, the best you can do is contain and defuse until it can be dealt with at a time when the person is sober and you are able to engage their will in the process.

About this time, I saw headlights in back of me as I was engaging the demon that had taken over Billy. I thought it was a cop or a resident – but it turned out to be Peter, one of our adult leaders. I was so grateful. He came out, Bible in hand, and immediately began to engage this thing with scripture and prayer. And it was *not* happy. I saw his Bible go flying and Peter being tossed to the pavement. I quickly helped Peter up, got the Bible and re-engaged Billy, trying to deflect attention off of Peter. Not that Peter wasn't prepared for this; he had faithfully attended my entire 22-week training class on spiritual warfare. In fact, he told me later that he had taken out his certificate of completion just days earlier to put on the wall, and said to himself, "This wasn't for nothing. I am going to need this."

Despite that, my instincts to protect took over and I tried to be some kind of a spiritual shield to protect Peter as well. He had never seen anything like this before. Frankly, neither had I. I had been in some pretty bizarre situations and seen some really startling manifestations, but the sheer depth of evil and the raw danger I felt was unlike anything I had dealt with yet. I had no doubt that if God had not been with me, I would have been badly injured or even killed.

Still, this thing began to direct its anger toward me, and I found myself leaning against Billy and moving him back as much as I could as he hit me over and over with his fists onto my chest. Billy was twice my size. I didn't feel much pain, but I could feel the rage and the determination to hurt me. I just kept praying, pushing, containing. At one point, it started to say, "I KNOW YOU, GREGORY REID! I KNOW YOU!" and then began uttering curses, weird tongues, and some very specific threats on my life. I began to mentally smokescreen the words, so as not to become distracted, but I couldn't help but hear the threat to stop my heart.

This went on for some time. At one point, I could feel Billy physically weakening from the alcohol and spiritual battle, and I began to move him back toward his apartment. Suddenly a cat screamed like it was being murdered. Peter and I both were startled but did not move.

Within a few moments, we managed to get Billy into bed and waited until he was nearly passed out before we felt the assurance that the worst of it had passed. For now.

I was unnerved to hear later that on a previous occasion, he had picked up a policeman with one hand and tossed him halfway across a street like nothing, waved a gun another time, and picked up a relative and tossed him across the room. This was no ordinary extraction. This had been a brush with a potentially deadly situation. I am so thankful I know the power of Jesus Christ. I have no power. I am not physically strong. Even if I were, I have seen demonized people pick up someone three times their size and toss them across the room like nothing. But I know there is a bloodline of Jesus that the enemy cannot cross. And by His grace, I was behind that thin red line of power.

I still pray for Billy, and I trust Jesus will one day deliver him and grant him peace from all his torment through deliverance in Jesus Christ.

Lessons from the battle:

1. Do not engage a demonized person to attempt extraction if the person is under the influence of drugs or alcohol without a specific command from the Holy Spirit to do so.
2. If engaged in such a situation you didn't expect, your goal, unless God tells you differently, should be containment. Under the influence of substances, the person's will may have been surrendered to the demon. If the person's will cannot be engaged, it will be very difficult to get them to leave since they were given a legal right to be there.
3. Do not be caught off guard if there is some physical engagement; try to avoid it but if you should find yourself injured in some form, don't lose heart. Paul was one of the greatest Apostles of the church, yet that did not always shield him from harm. Know that if you are covered in prayer and the blood of Jesus, nothing can happen that is not in God's ultimate control.

There's never a holiday in the spiritual realm…nothing but the full armor of God will ever suffice us in this terrible conflict in which we are engaged. There is no protection…against this wily, subtle, powerful enemy but the full armor of God himself.

- C.S. Lewis

Gregory R Reid

8 SATAN FROM ACTS TO REVELATION

Satan Can Fill Your Heart

"But Peter said, 'Ananias, why has Satan filled your heart to lie to the Holy Spirit and keep back part of the price of the land for yourself?'" (Acts 5:3)

Ananias and his wife were probably believers. At the least, they had attached themselves to the Christian community. But they lied about the big donation of land they were "giving" to God. And as a result, they were both struck dead. Satan had filled Ananias' heart. You see, we as believers may not be in fear of being "possessed" – but Satan can certainly fill our hearts with ungodly things! For Ananias, it was selfish greed. What is it for us? Bitterness? Rage? A hidden desire for revenge? Gossip? Arrogance and pride? Pharisaism? Anything we hide in our hearts from the Holy Spirit, Satan will feed, grow, and fill our hearts with until Jesus is completely submerged in our lives. How many Christians in their older age have you seen who have been in church all their lives who are so bitter, poisonous and ugly that they make the church and the pastor completely miserable? (And themselves!) Satan filled their hearts. Only Jesus can flush out whatever junk we have allowed the enemy to fill us with.

Satan has Jurisdiction Over Unbelievers

"I will deliver you from the Jewish people, as well as from the Gentiles, to whom I now send you, to open their eyes, in order to turn them from darkness to light, and from the power of Satan to God, that they may receive forgiveness of sins and an inheritance among those who are sanctified by faith in Me." (Acts 26:17-18)

We too often forget that the world, and the people in the world, are under the jurisdiction of Satan. Especially in the age we are in, we tend to get angry with unbelievers, and are ready to slam them and condemn them without remembering that they are in *darkness*. If you are not a servant of Jesus, you are a slave to Satan. As Bob Dylan so succinctly put it, "It may be the devil, or it may be the Lord, but you're gonna serve somebody." There are dozens of scriptures to attest to this fact, but although we know everyone has free will, those who are without Jesus have committed that will to Satan's pleasure by their choice to sin. Then they become puppets, marionettes for the enemy.

Have you ever noticed how people in the world parrot the same few lines over and over, just like a script? "All Christians are hypocrites!" "All paths lead to God." "Jesus said judge not!" (The only scripture unbelievers uniformly know.) "The Bible is full of contradictions." That's just them parroting Satan's favorite deceptions and lies.

Have you noticed how if you are a believer in a nonchristian setting and you mention the name of Jesus or carry a Bible, people get agitated? Stirred up? Angry? Hostile? Well, it's not them. It's the Puppetmaster, pulling their strings. Don't react in anger. Have compassion. Sinners sin, because that is what they do. Without Jesus, they cannot change, and they cannot break the puppet strings. Remember what Jesus said to the worst of them: "Father, forgive them, they know not what they do!" Don't allow the enemy to pull *your* flesh strings, turning them away from Jesus. Love them, tell them the truth. If they are angry, hostile, argumentative, just stay on point in telling them about the Good News of Jesus. We're here to proclaim, not explain. Be like a laser beam of truth, stay on point!

This verse tells us that we can turn them from darkness to light. If you have ever been sleeping in the dark and someone comes in and suddenly turns on the light, you are not happy! Those in darkness are accustomed to the dark. We are called to go in and set off light bombs of truth and the Gospel of Jesus to turn them from the darkness. Don't be surprised or shocked by the hostility you may face. But hang in there because some will turn from that darkness to the light of Jesus Christ and His salvation.

Dominion Over Satan

"And the God of peace will crush Satan under your feet shortly. The grace of our Lord Jesus Christ be with you. Amen." (Romans 16:20)

I love this verse because this shows that we *do* have dominion over Satan through Jesus. Jesus came to destroy the works of Satan. Because we are His body, we too take part in that. We are not only His hands and heart – we are his feet! This reminds me of the Genesis promise that the coming Seed (Jesus – and through Him, us) would bruise his head. Crush is one of the meanings there. We were going to crush him! The word in this verse is syntribo: shatter. Our posture in war should have that determined effort and authority. We are not in a defensive mode, but are going to be victors as the God of peace shatters Satan under our feet, in every area, and in every life He calls us to touch. Do not relent until this promise is secured in your life and in the lives of all we encounter!

Turning Someone Over to Satan?

"…deliver such a one to Satan for the destruction of the flesh, that his spirit may be saved in the day of the Lord Jesus." (1 Corinthians 5:5)

"…having faith and a good conscience, which some having rejected, concerning the faith have suffered shipwreck, of whom are Hymenaeus and Alexander, whom I delivered to Satan that they may learn not to blaspheme." (1 Timothy 1:19-20)

These are two of the most misused verses I have encountered in all my years of serving Jesus. I have heard of many pastors and elders who have turned someone over to Satan with their prayers and disfellowshipped them.

Is there a time to discontinue fellowship with someone? Absolutely! Paul needed Corinth to do this to a man who was having sexual relations with his stepmother. The problem wasn't just the sin, it was the fact that no one thought it was a big deal. Paul knew drastic action was needed, both to preserve the church and in hopes of saving the sinner. So he told them to deliver him over to Satan so that could happen. In other words, they were to take off all prayer cover, spiritual support and friendship so he could be thrashed by Satan until he came to his senses. It was a difficult – but redemptive – act.

The same act was done by Paul to two men who were hurting young Christians. Again – drastic, but necessary, done through the authority of Paul's Holy Spirit directed apostleship.

The most painful times in ministry for me have been the (thankfully few) times I have had to ask someone to leave. Every setting has been at youth groups that I was pastoring, where the need to protect the flock is extremely important. All but one instance involved someone older who tried to attach themselves to the youth group as "volunteers." In a short time, I was able to determine that they had other interests. Two were pedophiles. They were quickly gone. (Along with warnings sent out to the next churches they attempted to invade.) It is painful to have to do this, but it is sometimes necessary to protect the flock.

But not *once* did I feel I was to "turn them over to Satan."

I point this out because I have encountered a great deal of presumption and even arrogance among some people and even ministry leaders over the years, who just "turn people over to Satan" without blinking twice. Although we may at times be tempted in a moment of frustration with people, or when someone really hurts a person in church, to "turn them over to Satan," I caution you to be very careful. Are you Paul? Very few people I have ever met in my life have anywhere near the gravity or authority Paul had (although there are a few). Unless you are sure you are in his league, you better watch your steps here. Remember that Paul was giving specific instructions to a specific church regarding a specific issue. You cannot play fast and loose with the scriptures, just taking verses you like or verses that make you feel important or authoritative and use them for your own purposes. For example, you wouldn't take Saul's command to Doeg the Edomite to execute all the priests of God and think that you could also command that to be done, would you? It's an extreme example, but part of our commission as soldiers in this war is to not take commands out of context and simply use verses without understanding their context, their subject, and their targets. If Paul had said that all of us can turn people over to Satan when we so wish, then that's another thing. But he did not. Pastors and ministry leaders need to be quite sure that God Himself has spoken to them to take this most drastic step with someone, because it is serious, and God will hold you accountable if you misstep.

The reason this is serious is that I believe there is a lot of "Charismatic witchcraft" out there. By that, I mean those who pray for others out of the will of God. "Lord, teach them a lesson! Turn them over to Satan until they repent!" Or, "Lord, I know they are not supposed to marry that person. Wreck their relationship!" You get the idea. We must pray according to the will of God precisely because God is not the *only* one who answers prayer. You heard that right. If you pray for yourself or others out of the direct and explicit will of God or meddle with prayers in others' lives, there are plenty of demons more than happy to take your unbiblical or misplaced prayers and "answer" them!

Having said that, I do believe there are times that people – believers – are given over to Satan for a time to try and save them. I knew of one man who was in ministry who fell into sin, did not surrender to the right steps to be restored, and went on a several year nightmare trip where he was "indulged" by Satan in all the sins he had opened the door to. He became just a shadow of the man of God he was. Thankfully, when he repented and returned, God restored to him all the enemy had stolen and delivered him from the things he had become trapped in.

Others I believe are simply taken home. John said, "There is a sin unto death. I do not say that you should pray for it." (1 John 5:16) It is possible for you to go too far so that God in His mercy simply takes you home. We all pray that we never reach that point.

But let God be the judge of that; do not presume because of these verses you can do the same thing Paul did, unless God gives you overwhelming evidence, confirmation, and command to do so.

Satan Comes as An Angel of Light

"For such are false apostles, deceitful workers, transforming themselves into apostles of Christ. And no wonder! For Satan himself transforms himself into an angel of light. Therefore it is no great thing if his ministers also transform themselves into ministers of righteousness, whose end will be according to their works." (2 Corinthians 11:13-15)

There has never been a time in history, as we approach the end of all things when it has been more critical that believers get hold of this scripture. There has never been a time when the need for it is clearer, in the light of all the lies and deceptions of the occult and the new age that are running rampant today.

We need to understand this very clearly: Satan doesn't show up in red underwear and a pitchfork and a tail. He's not a Hollywood caricature. In fact, he loves that portrayal. It makes it easy for people to make fun of "the devil" or just dismiss him altogether.

He is, in fact, or was, one of the most beautiful creatures God created. We don't know how much the fall disfigured him. But this verse makes it completely clear – he transforms himself as an angel of light. And he can make his human messengers look like righteous people as well.

The word "transform" here is not the word used for believers – metamorphoo – metamorphosis of our minds to Christ. It is a word meaning a *complete disguise*. Satan puts on a perfect disguise of light, love and religiosity, or whatever else will deceive people.

I often tell our youth, "What does Satan look like? Whatever you want him to. Whatever will attract you and take you away from Jesus, he will look like that."

But we have been completely unprepared for the onslaught of lies, deceptions and delusions that have come to the church in this last hour, particularly to the Western church. It began with books that were written that no one checked for Biblical accuracy and credibility. Doors were opened to yoga in the church, then "contemplative prayer" eastern style, and numerous other "little foxes" that began to eat at the vine of truth.

It is important to understand some of the most recent progressions here. In the 1980s there was a huge movement to teach and equip the church in spiritual warfare. Some of it was very good, some completely off base, and some of it was downright silly. However, the basic idea that we were in a real war and needed to be prepared was essential. The best teachings were completely scriptural. But on the heels of that came a number of questionable books and teachings that had very little substance in scripture.

As a result, people burned out on the idea. Then, building megachurches based on corporate models and looking for signs and wonders became the new fads. In the wake of Charismatic and Evangelical excess, a whole new group emerged that knew all the excess was wrong, and wanted something authentic. From that was born the "emergent" movement.

By the time the new millennium had come, nearly all talk of spiritual warfare was forgotten, except as an occasional joke among people that now believed that spiritual warfare was nothing more than fad books, anti-Smurf campaigns and plastic warrior armors sold for children at Christian bookstores.

In its place, we were now reading books on how to build mega churches, how to think and grow rich, how to prosper, Christian romance and feel-good fluff books with very little Christian content.

There were two major movements that sprung up out of nowhere through the first decade of the new millennium. One was the "emergent" movement, which was never better exemplified than through a new and hip teacher, Rob Bell. His book *Velvet Elvis* was a "must read" for every youth pastor in America, according to those who read it. So I did, and it was truly frightening to see such a slickly written, feel-good book that subversively and systematically tore down faith in the scriptures as God's Word. But you only saw that if you had discernment and understood that Satan comes as an angel of light, and his servants as ministers of righteousness. After reading the book and watching some of Bell's *Nooma* DVD's, I raised a serious alarm. A documented alarm. A carefully prayed through and completely researched alarm. The reactions I got were disconcerting. Many e-mails and letters to me were vicious, ugly and ungodly. I knew we had a major problem.

Since that time, Mr. Bell has gone on to prove he has indeed bitten into the fruit of the forbidden tree, as he now supports gay marriage and questions whether there is a hell. But he was just the beginning.

Soon there were dozens of books coming out of the emergent church that were very similar. They were weak on scripture and strong on feelings-based Christianity, "mystic" experiences and a one-world mentality. An entire movement started to weaken and gobble up a generation of young people that had never been taught there was a real Satan and a real war. And unfortunately, many pastors, elders and parents were too busy building the megas to notice that they had lost the heart of the youth. These young people realized there was something very wrong with the mega-corporate mentality in church, but were drawn hypnotically to this new "authentic" faith movement called emergent that had all but abandoned scriptural truth and was now promoting the very things the scriptures said would accompany the last days.

The other movement that developed was a huge rash of "supernatural" events that included "angel feathers," gemstones appearing out of nowhere, gold dust, etc. Accompanying that was the "laughter" movement, that had thousands of Christians rolling on the floor in hysterics, which then devolved into people barking like dogs, roaring like lions, slithering like snakes and even oinking like pigs – which one teacher blasphemously called the "anoinking of the Spirit." I have recently seen some videos which are so frightening that they make me tremble – videos which show believers supposedly being touched by God but whose manifestation looks identical to voodoo ceremonies of possession.

I need to make it clear that I believe in all of the gifts of the Spirit, and I have seen God do many, many miracles, and a few very strange things! But all of the aforementioned "manifestations" are not the true "charisma" of God. Without discernment, the church has lost its ability to know if these things are really true. The Bible makes it plain that the antichrist, when he comes, will come "after the working of Satan with all power and signs and lying wonders." (2 Thessalonians 2:9)

Satan can imitate nearly perfectly almost all of the gifts of the Spirit. In an age where this verse from Ephesians is a warning for our time, we need to pay close attention: **All that glitters is not gospel.** Just because someone claims to be from Jesus does not mean that they are. Back in the 1970s an evangelist who preached the Gospel and saw massive revivals and real miracles in his crusades, denied it all. The movie Marjoe was a real shock. As a little boy, Marjoe Gortner was raised by extreme parents that used to half-drowned him to get him to perform, and as an adult he was a complete fraud disguised as a man of God. We cannot be too careful.

I pray for, and believe in, the supernatural power of God. But I will not, and you cannot, blindly accept things just because they are supernatural. "Beloved, believe not every spirit; but try the spirits to see whether they are of God, because many false prophets have gone out into the world." (1 John 4:1) It's not a suggestion. It's a command.

I recommend you obtain a copy of my book *The Trojan Church* for a complete understanding of these issues in these days.

Satan Is a Buffeter

"And lest I should be exalted above measure by the abundance of the revelations, a thorn in the flesh was given to me, a messenger of Satan to buffet me, lest I be exalted above measure." (2 Corinthians 12:7)

God allowed a "messenger" of Satan to buffet Paul. We don't know if it was a demon, a circumstance or a human who was allowed to continually assault Paul, or something altogether different. We just know it was something that battered Paul, and that God allowed it to keep Paul's pride in check. Again, it goes back to the understanding that for the believer, Satan is limited in what he can do. But it was very difficult, difficult enough for Paul to ask God three times to take it away. God said "No, Paul. Lean on my grace, and it will be enough."

The word buffet is kolaphizo. It means to strike with a fist. These blows hurt. When we are so assaulted, it makes us aware this is a real war. Sometimes we can rebuke it, and it goes away. Sometimes it will take prayer and even fasting. But if it is something God allows, for however long, and all the fasting and praying and binding and rebuking doesn't work, then rest in His grace. He is allowing it for your perfection and growth. And lean hard on Romans 8:28: "God is at work in all things to produce good." Even this! Sometimes these things are allowed, the attacks are permitted because it makes us stand like steel until it cannot even affect us anymore. It has moved us closer to Jesus, and Satan lost his goal. What he meant to hurt us, God allowed in order to deliver us out of the influence of his attack.

Satan Hinders God's Work

Anyone involved in real ministry learns very quickly that spiritual warfare is not a fantasy. The minute you set out to do the work of the Gospel, you will be opposed on every level. You need to be prepared for this, and not surprised by it. You are entrusted with the most life-changing, powerful message in all eternity, the message that has the potential to pull millions of Satan's slaves out of the pit and into the Kingdom of God. Do you not think he will do everything he can to tempt you, discourage you, distract you, fight you? Listen to Paul:

"Therefore we wanted to come to you—even I, Paul, time and again—but

Satan hindered us." (1 Thessalonians 2:18)

The word is enkopto – cutting off the way. As you advance the Kingdom, Satan will attempt to cut your way off – finances, gossip, discouragement – whatever it takes. It goes with the territory of Kingdom work. Never underestimate the battle to forward the Kingdom of God.

If Paul was hindered – we can expect the same. I wish we could divest ourselves of the Pollyanna view of ministry that it's an easy ride filled with perks. Real ministry is a Humvee hitting potholes trying to avoid landmines. It's serious. But if we recognize there will be hindrance from the enemy, we won't be caught off guard. We will stay armored up and be prepared to do the wrestling that is necessary to advance the Kingdom. The enemy will not surrender territory without a fight.

The Coming of Antichrist

"For the mystery of lawlessness is already at work; only He who now restrains will do so until He is taken out of the way. And then the lawless one will be revealed, whom the Lord will consume with the breath of His mouth and destroy with the brightness of His coming. The coming of the lawless one is according to the working of Satan, with all power, signs, and lying wonders, and with all unrighteous deception among those who perish, because they did not receive the love of the truth, that they might be saved." (2 Thessalonians 2:7:10)

Who is the "he" that must be taken out of the way? What does that mean? I don't want to get into the pre-mid-post tribulation rapture discussion. But some have said we will be raptured before the antichrist shows up, because the church is restraining the evil. But the church is a *she* – not a *he*. The He, I believe, is the Holy Spirit. And He has indeed restrained the lawlessness. But as of this writing, I see an unprecedented degree of lawlessness in the land – the breaking of marriage sacredness, the legalization of drugs, the acceptance of gay marriage, the unrestrained filth on the internet and in the media. I don't think the church is being taken out before we see the "lawless one" revealed. I think the Holy Spirit is simply letting evil prevail – ending His "restraint," because we have come to the place of disinviting God, Jesus, the ten commandments and all that is right and holy from our culture. And I believe at this moment, that lawless one is preparing to take the stage.

The antichrist will be accompanied by power, signs and lying wonders. The word lying is pseudos. It means counterfeits. And we must be, as I said before, just as careful in the church. How do we know the truth from a lie, a counterfeit?

I heard a story about new bank tellers in one of New York's top banks who did nothing for the first three weeks but count money. Over, and over, and over. Then, a counterfeit bill was put in the stack. And immediately, they caught it. Why? Because they had handled the real thing for so long that they could immediately recognize the counterfeit. It didn't look right. It didn't feel right.

How do we recognize the lie, the counterfeit, even if it is subtle? It is incredibly simple. Handle the truth of God's Word so consistently and diligently, that the minute a lie even gets near, you recognize it. Spend so much time in the Word with the Author, that His Spirit immediately warns you when there is a problem.

Satan Turns People Aside

"For some have already turned aside after Satan." (1 Timothy 5:15)

The word indicates that they were medically incapacitated, as in a dislocated limb. It is a spiritual crippling through sin, discouragement, bitterness, etc. Satan is always on the lookout to take us out by crippling us so that we are unable to get up. We must be like boxers or martial art fighters who are always looking for the unexpected thing that would injure us and take us out of the ring. We must always be on the lookout and on guard.

The Depths of Satan

"Now to you I say, and to the rest in Thyatira, as many as do not have this doctrine, who have not known the depths of Satan, as they say, I will put on you no other burden. But hold fast what you have till I come." (Revelation 2:24)

Jesus gave a long exhortation to the church at Thyatira here. The word "depths" is Bathos = Profundity, extent, poverty, mastery, extremity.

Whatever Jesus was referring to here, we can know that there are those who know Satan's ways in their profoundness, have experienced the poverty that following him and his ways lead to, (and they always do), the extremities. Anyone who has faced and survived the horrors of drug or alcohol addiction, or pornographic addiction, knows the depths of darkness and the extremities of them, and the way they take you to places you never imagined you would go, robbing you of everything precious in your life. Those are the depths of Satan.

Jezebel

Jesus said this before the passage above: "Nevertheless I have a few things against you, because you allow that woman Jezebel, who calls herself a prophetess, to teach and seduce My servants to commit sexual immorality and eat things sacrificed to idols. And I gave her time to repent of her sexual immorality, and she did not repent. Indeed I will cast her into a sickbed, and those who commit adultery with her into great tribulation, unless they repent of their deeds. I will kill her children with death, and all the churches shall know that I am He who searches the minds and hearts. And I will give to each one of you according to your works." (Revelation 2:20-23)

This is one of the most sobering passages in the New Testament. I often wonder what those believers, who think Jesus is a Care Bear, a Gandhi or a softball on sin, do with this. If you don't repent, He says, I'm going to kill your kids. Dead. Hardly the cozy image we like to have of Him. But He is, after all, not just the lamb of God but the Lion of Judah. And these are believers that He is talking to!

He refers to someone we know nothing about – at least, not the actual person – Jezebel. We don't know if that was her real name, or a figurative name Jesus gave her so we would be clear not to miss the connection to the horrible and evil Jezebel of the Old Testament, wife of the spineless and wicked King Ahab. Either way works, and we should not miss the meaning. She was teaching others to fornicate, and to bow the knee to idols in their dietary practices. He indicates she herself was sexually immoral. And then he pronounces her judgment, if she does not repent. Really weighty stuff!

But I think we need to look at an issue that has come up for decades: Is there a "Jezebel Spirit"? And "Ahab Spirit"? There has been a great deal of teaching, much of it scripturally unfounded, on this. It has been taken so far that it has become a tool for the enemy to use to hurt others. "The elder's wife has a Jezebel spirit!" "The pastor is a real Ahab! He's so weak!"

Be careful, beloved. I have seen many people greatly injured because we presume God has given us the ability to so judge and sentence people.

First, let's be clear: Jesus was addressing *one person* here. Second, there *was* a Jezebel in the Old Testament, and she was horrible. She completely dominated King Ahab. And rightfully so, she has come to represent any woman who usurps authority over men, is dominating, arrogant and leads people astray. And there was an Ahab, a whiny, compromised and thoroughly ungodly king who has rightfully come to represent all those who will not stand up for truth, but instead allow sins and ungodly trends and fear of people to rule their lives and even ministries.

And, yes, you can recognize those features in others. But also in yourself, which you better do if you intend to point at others. I think we all have some of these things in our hearts that need crucifying. So yes, there is a kind of "Jezebel" personality that exemplifies the nature of that queen of old. And there is an Ahab personality as well. But please be careful – not every strong-willed woman is a Jezebel, and not every mild-mannered man is an Ahab. You should walk with fear and trembling in making such evaluations, my friend. I have seen many a decent person ruined because of the "Jezebel" accusation. Be sure that *you* are not acting as an agent of the enemy by making false accusations about "Ahabs" and "Jezebels."

Having said that, I have in fact seen devil-driven Jezebel-type women in churches who are full of division, strife, gossip, anger and uncleanness. And I have also seen Ahabs in leadership who are mesmerized by them and do nothing to stop them.

And don't miss the big message here – this "teacher" was teaching God's people to violate sexual ethics and to be idolaters. I know plenty of modern "church" teachers of both sexes that are doing those things right now. Anyone who teaches contrary to these things, especially in the area of sexuality, needs to be dealt with swiftly so that they do not destroy young believers. It is *not* ok to have sex outside of marriage. It is *not* ok to indulge pornography with your spouse or in any other context. And homosexuality is forbidden, Old Testament and New, and it doesn't matter how many spineless Evangelical leaders and pastors have now decided God changed His mind and think that we must alter the scriptures to get it to say something it doesn't and never did. To teach that it is acceptable is the kind of lie that Jesus refers to here that will bring grave consequences indeed.

The Great Dragon

"So the great dragon was cast out, that serpent of old, called the Devil and Satan, who deceives the whole world; he was cast to the earth, and his angels were cast out with him." (Revelation 12:9)

"Therefore rejoice, O heavens, and you who dwell in them! Woe to the inhabitants of the earth and the sea! For the devil has come down to you, having great wrath, because he knows that he has a short time." (Revelation 12:12)

I don't pretend to understand much more than a fragment of Revelation. But I do know it is a clear picture of spiritual warfare, and of the end of days. Revelation is a companion book to Daniel and Zechariah, and reading all three gives you a greater understanding of the big picture prophetically. I just wanted to touch on two things here: One, Satan is referred to as the great dragon. The word dragon here, drakon, means, "To look; fabulous kind of serpent; fascinator." We go all the way back to the garden picture! He is a serpent, a fascinator. He's a mesmerizer and a deceiver who deceives the whole world.

Two, at some point, he will lose access to heaven. (Some think he already has.) When he does, (and it does seem to be in the context of these final days) he will come down with great wrath because he knows he's running out of time.

My own understanding of this came to me a number of years ago when I realized that as we approached the return of Jesus and the end times, things were going to get horrible. The Bible mentions in Daniel that this antichrist force would "wear out the saints of the most high." (Daniel 7:25) It also says he will make war against God's people and prevail against them for a time. (Daniel 7:21) It will be a time of great persecution. Much of the world is experiencing it already, especially in Islamic countries and in countries like North Korea and China.

I saw a clear picture of Satan coming to earth enraged, because he knew the end was coming, but like the evil Hitler, when he was told clearly that he was going to lose, he did not quit. His insanity only got worse, and he made the fateful decision that if they couldn't win, he would destroy Germany himself so that the allies would never have it. It was called "The Scorched Earth Policy." Satan's frantic and failing effort at world worship and domination will end in his own "scorched earth" effort at Armageddon.

Satan has the same design in the end. He is enraged against the remaining believers who insist on evangelizing "his world," and the more obvious his defeat is, the more he will turn his wrath on all who stand for truth in Jesus' name. But we must hold fast to the end. Do not let anything take you away from Jesus! Paul said, "I was not disobedient to the heavenly vision." Do not back down! As a song written by the Sojourners said,

> Keep the fire burning, the fire of your faith
>
> The master is coming, the hour is so late
>
> In moments of silence, you almost can hear
>
> The sound of the trumpet, the climax is near
>
> Fan the flame, and add the Spirit's fuel to it,
>
> Lift up the lame, when they themselves can't do it
>
> Prepare, prepare to meet Him in the clouds!
>
> Keep thyself holy, look full in His face,
>
> Be yielded completely, with joy run the race
>
> The battle grows savage, He told us it would!
>
> That Christ is the victor, must be understood!
>
> Hey world, you've got to understand,

It's the midnight hour on the eve of man

The hour is late, but not too late to pray.

Amen! The hour is late, but we will be victorious to the end!

FROM THE FRONTLINES: INTERRUPTIONS

1 was on the last night of a three-day outreach at a church. It was a youth rally where I was sharing my testimony. The Spirit of God was very present, and the church had nearly three hundred who had come to hear. I felt the power of the Holy Spirit in my testimony, and as always, it confirmed to me the word that they would "overcome by the blood of the lamb and the word of their testimony." Satan hates it when the "redeemed of the Lord say so."

I gave the altar call, and the altar was quickly packed with kids who had come down to receive Jesus. I was about to lead them in prayer, when from halfway in the back of the church came a terrible demonic scream, and I watched someone fall out of their seat and writhe on the floor in a horrible demonic takeover.

Human compassion would have dictated that I go and pray to see this prisoner freed.

But God stopped me before I did, and instead I said, "Can the elders please help get this person to the prayer room and deal with this?" They acted immediately.

I looked and saw all these kids with looks of abject fear on their faces. "Don't pay attention to that!" I admonished. "It's a distraction meant to keep you from Jesus tonight. Do not fear demons. They fear Jesus!"

We proceeded from there to lead them all to the Cross and to eternal life.

Satan is always trying to disrupt the work of the Kingdom and of salvation. He hates the true Gospel, and he hates when people come to Jesus. Stand your ground, and never let the enemy steal people away from salvation through fear!

Gregory R Reid

Many do not recognize the fact as they ought, that Satan has got men fast asleep in sin and that it is his great device to keep them so. But if we awake the sleeping sinner he will gnash on us with his teeth."

- Catherine Booth

9 FALLEN ANGELS AND DEMONS

Now we are coming to one of the more precarious subjects in scripture and in our study on spiritual warfare. We have to tread very carefully so as not to stretch beyond the bounds of scriptural truth into places that become unscriptural. Second, the enemy is very aware of those who seek to learn his weaponry and rank and file – and will attempt all manner of confusion, misinformation and even deception.

So I will attempt here, humbly, with a great sense of my own inadequacy and yet a great sense of need to give insight into the world of fallen angels and demons. We really know so little! But there are things we can know in order to help us battle effectively, based on the truth of His Word.

The Sons of God

"And it came to pass, when men began to multiply on the face of the earth, and daughters were born unto them, That the sons of God saw the daughters of men that they were fair; and they took them wives of all which they chose. And the Lord said, 'My spirit shall not always strive with man, for that he also is flesh: yet his days shall be an hundred and twenty years.'" (Genesis 6:1-3)

There has been considerable debate about these verses. There are many sincere teachers and Bible scholars who believe that the "sons of God" refer to the sons of Seth, and the daughters of men to the children of Eve. But I don't think this holds up under scrutiny.

First, the Old Testament consistently uses the phrase "sons of God" to refer to angels – both those who remain with God, and those who fell into darkness with Lucifer. All the Jewish writings I have read support this.

Second, there is a clear distinction between three groups here: Sons of God, daughters of men, and man.

Let's read on about this terrible time in which Noah was to build an ark:

"There were giants in the earth in those days; and also after that, when the sons of God came in unto the daughters of men, and they bare children to them, the same became mighty men which were of old, men of renown." (Genesis 6:4)

This makes it very clear that these sons of God (angels) had sexual relations with human women, and gave birth to a race of giants.

While this may seem inconceivable to us and beyond understanding, most Jewish teachers have *always* taught that this is what happened, and even had a word for these miscreant and damned children of angelic/human interbreeding: The Nephilim. Most Jewish scholars would shake their head if you tried to put another interpretation on it.

There is much to be said about the giants, but first, let's lay a little more groundwork on these events. The book of Jude is very instructive here:

" And the angels which kept not their first estate, but left their own habitation, he hath reserved in everlasting chains under darkness unto the judgment of the great day." (Jude 1:6)

Jude says these angels did not guard their first "arche," their first estate – their origin, first beginning, or rule, or magistracy – but left (deserted) their own habitation (of the body as a dwelling place for the spirit). They abandoned who they were created to be to apparently go outside the bounds of their God-given species, seeking human sexual contact.

Sexual lust and depravity is not just a human thing - fallen angels lusted as well. And apparently, this angel-to-human lust and co-mingling was known and sought after in Sodom and Gomorrah. Surprised? Let's look at the story:

"But the men of Sodom were wicked and sinners before the LORD exceedingly." (Genesis 13:13) (Wicked: Evil, malignant, worse than worst.)

We know that two angels entered Sodom and lodged with Lot and his family. The men of Sodom demanded that the angels be brought out of the house so they could rape them.

We often point out homosexuality as the prime sin of Sodom and Gomorrah – and it surely was the notable and pervasive sin of the men of those cities. But Jude seems to indicate they knew full well that these were angels they were seeking to violate:

"Even as Sodom and Gomorrah, and the cities about them in like manner, giving themselves over to fornication, and going after strange flesh, are set forth for an example, suffering the vengeance of eternal fire." (Jude 1:7)

The word "strange" of "going after strange flesh" is not what you would expect –it is not "homo" – the *same* flesh (though they evidently went after that) – but it is "hetero" – wholly other flesh, wholly other species. Angels. I believe angel or demon to human sexuality was not just known (because of the Nephilim) but rampant, so it was nothing for the men of Sodom to seek to defile God's purest. They were beyond conscience. For this they were annihilated.

In our times – and as of this writing – we are on the precipice of just such things once again. The internet and media have escalated pornography from Playboy magazines to R and X rated movies in the '60s, to anything goes now — gay sex, group sex, incest, child sex, bestiality, infant pornography and even necrophilia. What's next?

As of this writing, our media and nation are obsessed with vampires, werewolves, shape-shifters and "the undead" – zombies. There is a new and disturbing trend to include sexual relationships with the "undead" (vampires) in literature and television and movies, and now they are starting to hint at sex with the dead - with "spirits." (demons). "Spirit" (demon) to human sex will be the next wide open door and we will have returned to Sodom and fast forwarded to annihilation. Demons who attempt to engage in sexual contact with sleeping humans will soon have free reign over an occult overtaken generation.

Before Sodom, there was an annihilation of the entire human race save for Noah's family:

"And God saw that the wickedness of man was great in the earth, and that every imagination of the thoughts of his heart was only evil continually. And it repented the Lord that he had made man on the earth, and it grieved him at his heart. And the Lord said, 'I will destroy man whom I have created from the face of the earth; both man, and beast, and the creeping thing, and the fowls of the air; for it repenteth me that I have made them.'

But Noah found grace in the eyes of the Lord. These are the generations of Noah: Noah was a just man and perfect in his generations, and Noah walked with God." (Genesis 6:5-9)

It is possible at least part of what is implied here – that he was "complete" in his generations - is that his line was uncontaminated from the mixing of species which the fallen angels had produced.

If part of the purpose of the flood was to destroy this twisted, genetically and spiritually corrupted race called "Nephilim," the product of human and angelic intermingling, then what happened to these children of corruption?

This is my speculation - and I cannot tell you it is 100% Biblically provable, though there is nothing scripturally to deny it, and many things to support it - I believe these damned souls became what we now call demons.

This is why they seem to know what it was like to once have a body. They seek a body in which to act out sinful lusts and actions which they can no longer commit without a body. It is why their entire goal seems to revolve around getting a body to inhabit. They fear not having one! That is why the demons in the man of the tombs begged Jesus to send them into any physical body, even if it were pigs.

Contrary to common assumption, fallen angels are *not* demons. They are angels. Their body and substance is completely separate from what demons are. The way demons act is very humanlike, and some I have confronted act and sound like evil corrupt little children, whimpering and begging when they are sent away, terrified of facing Satan and admitting that they failed. Again, I cannot 100% prove it, but it makes sense to me that the disembodied souls of the flood, damned forever, would seek human bodies to continue to corrupt, pervert, and vicariously sin.

In a few demon extractions I have been in, we were near the expulsion of a demon when it called on a higher principality for backup strength and support – a fallen angel – and the entire nature of the extraction took a dramatic turn for the worse, turning a simple extraction into a dangerous and serious battle for the person's deliverance.

If this is a true reading of the flood, then why did there continue to be giants *after* the flood?

Why would Satan stop trying to create his own special hybrid race? Apparently, he did not stop. The children of Israel were faced with entire populations of giant inhabitants in the promised land, such as the Emims (translated "frightening beings") and the Anakim, etc.

Might there have been a very good reason God required the elimination of an entire tribe of giants?

And although during that period the last of them appear to have been extinguished, "For only Og king of Bashan remained of the remnant of giants; behold his bedstead was a bedstead of iron; is it not in Rabbath of the children of Ammon? nine cubits was the length thereof, and four cubits the breadth of it, after the cubit of a man (Deuteronomy 3:11) it is clear that Satan did not stop his attempts at human/angelic crossbreeding. David had to fight them later! David fought the giant Goliath and his brothers, also giants. And the Bible mentions at least one description of these giant creatures and their deformed state:

"And yet again there was war at Gath, where was a man of great stature, whose fingers and toes were four and twenty, six on each hand, and six on each foot and he also was the son of the giant." (1 Chronicles 20:6)

If Satan kept trying, is there any doubt he is *still* trying to carry out this crossbreeding abomination? Could not, in fact, this explain what we call aliens? The UFO phenomena, even stories of "alien abductions" cannot be dismissed without considering the possibility that they may be a product of demonic activity in the highest level, a continuation of Nephilim activity. Whatever these things are, they are not from God, they are *not* our "space brothers," "ascended masters" or "extraterrestrials" but more likely, extra-dimensional – the return of the Nephilim, as a friend has called it. We shall see.

Although what I have proposed is somewhat speculative, I have been careful not to go beyond any clear scriptural principles of truth or understanding of truth. I trust that some of this may have answered some questions about the origins of that which we fight against, without causing undue curiosity; in fact, my recommendation is that you be very careful *not* to spend much time investigating these "Nephilim/alien" subjects, lest you be sidetracked and caught up in that which is not profitable.

Demons in the Old Testament

Now we turn to the scriptural mention of demons or "devils" in the Old Testament:

"And they shall no more offer their sacrifices unto devils, after whom they have gone a whoring. This shall be a statute for ever unto them throughout their generations." (Leviticus 17:7)

"They sacrificed unto devils, not to God; to gods whom they knew not, to new gods that came newly up, whom your fathers feared not." (Deuteronomy 32:17)

"And he ordained him priests for the high places, and for the devils, and for the calves which he had made." (2 Chronicles 11:15)

The word "devils" in Deuteronomy translates as devil; demon. The word in the Leviticus and Chronicles verse is "saiyr," translated as a he-goat, a faun, a satyr, a demon-possessed goat.

These show that man was obsessed with idolatrous worship of demons, and the image of a goat. You can see this thread all the way through to the times of Greece and Rome with their Satyr worship, the goat worship or Pan worship of Jesus' time. In fact, the very place where Jesus told His disciples that He would build His church and the "gates of hell" would not prevail against it – Caesarea Philippi - was the site of a cave literally called the gates of hades or hell, a place where Pan worshippers gathered because it was believed that Baal would enter and leave the underworld through places where water came out of it. According to one writer, "In first-century Israel, Caesarea Philippi would be an equivalent of Las Vegas – Sin City – but much worse than the modern city in the American West. In the open-air Pan Shrine, next to the cave mouth, there was a large niche, in which a statue of Pan (a half-goat, half-human creature) stood, with a large erect phallus, worshipped for its fertility properties. Surrounding him in the wall were many smaller niches, in which were statues of his attending nymphs. On the shrine in front of these niches, worshippers of Pan would congregate and partake in bizarre sexual rites, including copulation with goats – worshipped for their relationship to Pan." (From the website, "Fishing the Abyss" http://www.fishingtheabyss.com/archives/44).

Disgusting, but there again, Satan and his fallen ones and demons are the authors of all sexual debauchery.

And Jesus said in the very presence of such wickedness, His church would prevail. Isn't that amazing? We should not fear these things, but stand and challenge all those things which seek to usurp Jesus' authority and enslave that God loves, and Jesus died to redeem!

The "goat worship" extends into modern times, as people who practice black magick and blasphemous Satan worship use the goat as their "god" symbol – "Baphomet" – no doubt partially in mockery of the "lamb of God," but unwittingly, because they are literally worshipping goat demon creatures!

Anything we see in our modern times can be traced back to ancient origins. Today these ancient corrupt practices are still being practiced, only in modern guises. "There is nothing new under the sun." (Ecclesiastes 1:9)

Gods, Goddesses and Child Sacrifice

"Yea, they sacrificed their sons and their daughters unto devils…" (Psalm 106:37)

Every demon god of the Old Testament had one common feature – the demand for the sacrifice of infants and children. The Bible often refers to this as "passing your children through the fire":

"But he walked in the way of the kings of Israel, yea, and made his son to pass through the fire, according to the abominations of the heathen, whom the Lord cast out from before the children of Israel. (2 Kings 16:3) (See also Leviticus 18:21, Deuteronomy 18:10, 2 Kings 17:17)

Baal, Moloch, Chemosh, Ashtoreth, all demanded the blood of a child, usually a firstborn. The idol statue of Moloch was heated white-hot, and the live infant was placed into its belly until it was cremated – all while the worshippers – including the family of the infant – reveled in sexual debauchery. (See page 180 also)

Again, Solomon was right; there is nothing new under the sun. Abortion is the new demon god, and abortion of our babies is the new form of human sacrifice. And we have slain more at the altar of abortion tables and clinics than through every demon god idol put together in all of history.

Winkie Pratney wrote a book years ago called, *Devil take the Youngest*. He showed historically and scripturally how Satan has systematically slaughtered innocent infants and children – often just before a great move of God or God's intervention in our world. Satan began slaughtering Hebrew firstborn children in Egypt when Moses was born. Also after the birth of Jesus, Satan attempted through Herod to kill Jesus by slaughtering all the young ones. Satan is corrupt, evil and cruel. Babies and children are the height of innocence. He hates them. He craves their destruction. Nothing has changed but the face of the sacrificial altar. Once it was the altar of Baal. Now it's Planned Parenthood.

The great destruction of infants, children and young people in this age tell me that God has yet one major move He will make on this generation. We must be ready to reach and receive them!

You must keep in mind that Satan, since his fall, has only craved worship for himself, to "be as God." He doesn't care whether foolish humans call him Baal, Diana, or anything else – he ultimately gets the evil power from such human sacrifices and worship. All the gods of this world, from Pan to Shiva, are simply vehicles through which he and his demons can suck the very life out of their human worshippers and send them to hell.

Speaking of Solomon – what a gifted, blessed young man! He was David's heir. He realized he needed God's help to rule. God asked him what he wanted; he said, "Wisdom." God told him that he could have asked for riches, but he didn't; so, God was going to give him riches *and* wisdom. He was wealthy beyond belief. With those resources, he did what his father David was not allowed to do - build the temple for the Living God. And although God does not dwell in houses built by human hands, He showed up at the inaugural prayer for that temple, and the glory cloud of the Spirit of God was so overpowering that the priests could not stand to minister because of the glory of the presence of God. (1 Kings 8:10-11)

He had it all. But, he had something else – something that destroyed him and his Kingdom. He had an insatiable lust for women:

"But king Solomon loved many strange women, together with the daughter of Pharaoh, women of the Moabites, Ammonites, Edomites, Zidonians, and Hittites: Of the nations concerning which the Lord said unto the children of Israel, Ye shall not go in to them, neither shall they come in unto you: for surely they will turn away your heart after their gods: Solomon clave unto these in love. And he had seven hundred wives, princesses, and three hundred concubines: and his wives turned away his heart. For it came to pass, when Solomon was old, that his wives turned away his heart after other gods: and his heart was not perfect with the Lord his God, as was the heart of David his father. (1 Kings 11:1-4)

It wasn't just a little bad; it was really bad. He eventually consented to the building of pagan altars and the worshipping of Ashtoreth, Chemosh, Moloch, and Milcom.

It is interesting to me that even the pagans trace their "goddess of wisdom," Sophia, back to the worship of Asherah (Ashtoreth) and Solomon! They claim him as one of their own in a sense, and in part, they would not be incorrect.

Later we will go into the Masonic Order in detail, but one of the ways they persuade Biblically uneducated people to join their order is to show them Biblically how Hiram (Abiff, as they have given him a last name) was Solomon's chief architect, and how their whole order of Masons is rooted in Solomon and Hiram, and therefore, God. But I assure you, it is not the God of the Bible. As with pagans, they may rightfully claim Solomon as one of their own (because of Solomon's last years spent in idol worship) but that's not a *good* thing. The Masonic symbology and ritual are completely immersed in occultism. If the Masons have any claim to Solomon, it's that he swung wide the doors of darkness and demon worship into Israel, causing judgment and the division of the nation.

The worship of demons and fallen angels have only changed names and faces over the centuries. In the beginning, there was the worship of King Nimrod, and later his wife Semiramis and her baby Tammuz, who they believed to be the reincarnation of Nimrod. Later came the worship of Isis and Horus…then Diana and her child…all pushing into our current age with Wicca and modern paganism in which all the goddesses and gods are worshipped. If they only knew that what they were worshipping were not benevolent beings but malevolent, malignant beasts of hell disguising themselves behind the faces of these false gods and idols.

Satan still longs for worship to himself. He still desires to usurp God and rule over man. He has an agenda that has never changed. All of mankind's history is leading to this present age. I am quite confident that "Lucifer" is finally ready to take the stage embodied in the Lawless One (antichrist) to take control of a one world, one religion order in which "Enlightenment" (Lucifer=Light) will be the "true" religion, and all religions will be welcomed – except those that claim Jesus Christ as their sovereign Lord and the only way to be saved.

And demons still crave a body – one of the indications to me that they once inhabited flesh like ours. In every demon extraction I've ever done, they will lie, they will cry, they will beg, they will do anything they need to in order to avoid being disembodied from their host. They are vile creatures who seem to have once indulged every filthy sin and lust in flesh form, and now seek to use humans as a vehicle in order to vicariously feed on their sins. They are spiritual vampires. As the last days approach, they will be escalating their human invasion as they seek to kick in every open door they can to create a vast "net" or network of human vehicles to use, corrupt and destroy.

Remember that Jesus Christ is still Lord over all of them, and there is no reason to fear them. We have His authority to shatter Satan's work under our feet in His Name.

Remember also that the world, its ways, and what is transpiring in this wicked world are going to make little or no sense unless you understand the spiritual world and the warfare behind all we see and hear in this hour. Whatever you think the issues are about, they are not what they are *really* about. Legalizing drugs is not a medical issue. It is an attempt to open the doors to the demonic world to the masses. Abortion is really about human sacrifice. Gay rights is really about mocking God and reversing the course of a culture toward destruction. You have to be willing to see beyond the veneer of the cultural anti-biblical changes and see the forces and principalities that drive them. That is how we know to pray, not against people, but the powers that move and control them.

In light of the times we will shortly face, it's important to look in the next chapter at world rulers throughout history in order to understand a little of how this present world system works, so that we may be diligent and discerning watchmen for these last times.

FROM THE FRONTLINES: A CONVERSATION WITH THE ENEMY

It had been a hard year, and I was exhausted. I finally made it to my yearly vacation destination. I was looking forward to some distraction and fun. I settled into my movie seat. The theater promo was shown. It showed young people settling into their theater seats. Suddenly the seats became stone, vines grew up around them everywhere, and beautiful, twirling plant lights appeared everywhere, transforming their surroundings into a stunning virtual paradise.

My old enemy Lucifer, creator of false light, sat next to me. "This is the world I have created for this generation. What can YOUR God do?"

The intrusion – interrupted when I told him to shut up in Jesus' Name and stop bothering me on vacation – caused me to consider many things. It occurred to me that the god of this world, who used to be the Light Bearer, has enthroned himself in the center of our digital world. For all the "good" that technology has produced, we believers fail to understand the big picture. We are living in an increasingly unreal world of illusion and tricks and light magick. Entertainment is now the altar at which we bow, as we offer sacrifices of time, money, family and our own souls with televisions and computer screens acting as the new altars of Baal.

We are addicted to video screens, games, movies, pods, pads, and porn.

But none of it is *real*.

I remember the movie Soylent Green, in which old people and people who just didn't want to live anymore were euthanized while watching pretty movies of meadows and peaceful pastoral and nature scenes. They were unaware that they were about to become food.

What an apt description of our age.

We have recreated the tower of Babel. For the first time since its fall, the world is once again one language. It is the language of ones and zeros – the language of the computer.

Maybe there is a reason the first personal PC sold for $666. Maybe there is a reason that the largest and most innovative computer and tech company uses a half-eaten apple as its logo, as we eat of the tree of the "knowledge of good and evil."

In any event, here we are. As believers, we need to do two things. We need to make sure that we are not so much a part of the tech age that we are nothing more than a spiritual cyber-attachment to all our devices and media addictions. Secondly, we need to not be fooled to think that if we just get more high-tech entertainment, we can reach the masses for Jesus. Media and tech are just tools. But without the powerful message of the Gospel, the Cross, the Blood, and the anointing of the Holy Spirit, then all we are doing is becoming a part of Satan's sideshow for anesthetizing the masses. God forbid. See it for what it is, and see him for who *he* is – a deceiver, a creator of false light, one who will come as an angel of light to deceive many. All that glitters is not gospel in the big, brilliant world of Christian church and media superstars, and all that shines and is attractive, exciting and can draw a crowd – even in church – is not necessarily from God. Try the spirits. Not everything that is creatively designed to emotionally stir is from God.

We are on dangerous territory in a world where tech is god. Learn to exploit its weaponry without bowing the knee to its allure and seductive power. Keep yourself from the trap of it, the addiction of it and the lie that we cannot do the work of the Kingdom without it. Nonsense. Paul was perfectly able to preach to the thousands without a microphone.

I leave this with a challenge: If we went to church one Sunday and had no computers, no PowerPoint, no videos, no sound system, and no microphones – could we still have church? Would we? And would it be just as anointed – and perhaps more so – if we did?

To those who seek to use the very tools that the enemy is using so well to devour a generation with false light – use those tools with diligence, without compromising with the world and the culture, and with the sure knowledge that the "prince of the power of the air" allows no competition without a battle. May God raise up communications people who are so bathed in prayer that the enemy cannot stop them, who are so gifted with God's creativity that they make Lucifer's circus entertainment look like a cesspool, and may they be mightily used to draw people to the *true* source of life and Light – the Light of the world, the Lord Jesus Christ.

Till we sin Satan is a parasite; but when once we are in the devil's hands he turns tyrant.

- Thomas Manton

10 WORLD RULERS

Because our battle is not just local but global, not just individual but against vast spiritual networks of darkness in this present age, it will help to get a sense of how the enemy has worked on the world scene over the course of man's history. We will look at some of the most influential people throughout history that have been used by the enemy to turn man away from God.

When I taught law enforcement classes on cults and occult-related crimes, a large segment of my class was given to the forensics of "connecting the dots." Sometimes when they were looking at a case, they would see it in a very narrow vision range - just what was in front of them. It was important for them to broaden their view, include other factors, individuals and possibilities. By connecting the dots between cases, states, suspects and crime scene clues, they might possibly uncover a much bigger picture and thus open up the possibility of more convictions and case closures.

That is what we must do here. We have to get the big picture – the spiritual and historical picture – of what the enemy has done and is doing so we can be equipped to fight this battle well.

Nimrod

Nimrod was one of the first real-world leaders of man's history. He was the son of Cush, and great-grandson of Noah. He was King of Shinar, and of Babel. His name can be interpreted, "he who made all of the people rebellious against God," which may give us some insight into his nature. And rebellion, the scriptures tell us, is as the sin of witchcraft. (1 Samuel 15:23) He was the first to wage war.

There are a number of different historical views concerning Nimrod; One, that he had a wife, Semiramis, who was later deified as a goddess or "queen of heaven," and she had a son named Tammuz whom she claimed was the reincarnation of the dead Nimrod. Some claim this was the beginning of goddess worship, to be followed over the centuries by a succession of similar mother/child goddesses and gods, including Isis/Horus, Aphrodite/Cupid, and Asherah/EL. One certain thing is that Nimrod turned people from the living God to idolatry. Paganism and occult worship of the stars flourished under him.

The story of Babel is found in Genesis 11:1-9:

"Now the whole earth had one language and one speech. And it came to pass, as they journeyed from the east, that they found a plain in the land of Shinar, and they dwelt there. Then they said to one another, 'Come, let us make bricks and bake them thoroughly.' They had brick for stone, and they had asphalt for mortar. And they said, 'Come, let us build ourselves a city, and a tower whose top is in the heavens; let us make a name for ourselves, lest we be scattered abroad over the face of the whole earth.'

But the Lord came down to see the city and the tower which the sons of men had built. And the Lord said, 'Indeed the people are one and they all have one language, and this is what they begin to do; now nothing that they propose to do will be withheld from them. Come, let Us go down and there confuse their language, that they may not understand one another's speech.' So the Lord scattered them abroad from there over the face of all the earth, and they ceased building the city. Therefore its name is called Babel, because there the Lord confused the language of all the earth; and from there the Lord scattered them abroad over the face of all the earth."

This is a simple story if you just read it on the surface. But it doesn't make sense if you use human understanding: Why would God be threatened by people building a tall structure to reach into the sky?

But it was neither tall, nor meant to reach into the sky. It was known as a Ziggurat, and it was a spiritual center, meant for worshipping the gods and the stars. Its intent was not to "reach heaven" in height but rather to "reach into the heavenlies" – i.e., breach the forbidden dimension between where we dwell, and where God and His angels have dominion.

I contend that the occult world, beginning in this time, was attempting to open the doors that God forbade in Eden when man was expelled:

"So He drove out the man; and He placed cherubim at the east of the Garden of Eden, and a flaming sword which turned every way, to guard the way to the tree of life." (Genesis 3:24)

This indicates that God blocked the way for man to return to that place. It was guarded by angels. It was a literal place, still somewhere, but hidden beyond our seeing.

There is a Jewish mystical (I believe forbidden) practice known as the Kaballah. Those who practice Kaballah seek to "get around" the guarding angels of Eden and work their way up through the "tree of life" to "partner with God" through the agency of the angels to 'heal the world" (Tikkun Olam). But God did not change His mind. We are still forbidden to access that place, and those who do are *not* working with those who stand by His throne but rather with fallen angels who are counting on human agencies to break down the wall between their world and ours in an ever-greater way, to give them more power to influence nations and kings and people and history.

Nearly all true occult workings are designed to break down that forbidden wall. Black magicians have used the reverse Kaballah for the same reasons, but more openly calling on the fallen ones.

I believe that the tower of Babel was just such a vehicle, humans using occult means to pry open the doors between the heavenlies where fallen angels dwell and our human world. To do so is not just forbidden, but dangerous. God confounded the people of Babel to prevent them from entering a realm that would – and always does – create chaos, evil, rebellion, and destruction.

Pharaoh

When the children of Israel were enslaved in Egypt, Pharaoh was one of the first Biblical examples of a world ruler who was empowered, at least in part, by occultism and pagan idolatry. When Moses demanded that the people be set free and threw his rod to the ground and it became a snake, the Egyptian magicians did the same. But Moses' serpent ate theirs, proving that while Satan has some interesting parlor tricks, they are all only weak imitations of the real power of God.

When God pronounced judgment on Egypt, he pronounced judgment on their demon gods as well. Every plague was a direct attack on the "power" of Egypt's gods – blood in the Nile to judge the "god of the Nile," a plague of frogs to judge their "frog god" Heket, the lice plague as a judgment on their "god of the earth," a plague of flies to judge their god of rebirth represented by the dung beetle, a plague of death to cattle and livestock to judge their goddess of protection, a plague of ashes and boils to judge their goddess of medicine and peace, a plague of hail to judge their god of the sky, a plague of locusts to judge their god of storms and disorder, a plague of darkness to judge their sun god, and finally, a death of the firstborn – and pharaoh's son – as a judgment on he who was called "God, and Egypt."

God will not be mocked. The gods and goddesses of this world are nothing more than demonic entities and fallen principalities taking on the masks that we give them so that they can receive our worship and then share their fate – eternal damnation.

Pharaoh learned that there is no one like our God and that all the magickal and mystical powers of this world are nothing but cheap imitations of the real thing.

Nebuchadnezzar

King Nebuchadnezzar of Babylon was the ruler of one of the vastest and most powerful kingdoms in all of man's history. His was also a kingdom that was filled with occultism and false pagan gods. It was into this world that Daniel and his friends Hananiah, Mishael, and Azariah – young teens that were taken as slaves and forced to serve in Babylon – had to adapt in order to survive.

The story of Nebuchadnezzar and Daniel and his friends is a tremendous encouragement to those who are engaged in spiritual warfare. These young men were surrounded by some of the deepest, darkest demonic occultism ever known. Yet even in the midst of it, God raised them up to demonstrate His power and strength. When Nebuchadnezzar had a dream, not one of his useless magicians could interpret it. God sent Daniel who not only told him what his dream was, but what it meant. In one moment, he was elevated to one of the most powerful positions in Babylon, and he went on to serve Nebuchadnezzar's successors well into his older years.

The lessons of this world leader are that even when we are under their rulership, we can still thrive and survive and glorify God, and again, that there is no contest between the real power of God and the ridiculous chicanery and fraud of slight-of-hand occultists or even the real occultists that have tapped into demonic powers to do what they do.

The Catholic Reversal

In the period of time between the 1400s and the 1600s, there arose a demonic manifestation known as The Black Mass. Although the actual beginnings and sources and history of it are somewhat unclear, it appears that a group of knights known as the Knights Templar, who once fought for the Pope, were turned on by him. Many in turn rejected the church and created and practiced "The Black Mass." It was a satanic rite that reversed all of the Roman church rituals and blasphemed God with it. An upside down cross was used, a goat to mock the Lamb of God, and defiled substances instead of communion elements were consumed. Sexual debauchery of the worst kind was performed on the church altar. Prayers were repeated backward. (Reversal remains one of the prime principles of Satanism and black magick. Notorious black magician Aleister Crowley would write that the black magician must walk backward, speak backward and play music backward. There IS something to some of the "backward masking" concerns in rock music.)

Gilles de Rais was one of the early practitioners of the Black Mass, having turned away from God after his lifetime love Joan of Arc was not spared death by fire. Before he was arrested, he had sodomized and murdered hundreds of little boys and buried them in his backyard.

There were many who were priests by day but performed the Black Mass in basements at night, a practice which, according to Malachi Martin in his book *Windswept House*, continues to this day in many Catholic churches around the world.

Blavatsky, Bailey and Luciferianism

Although there have been many different manifestations of the fallen one's hand in human affairs since Babylon, from Rome to the rise of black magick in France in the 1600s, I need to fast forward to a key occult figure who was greatly used by the enemy to bring unity to Satan's world domination plans. Her name was Helena Petrovna Blavatsky, and she founded the order of Theosophy in 1875. Blavatsky was a Russian "trance channeler." (A trance channeler is a medium - one who lets "spirits" (demons) talk through them.) She developed, through her communications with the "ascended masters" - whom she had been taken over by during her time in Tibet - a whole religion based on the idea that Lucifer is really the rightful god of this world, and that all of history is moving toward unity under his "light." She wrote this:

"Lucifer represents Life, Thought, Progress, Civilization, Liberty, Independence…Lucifer is the Logos, the Serpent, the Savior. It is Satan who is the God of our planet and the only God." (From *The Secret Doctrine* by Helena Petrovna Blavatsky.)

Theosophy published the magazine "Lucifer" for a time.

Blavatsky taught in her book "The Secret Doctrine" that there were seven evolutionary stages of man, including an earlier Atlantis. One of the stages was the Aryan race. Make no mistake about it – the rise of Hitler was not by chance. After her death, her husband continued her work. He claimed that a few years prior an unnamed disciple had tried to "unite the people of Europe by the Rhine River" and had failed. More on Hitler in a moment.

Blavatsky and her later followers, including Annie Besant and Alice Bailey, would set the template for both the New Age movement and the hidden Luicferian agenda behind it.

Remember – Satan still thinks he's Lucifer and he is determined to rule over man and receive his worship. He – and those who follow him – know that in order for that to happen, there has to be a "One World Order," "One Religion" and One to Rule Them All - Satan incarnate – or as the Bible calls him, the antichrist.

I truly believe that Hitler was a trial run for the antichrist. Satan wanted to see how much he could accomplish through one person to dominate all of mankind. He wanted to see how close could he come to embodying one human. Hitler came close. But he wasn't "the one" the Theosophists and Luciferians were seeking. He is yet to come. And he is almost here.

Darwin: Satan's Unwitting Social Engineer

Charles Darwin, a former Cambridge student with the intent of being a clergyman, instead became the architect of the theory of evolution through his book, *On the Origin of the Species*. Few other single events have more powerfully molded the world toward Lucifer's endgame. What began as a theory eventually became a god of science that no one dares contend with without mockery, ridicule and even unemployment in the educational, academic and scientific world.

But let's look beyond the man and the theory to its effects. The idea that there was no God intervening in human fate and that all of our world was a matter of the "survival of the fittest," became the foundational belief of Karl Marx, a failed seminary student whose father believed he had "sold his soul to Satan." Marx co-wrote *The Communist Manifesto* and produced a system so sinister and so destructive that millions upon millions of people were murdered in its wake through Marx' spiritual children Leo Trotsky, Mao Zedong, Vladimir Lenin, Josef Stalin and those who have held this bloody system in place for nearly a century now.

Many, many Jews and Christians were slaughtered under this system that makes perfect sense if you believe that (1) "Religion is the opiate of the masses" and (2) Man is only an animal - no more and no less, that (3) The survival of the fittest is simple evolutionary logic, and (4) If there is no God, it doesn't really matter if masses of humans are eliminated in order to push forward evolutionary human "progress." All of this was the brainchild of Satan, using the former clergy hopeful Darwin to lay the foundation for a society devoid of God.

Now let's connect a few more dots. Darwin had a cousin, Francis Galton, who was so enamored with his cousin's evolutionary theory, that he took it to the next level and developed the eugenics movement. Simply put, it was the idea that we should "improve human stock by gaining knowledge and instituting public policies that would help 'the more suitable races' prevail over 'the less suitable races' in order to maximize intelligence and to prevent feeblemindedness." (From Christian Medical and Dental Associates, http://www.cmda.org/wcm/CMDA/Issues2/Other1/Genetics1/Ethics_Statements11/A_History_of_Eugenic.aspx)

He advocated scientific marital arrangements to breed "intelligent children." Galton favored selective breeding "...to give the more suitable races or strains of blood a better chance of prevailing speedily over the less suitable." He also said, "It (eugenics) must be introduced into the national consciousness as a new religion."

Margaret Sanger and American Eugenics

Across the pond, the biggest supporter and advocate of the eugenics movement was Margaret Sanger. She believed that "The most merciful thing that a large family does to one of its infant members is to kill it." She called blacks, immigrants and indigents, "...human weeds, reckless breeders, spawning...human beings who never should have been born." (Margaret Sanger, *Pivot of Civilization*.) She believed she was "working in accord with the universal law of evolution" and quoted Darwin frequently. She was a pioneer in pushing early teen sexuality, and wrote this on the back of her book, *What Every Boy and Girl Should Know*:

"Stop bringing to birth children whose inheritance cannot be one of health or intelligence. Stop bringing into the world children whose parents cannot provide for them."

America, aided through the efforts of Sanger and other pro-eugenic writers and speakers, soon was on the cutting edge of "selective breeding." We soon became enmeshed in Immigration restrictions, genetic fitness testing, and compulsory sterilization of those deemed "unfit" – including the mentally challenged, and at times, whomever they deemed unfit. All these were the demon children of Darwin, and of Satan, who hates innocence, and longs for the blood of the innocent and the destruction of children.

Margaret Sanger was the founder of the American Birth Control League. And that became Planned Parenthood, the largest abortion provider in America. Given Sanger's feelings about blacks and minorities being "human weeds," is it any wonder that 78% of their clinics are in minority communities? Getting the big picture? From Darwin to Galton, Galton to Sanger, Sanger to Planned Parenthood: The result is now well over 55 million abortions since 1973.

The Bible says "the blood is the life." (Deuteronomy 12:23) Satan is a murderer and he revels in stealing life from the creation God loves.

An Admirer in Germany

Adolph Hitler took great notice of Sanger and her work. "There is today one state," wrote Hitler, "in which at least weak beginnings toward a better conception [of immigration] are noticeable. Of course, it is not our model German Republic, but the United States." (From *Mein Kampf*) "I have studied with great interest," Hitler told a fellow Nazi, "the laws of several American states concerning prevention of reproduction by people whose progeny would, in all probability, be of no value or be injurious to the racial stock."

Telling his fellow Nazis that they were falling behind the American model, he began to institute his own eugenics program. It quickly turned into a breeding program for the super Aryan race. It became a systematic, and at first medical, sterilization and then liquidation of the mentally retarded, the infirm and disabled. It then became the Final Solution – resulting in the murder of over six million Jews and millions of others not considered fit to live. All of this was a spiritual byproduct of the demon of Darwin's theory of evolution.

Hitler's Formation

Hitler did not happen in a vacuum. He came to power in a time very similar to ours – a time of national weakness, a departure from Biblical Christianity, and a national obsession with the occult and the supernatural. He was a leader whose time had come. But he was also a leader well-trained in the ways of the occult, including, among other things, Blavatsky's Theosophy and root race theories:

"The German Brotherhood of Death Society is the Thule Society. Adolf Hitler joined this society in 1919, becoming an adept under the leadership of Dietrich Eckhart. Later, the Thule Society selected Hitler to be their leader of the New World Order, as Eckhart revealed on his deathbed, saying, 'Follow Hitler; he will dance, but it is I who have called the tune. I have initiated him into the Secret Doctrine, opened his centers in vision, and given him the means to communicate with the powers.'" (Trevor Ravenscroft, *The Spear Of Destiny*, p. 91).

Hitler was an occultist, steeped in the legends of the old Norse gods, rumored to be an initiate of the occult Vril Society as were Himmler and others close to him. I recommend Gerald Suster's *Hitler: The Occult Messiah* for a more thorough understanding of his background and practices. It is a fact that his SS officers regularly practiced ritual human sacrifice at the Wewelsburg castle during Hitler's reign. The sacrifice of millions of people under Hitler was nothing less than the greatest act of human sacrifice to demon gods ever committed up to that time.

Following Hitler were the mass genocides of Stalin who was responsible for killing over 40 million people, and closing down over 48,000 churches in an attempt to liquidate the entire Christian Church. Then came China's Mao Zedong who launched the "Great Proletariat Cultural Revolution" which has been called "History's most systematic attempt ever, by a single nation, to eradicate and destroy Christianity." Mao was responsible for murdering about 72 million people.

All this had its genesis in Darwin's theory. Darwinism produced a stark reality that played out in the horrible acts of mass murder that followed. The logic of Darwinism produced certain inevitable conclusions: "Without God all activities are equivalent…" (Jean-Paul Sartre), and, "If God is dead, then all things are permissible!" (Dostoevsky) So, "professing themselves to be wise they became fools, they worshiped and served the creature rather than the creator." (Romans 1:22-23) In so doing, they unknowingly worshiped and served Satan and brought horrible holocaust down on mankind.

The Aftermath and the Preparation for the Final Battle

After "the war to end all wars" came the explosion of a bomb that ripped the fabric of atomic reality and caused its architect Robert Oppenheimer to quote a Hindu god, Vishnu saying, "Now I am become Death, the destroyer of worlds."

More wars – and more death – followed. In the midst, the League of Nations was born, the precursor to the United Nations, another human effort to bring human unity and peace – (a Luciferian dream) – without God. The United Nations is a supreme antichrist organization whose goals are the same as the enemy's – one world, one government, one religion, without the God of the Christians and the Jews. Almost everything they do moves toward this goal.

A number of world leaders entered the post-WWII scene to continue to move the world toward this goal of Luciferian rule. They included Mikael Gorbachev, the last leader of the Soviet Union who has been a key player in New Age spirituality and governance, and Jimmy Carter, former president, and Baptist Sunday School teacher and lately a model of the "new age Christian." He no longer accepts Jesus as the only way to God, no longer accepts the biblical prophetic worldview, opposes Israel and can no longer realistically be considered the "born again" believer that he portrayed in his presidential years.

Other occult leaders have included Manuel Noriega who was steeped in Santeria and ugly black magick religions, Jean-Paul Aristide and "Baby Doc" Duvalier of Haiti who are devoted to the Voodoo gods and goddesses, Joseph Kony of the Lord's Liberation Army who is a mass murderer and practices witchcraft, and the list goes on. Even Tony Blair of Great Britain is becoming a key player in bringing world governments and religions together for this final "beast" configuration spoken of in Daniel and Revelation. George Bush Sr. is only one of *many* to announce the coming of a "new world order."

Of Presidents, Bankers and Kings

When you take the long view, you begin to realize that not all is as it seems in the geopolitical world, or even in our country.

Without getting into some of the outlandish conspiracy theories that are out there for anyone to read and guess about their accuracy, it is important to have at least a bare-bones understanding that there is a spiritual world system that has become flesh, so to speak, in the last few centuries through various organizations of lesser and greater influence and power.

One is the much-discussed "Illuminati." Founded by Adam Weishaupt in late 1776, it was a secret group of elitists which was steeped in occultism, Masonry and a belief in a one world system. From there, the thread gets fairly lost. Most of what we do hear about is rumor. However, after careful research and debriefing a number of ex-occultists, I can tell you that the

Illuminati is real. I can also tell you that about 80% of what you hear about it in the media is half-truth and a *planned distraction* from finding the truth about the real group. Luciferians are the *real* power-players in the world, whether they are called Illuminists or some other name, or no name at all. My well-researched guess is that they are in fact above the Illuminists, and you will never know who they really are. They are the bankers, politicians, kings and influencers that treat the world as their personal chessboard and dream of world control under the rulership of Lucifer. (Again, I recommend Malachi Martin's *Windswept House* for further understanding.)

We will likely never know who the real rulers are at that level. And have pity on the JZs And Beyoncés of the world who are so committed to this "Illuminati" occultism either for money, fame or publicity – or because they really *do* think they are "club members" – for they are merely throwaways and the gum under the shoes of the *real* rulers of that world. The law of Lucferianism is that "the guarantee of our tomorrow is today's perception that we do not exist."

One can get a glimpse, but only partial, of how the world is run by powers other than the vote of people by doing a little research into what is called the Bohemian Grove. Again, I ask you to be careful and selective in researching it, because too many people become obsessed with it and cannot focus on Kingdom work.

However, there is an actual retreat center in Northern California that is host to great "world leaders" – bankers, media moguls, Presidents, politicians, and kings throughout the year. The Bohemian Grove is a weekend party retreat for the rich and powerful, including nearly every president that we have had in this century. They show up for a weekend of partying, making world decisions and who knows what else. The weekend always concludes with the "Cremation of Care" ceremony in which twelve men in black robes cremate a wicker effigy of a human being before a stone god that resembles an owl. (Some say it hearkens back to Moloch that was once represented by an owl in modern symbology.)

This is what I do know. It does exist. And presidents and world leaders attend. It is one of the most secretive places on earth – it is even blurred out on google earth. It is an extremely well-guarded, members-only club, and nearly every president since Hoover, and others like Henry Kissinger are part of the club. And they *all* participate in that sinister ceremony. No one will talk about it, or acknowledge their participation, even when it has been recorded. For example, George W. Bush gave his acceptance for his first nomination by phone from the Bohemian Grove. Members of Clinton's staff have been videotaped coming and going, and angrily reacted to a reporter later asking about their involvement.

Why does any of this matter? Because the world is now moving toward a decisive and deliberate antichrist, antichristian one-world, one religion mode, and I firmly believe that the decisions on the rise and fall of kings and empires, wars and economies are being decided by a secret cabal of world players that treat the ordinary citizen as simply cogs in a wheel moving the world toward a Luciferian order. Anyone involved in the real world of geopolitical and economic movement knows that this other hand is in the shadows behind everything.

That is the short version, the one I can give to you without getting us distracted or out of focus from the matters at hand. To fight spiritual warfare, it is absolutely necessary to understand that it is the powers and principalities behind the wicked rulers in this world that we battle. And that is where we do warfare, against those Princes. And remember always – Satan may be the ruling power of this present world system, but Jesus is the Prince of Peace, the Everlasting God, the father of the eternities. He is Lord! As we move out under His Lordship, no power on earth or principality of darkness can stop us from forwarding the Kingdom of God and the Gospel of the Lord Jesus Christ!

Jesus laid out a clear progression of things to watch for in Matthew 24 and the other Gospels. Both Peter and Paul spoke plainly about what to watch for in the last days – a falling away, deception, signs and lying wonders, a revealing of the lawless one and the turning away from truth. Can anyone deny that we are there?

Israel is – and always has been – and will be until Jesus' soon return – God's timepiece. The entire world will center in this last hour on the Middle East conflict because that is where the conflict began between the powers and principalities. It is the birthplace of Abraham and the birth of the nation of Israel. It is the place of Israel's rising and falling, its idolatry and then banishment to Babylon. It is the place of its restoration and return to God, the rejection of the Messiah, and the destruction of Jerusalem. Still God's heart pursued Israel through the worldwide exile for centuries, the attempt at complete annihilation first under Isabella and Ferdinand in Spain in the Inquisition that went worldwide, then the horrible holocaust under Hitler, which led to the birth of Israel in 1948 which fulfilled the scripture, "Shall a nation be born in a day?" (Isaiah 66:8) Israel is proceeding exactly according to God's timing, and it will culminate in the battle of all battles in Megiddo, where a demonized remainder of humankind will fight against Jesus Himself and the armies of heaven, and the armies of darkness and Satan himself will be locked in chains for a thousand years.

Satan knows it's coming, and he's fighting furiously to hold on to what he's got. So must we. We have the overwhelming victory in Jesus. Defeat is unacceptable; we will not lose because we cannot lose.

How diligently the cavalry officer keeps his sabre clean and sharp; every stain he rubs off with the greatest care. Remember you are God's sword, His instrument - I trust, a chosen vessel unto Him to bear His name. In great measure, according to the purity and perfection of the instrument, will be the success.

- Robert Murray McCheyne

11 CULTURAL CONSEQUENCES, SOCIAL BREAKDOWN AND SPIRITUAL OPEN DOORS

There is a progression to sin, both culturally and personally. It is a regression, really. James speaks very clearly to this:

"But every man is tempted when he is drawn away of his own lust, and enticed. Then when lust has conceived, it brings forth sin; and sin, when it is finished, brings forth death." (James 1:14-15)

The word conceived – syllambano - means "when it is perfected."

There is a germination, a gestation and a progression of sin that leads to death.

In the same way, sin regresses a culture; it starts with a small breakdown of the law, little compromises, and justifications for sinful actions. It starts in a culture as a departure from the truth of God's Word.

We see this from the very beginning of man's history:

"And God saw that the wickedness of man was great in the earth, and that every imagination of the thoughts of his heart was only evil continually." (Genesis.6:5)

Man had become consumed by wicked thoughts. Not in the mind alone but in the heart, the very core of him was consumed by evil inclinations.

"And God looked upon the earth, and, behold, it was corrupt; for all flesh had corrupted his way upon the earth." (Genesis 6:12) They had corrupted God's design, and the image and likeness of God they were created in were being marred and defiled by sin, rebellion, and perversion.

"And God said unto Noah, The end of all flesh is come before me; for the earth is filled with violence through them; and, behold, I will destroy them with the earth." (Genesis. 6:13)

We can see how unrestrained sin led – and leads inevitably – to violence, and then death.

Why is this picture important? Because Jesus said, "As in the days of Noah, so shall the coming of the Son of Man be." (Matthew 24:37)

He said people would be eating and drinking, marrying and giving in marriage – business as usual. He also said they would be blind to what was coming – they "knew not till the flood came, and took them all away." (Matthew 24:39) They were completely blinded by their sins so that they had no idea, until it was too late, that the end was coming.

I believe the earth is becoming filled with violence once again, just as in the days before the flood. Can anyone deny it? We are witnessing terrorist butchery, crucifixions and beheadings of Christians in Islamic countries, random deadly shooters almost every month in the U.S.A. We suffer from a national fixation with zombies, violent video games and death themed movies. And we have a complete failure to connect the dots as to why there is so much violence and death. The government calls for gun control, negotiating with religions who wish us harm, more therapy and excuses for people who commit horrendous acts of murder, rape and torture, thinking that more psychological understanding and intervention will stem the tide. And none of it will work, because all of this chaos is the natural regression of humankind when separated from God. It is the simple law of progressive evil.

Evil, left unchecked, grows. It produces spiritual numbness and what the Bible calls a seared conscience:

"Now the Spirit speaketh expressly, that in the latter times some shall depart from the faith, giving heed to seducing spirits, and doctrines of devils; Speaking lies in hypocrisy; having their conscience seared with a hot iron." (1 Timothy 4:1-2)

If you have ever had a severe burn or scar, you know how that part of your flesh has been effectively seared – the nerve endings have been destroyed – so that you cannot feel anything on that part of the skin. That is what sin does to our hearts and consciences. It destroys our ability to feel guilt, conviction or consequences.

In a culture, this progressive sin over the course of generations naturally leads to an abandonment of the truth of God's Word, and God eventually sends "a strong delusion that they would believe a lie." (2 Thessalonians 2:11)

In a culture where sin is allowed to go unchecked year after year and walls and boundaries given by God's Word are broken down at every level, the entire fabric begins to unravel.

It does not happen overnight. Satan moves the goalpost of sin in a culture and in our individual lives slowly, almost imperceptibly. One little change there, a little compromise here, and we become like the frog in the pot, happily swimming away, not knowing that the water is being slowly turned up a half a degree at a time over a long period, until we boil to death without even knowing it – because we were conditioned to receive the changes so gradually. Can anyone deny we are there, in a culture in which divorce was a last resort a hundred years ago, but is now the norm – even among Christians? A culture that once looked down on unrestrained consumption of alcohol but now celebrates it with parties, football games and any holiday they can? A culture that had prayer in schools, honored the ten commandments, but is now completely stripping the nation of these things? A culture that has been so numbed that the abortion of over 50 million infants doesn't even phase this young generation? I could go on, but I think you see the point. We are regressing as in the days of Noah. And as in every culture, the departure from truth and righteousness inevitably leads to spiritual decay, moral depravity, and cultural extinction. It is the Galatians Principle which is at work in every area, culturally, personally and nationally:

"Be not deceived; God is not mocked: for whatsoever a man soweth, that shall he also reap. For he that soweth to his flesh shall of the flesh reap corruption; but he that soweth to the Spirit shall of the Spirit reap life everlasting." (Galatians 6:7-8)

It is a promise, and a warning. First, we must understand how it has worked in our present day, and then we can go on to personal application later.

The Path of Cultural, Social and Spiritual Destruction

Phase One: Fallen Foundations of Truth

"Shout against her round about: she hath given her hand: her foundations are fallen, her walls are thrown down: for it is the vengeance of the LORD: take vengeance upon her; as she hath done, do unto her." (Jeremiah 50:15)

"If the foundations be destroyed, what can the righteous do?" (Psalm 11:3)

No culture can survive the regressive nature of sin and destruction unless they have a foundation of truth. The Word of God is the foundation of truth that has always ensured the survival and blessing on any land that upholds it, whether it was Israel, Great Britain, the United States, or any other country at different times in history. God's ten commandments have withstood the centuries as the proven framework for a healthy society and a blessed people. And, contra-wise, you can see how once mighty nations have brought decay and destruction on themselves when they removed that vital foundation of truth.

We share with Great Britain the unfortunate experience of watching the truth of God's Word systematically rooted out of our courts, our schools, and our very foundation, and watching the decline of our nation in every way as a result. The sun began to set on the British Empire about the same time they began discarding the Word of God in exchange for other gods and the law of "every man did what was right in his own eyes." America is following that same path even now.

Phase Two: Breaking Down Walls and The Erasing of Boundaries

"For it is a day of trouble, and of treading down, and of perplexity by the Lord GOD of hosts in the valley of vision, breaking down the walls, and of crying to the mountains." (Isaiah 22:5)

Walls, in the scriptures, always represent a defense against invasion. That picture is applicable in spiritual warfare, to us as a culture, and as individuals. When we begin to erase the boundaries of God's Word - when we begin to call that which is sin in God's eyes, *not* sin - when we begin to ignore the plain and non-negotiable boundaries regarding occult practices, greed, substance abuse, sexual practices, and other clear scriptural principles - then we have set ourselves up for "a day of trouble and treading down, and crying." We have invited the enemy to invade, plain and simple. And while a godless society merely views these changes as "social evolution and enlightenment," Satan sees it as the open doors he needs to move his demonic troops into the land and begin to occupy both places and people.

Phase Three: Truth is Publicly Disregarded

"And judgment is turned away backward, and justice standeth afar off: for truth is fallen in the street, and equity cannot enter." (Isaiah 59:14)

The next step in the destruction of a culture is when truth becomes something to be mocked, something that is beneath us, something we just trample under our feet. When truth has "fallen in the street" – when it is not received, but falls to the ground like leaves from a tree, then our ability to judge correctly is suddenly gone, and the ability to bring justice fairly in the land has departed from us. That is why our justice system – even though it is at this moment still the best in the world – is beginning to become corrupt, confounding and increasingly anti-Christian.

Nowhere was this falling of truth to the streets more vivid to me when at one of our last political elections, when nearly an entire convention of our two-party system engaged in loud and angry "boo-ing" when the vote for allowing God on the party platform was brought to the podium. It was one thing to reject God in individual lives, quite another for the representatives of an entire branch of our political system to express their rejection of Him in such a public and hostile way.

Phase Four: Truth is Socially Discarded

"It is time for thee, Lord, to work: for they have made void thy law." (Psalm 119:126)

The words "make void" mean to break apart, frustrate, make ineffectual. When truth as a foundational necessity for living and preserving a land are socially discarded, then we have come to a place where the enemy has free reign.

And his end game is takeover, control, and possession.

Six Arenas of Regression

There are six major areas that are part of the destruction of a society and culture:

Prosperity

"When they had pasture, they were filled; They were filled and their heart was exalted; Therefore they forgot Me." (Hosea 13:6) Letting abundance and ease turn our hearts from God is a danger in any culture, as well as personally. Israel is our example here: when they were being persecuted and enslaved, they sought after God. When they prospered, they forgot Him. When they began to forget where their blessings came from, then sin entered in the gates.

Iniquity

"For the mystery of iniquity doth already work: only he who now letteth will let, until he be taken out of the way." (2 Thessalonians. 2:7)

"And because iniquity shall abound, the love of many shall wax cold." (Matthew 24:12)

Iniquity is a kind of sin that is very prevalent in a decaying culture. Iniquity is "anomia" – without law. It is not just individual sin, but the kind of sin that eats at the soul of a person and a people. In the last days, that iniquity – lawlessness - will be unrestrained. All the things that were once commonly acknowledged as sin will suddenly become acceptable, and the world will begin to revel in the kind of demonic darkness that only comes when people have abandoned themselves to their carnal nature to do whatever their flesh wishes to do.

Deception

"Woe unto them that call evil good, and good evil; that put darkness for light, and light for darkness; that put bitter for sweet, and sweet for bitter!" (Isaiah 5:20)

The next regression comes when the standard of truth is discarded so that, as Romans 1 says, "…even as they did not like to retain God in their knowledge, God gave them over to a reprobate mind…" (Romans 1:28)

One of the definitions of a reprobate mind is the inability to tell right from wrong. Isaiah told us clearly that people would call good evil and evil, good. The nature of unrestrained sin is that our sinful nature begins to reject truth seeing it as not being relevant to our lives. We begin to justify our sins one after another until it has altered our entire perception of truth.

Without any disrespect concerning those who struggle with mental illness, I recently saw a bit of a picture that helped me understand where we are going as a nation. I have known several people in my life with delusional mental illness. One often encounters people in street ministry with such a struggle. It occurred to me that they are often able to talk with great lucidity and clarity about things that are completely delusional. And you realize after a while that it makes complete sense to them. They can't understand why *you* don't understand the "truth" they are telling you.

I realized that we are entering a time of national insanity in our nation. There was a time when the majority of Americans, even if they didn't necessarily believe in the Bible, or Jesus as the Son of God, were at least somewhat respectful of those beliefs. But in the last two decades, there has been a seismic shift in our national mental state to where Christian thought, Bible truths, and all the Bible stands for is disregarded, disrespected, and increasingly despised.

Worse, this national insanity has created a socially engineered "language" in which people talk about what is important and what is "real," and it makes no sense at all to those who know Jesus. It's crazy talk. But they look at *you* as a believer and wonder what's wrong with *you* that you don't get it! The world, fast heading towards a New Age rulership of one-world antichrist government, is beginning to view Christians and their "extreme teachings" as a cancer on the "body politic," a hindrance to the spiritual and secular evolution of man. We are living out the reality of the spiritual insanity that overtakes a people when they begin to call evil good and good evil.

Idolatry

The next phase of cultural deterioration is a giving over to idolatry.

Even though the Old Testament idols looked different and their practices were different, they have their modern counterparts. Moloch and Baal still receive infant sacrifices today. Abortion clinics have become modern altars for infant sacrifice.

But idolatry is more than worshipping a false god. Idolatry is *anything* that you give your time, attention, money, or affection to that replaces God in your life. Today, the idols are numerous: Entertainment (movies, television, video games) the internet, technology, career, sports obsession, pornography. They all end up as idols when we let them absorb the time and devotion due to God alone.

There's a reason they call Hollywood movie stars "idols." And there is a reason they are called stars: Aleister Crowley, world-infamous Satanist from Great Britain, said, "Every man and woman is a star." (Book of the Law 1:3) We shouldn't be surprised. Hollywood is all about the most satanic principle of all: Do what thou wilt. Selfishness and self-will is the religion that fuels the industry.

Division

As the culture and society begin to slide toward oblivion, division becomes the ruler of the day. Divorce has skyrocketed to the point where the Christian divorce rate equals the world's divorce rate, the result of two or three generations of these cultural and biblical compromises and sins being injected into our landscape. Each generation is more broken, more divisive, more incapable of sustaining the core unity God designed for the human family. So fragmented is our society and family structure now, that Satan has been able to create his own legally recognized gay/bisexual/lesbian/transgendered counterfeit of a family, complete with an ever growing number of children either adopted into or created through genetic or invitro means into those families. In time, anything will pass as "family" and what's left of God's will and structure for family will be just shards and fragments.

Sorcery

Occultism and drug use is the acid that disintegrates the spiritual wall of protection and gives demonic spirits direct access into one's conscious mind and spiritual life. The Bible couldn't be clearer about this: The occult, in any form, is dangerous, spiritually poisonous and provides direct open doors for demonic influence, demonization, and even possession. Occultism includes astrology, divination, witchcraft, séances, Ouija boards, trance channeling, numerology, necromancy, fortune telling, etc.

The word sorcerer in the scriptures (Revelation 21:8) is *pharmakeus* – yes, that is where we get the word pharmacy. There are medical drugs used for healing, but here it is referring to the use of drugs, not for healing, but for magical purposes. There is a reason Aldous Huxley experienced the drug mescaline as the drug that opened the "doors of perception." (The rock group "The Doors" named themselves after his idea.) Psychedelic drugs, marijuana, etc. all are open doors into the spiritual world. But not God's world. The reason that sorcerers used drugs was specifically to open those doors. Even today some religious groups use peyote and other hallucinogens to do occult workings.

And no, you don't have to work an Ouija board to open those doors to the demonic world. Just smoke something, drop a tab, ingest a recreational drug in any form and spiritual doors will open, and you will have much, much more than you bargained for.

The Progression

Solomon said there is nothing new under the sun. If we look at how sin and darkness have overtaken us, we can look back at history and see that what we do is not new, nor are we the first: In the time of the Greeks and Romans, there were specific gods and goddesses: Dionysus, Aphrodite, and the Muses. The god of drunkenness and debauchery; the goddess of sex and love; and the gods of the arts.

Fast forward to the first half of the last century, when Hollywood was born, prohibition was defeated, and sexual permissiveness first found a foothold in our culture – and remember what the embodiment of the "good life" was – wine, women, and song.

Which became, in the 1960s, sex, drugs and rock 'n' roll.

Same spirit, different eras. Same corruptions, different cultures. Satan is really not that creative or clever. But from his standpoint, if it ain't broke, don't fix it. Sinful humans always fall for these same temptations and open doors.

A note on "wine, women, and song" – as we spoke of noted Satanist Aleister Crowley previously, it might be eye-opening to include his thoughts on that. He suggested that "'wine, women, and song" may be utilized towards "the development of genius in the individual or the attainment of mystical states." These pivotal cultural obsessions – substance abuse, sexual promiscuity, and addiction to entertainment - are cornerstones for the enemy to build a godless society on.

You can see this in our own history in the last century. The 1920s and 1930s saw a lowering of godly standards, an increase in drunkenness, an increased interest in the occult, and of course – the flourishing of Hollywood. In fact, pre-Hitler Germany saw an unprecedented increase in occult interest, which I believe opened the door for a supernaturally driven man to take over the minds of a people who had become supernaturally conditioned to receive a lie.

The 1940s caused us to refocus because of the wars and the need to fight a new and terrible evil that had been unleashed on the earth. But with the cessation of the war came a time of unprecedented prosperity. And prosperity, as we said earlier, can cause people to forget God. It did not happen all at once, but with prosperity came prosperous ease, and entertainment, music and television began to replace family time at the table, Sunday church and Bible studies.

With it, the divorce rates began to rise.

In the 1960s, a cluster of subversive satanic influences came into our culture which were like Trojan horses. They brought small changes at first, creating some clamor, which was followed by bigger changes whose place had been secured by the small changes.

First, prayer was taken out of school.

Abortion was legalized.

Rock and Roll became the central focus of youth. Rebellion became the generation's call: James Dean, the Beat Scene, things we look back on in amusement now, but they had the seeds of rebellion at their roots.

A Hindu guru from India, Maharishi Mahesh Yogi, mesmerized the Beatles, and his teachings - "TM" or transcendental meditation - opened a door into the schools and family life as a "healthy lifestyle" practice, unwittingly opening the door to all of the demonic influence that comes with Hindu god and goddess worship. Today even Christians smirk if you suggest yoga is spiritually dangerous.

Drugs began to infest the young generation, giving birth to the decade of sex, drugs and rock and roll – the "Love Generation" in which all Biblical moral principles were cast off and people "turned on, tuned in and dropped out." A bloody, fruitless war fueled the anger of youth and created an environment where everything their parents stood for was mocked, discarded, and detested – especially Biblical faith.

God moved mightily during this time, pouring out His Spirit everywhere in what was known as the "Jesus Movement," which I believe gave us a cultural reprieve from a complete godless collapse, as well as proving that "Where sin abounded, grace did much more abound." (Romans 5:20)

The Church of Satan and the Satanic Bible were birthed during this time, a directly blasphemous entity that shook its fist at God and mocked Jesus and all He was about.

Free sex gave way to a glut of street pornography as we had never seen – including child pornography, which, believe it or not, was for sale right out in the open on the newsstands in Hollywood in the early 1970s. R-rated movies became X-rated movies. Sexual boundaries were being crossed in every way. The gay rights movement was born and established. Women were encouraged to do away with the need for men, burn their bras and pursue their "inner goddess."

The 1980s gave birth to disco, the blurring of sexual identities, sexual abandonment, popularizing drugs such as cocaine and marijuana, and a complete obsession with sports, rock and roll and the party life. In the mid to late 1980s, death metal and a national epidemic of occult and Satanically motivated crimes swept the nation. (See my book *Diary of a Devil Hunter* for the *true* story behind what many called "Satanic panic." Information on www.gregoryreid.com) Blaspheming Jesus became the cool thing to do.

There was a new school agenda underway which was outlined by a keynote speaker at a national educator's conference in Colorado in 1988 who said, "Our job as educators is to sweep away the last vestiges of Judeo Christian thought from the schools." And they have succeeded beyond their wildest dreams since then.

Then the internet was born, and the personal computer created.

From that, a door opened up. It was not just a fulfillment of Daniel's prophecy that in the last days, "Many shall go to and fro [mass transportation] – and knowledge shall be increased," (Daniel 12:4) but it opened the electronic era in which knowledge, connectedness, and virtual reality burst into our world like a conqueror. Within just three short decades, digital technology became the life-force and life-blood of our culture, our social interaction, and our meaning in life. As they say, this was a game-changer. The personal computer and the internet have completely changed how we live, much of it not for the better. We have become digital addicts.

By the time we entered the 1990's, everything that was planted over decades began to bear fruit. Goddess worship came into the public eye. Harry

Potter introduced a whole generation to witchcraft in a way nothing ever had before.

To raise any alarm about Harry Potter made you an object of ridicule and mockery. Harry Potter, a character that single mother JK Rowling said simply "fell into my head," became a role model for an entire generation, and was the vanguard for erasing all fear and caution about the world of wizards, witches, and the occult. Suddenly, no one was afraid to touch these things anymore. Suddenly, God's commands concerning these things were discarded like yesterday's trash by an entire generation of children *and* their parents – even Christian ones.

The internet slowly took possession of everything in our lives – banking, media, communications, education. But at the center of the internet was a Satanic heart of darkness that drove, fueled and financed it – pornography. What was once the domain of sleazy side alley "adult" stores and material that youth could only obtain by finding a Playboy somewhere, was now open, plenteous, and accessible to anyone of any age, and it poured poison into an entire digitally raised generation.

This is not a minor issue. One of Satan's most crucial goals is to destroy mankind's God-given sexuality. Satan is neutered. He cannot produce children. He cannot love, and is not capable of intimacy. He hates the people that God created. He envies them. He knows if he can destroy a person's God-given sexual image and makeup, he can destroy that person, their family, their future.

Someone recently and rightly pointed out that the fallen state of man without God is completely sexually depraved. In fact, until God gave Israel the Ten Commandments, cultural sexuality was animalistic, unrestrained and abusive to women and children. God gave a set of boundaries, particularly marriage, that would preserve Israel and set a standard of holiness before God. It forbids bestiality, homosexuality, adultery and every aberration that deviated from the union between a man and a woman, "as it was in the beginning." The result was family integrity and social wholeness. Violation of those boundaries *always* brought spiritual chaos, family destruction and national fragmentation. The pattern is clear – the breakdown of the family brings the breakdown of the entire culture.

Internet pornography, quite simply, blew a gigantic hole in our cultural and spiritual integrity that is nearly irreparable and has created societal chaos and moral insanity.

You can literally get anything on the internet, from homosexual pornography to bondage, child pornography of the worst sort, bestiality and even necrophilia. The newest "trend" is infant rape.

How much more depraved can we get?

Internet pornography is now an integral part of young people's reality, especially for boys and young men, but increasingly, girls and women are also becoming addicted to pornography.

If you want to know how an entire country bowed to normalizing homosexuality and approving gay marriage, then do the math: From the time the gates to internet pornography opened – around 1989 – until the widespread acceptance of gay marriage – 2014 – is about 25 years. An entire generation was exposed to and indulging in no-restraints pornography. And it is a fact that the vast majority of boys who have viewed pornography have also crossed the line into homosexual pornography. It did not, for the most part, alter their sexual "preferences" – but it most certainly altered their sexual perceptions about what is right and wrong. 1+1=2. Acceptance of homosexuality didn't happen in a vacuum. It happened in a demonic workshop and a spiritual sewer. I know that is harsh, but that is spiritual reality.

You cannot in fact understand how homosexuality became *the* issue of the day and how a tiny group of people known as gay activists became so powerful that they are making politicians tremble for fear of them and churches ready to appease them unless you understand that behind all of it is a powerful principality that is determined that we will bow the knee or be destroyed. The force driving this issue is supernatural. We need to be prepared to battle this principality in prayer.

Unrestrained sexuality is the name of Satan's game because it completely mars, destroys and ruins the precious singular gift of naked oneness God gave to be a lifetime gift to be shared with one person.

The second part of the digital equation is video games, which have also succeeded in changing our social climate. If we are around long enough, some experts will eventually make the connection between emotional numbness, violence, and a culture where horrible acts of violence in real time are becoming more frequent and more senseless, and a culture that is addicted to violence in the media and to video games. It's a simple computer principle – "GIGO" - which stands for "garbage in, garbage out." If you ingest a large diet of video violence, occultism, and sexual perversion, it will come out in your spiritual and natural life in a whole host of destructive ways.

We have lost the ability to connect the dots. All the little sins and compromises, all the broken-down walls and disregarding of the Word of God have borne fruit. Our culture has become one massive open door into the Kingdom of Darkness.

God gave the late David Wilkerson a vision in 1973 that there was a baptism of filth coming that would make it seem that the very gates of hell had opened up on the earth, and "abominable filth" would overwhelm us. (Nahum 3:6) He could not have known how completely his vision would be fulfilled.

The full fruit of it has not yet reached maturity. This is what I see on the horizon:

- -Lowering the age of consent for sex between adults and youth

- -Complete legalization of drugs

- -Decriminalizing incest and bestiality

-Removal of the 501c3 nonprofit tax status from non-compliant churches that will not accept these changes, and who continue to stand against abortion, homosexuality, Islam, etc.

- The mainline churches will begin to marginalize, ostracize and dissociate from Christians, churches, and pastors who believe, preach and stand on the whole Word of God.

-Criminalization of evangelism in all forms

And finally, there will be a push to classify believing in the Bible as the only Word of God and believing that Jesus is the only Son of God and the only way to salvation as a form of mental illness.

Persecution in the West won't start with jails, but treatment in clinics and mental hospitals in an attempt to reprogram Christians so they cease to be a "threat" to social peace and harmony.

Habitation of Demons

America is beginning to fit this Biblical description:

"Babylon the great is fallen, is fallen, and is become the habitation of devils, and the hold of every foul spirit, and a cage of every unclean and hateful bird. For all nations have drunk of the wine of the wrath of her fornication, and the kings of the earth have committed fornication with her, and the merchants of the earth are waxed rich through the abundance of her delicacies. And I heard another voice from heaven, saying, Come out of her, my people, that ye be not partakers of her sins, and that ye receive not of her plagues. For her sins have reached unto heaven, and God hath remembered her iniquities. Reward her even as she rewarded you, and double unto her double according to her works: in the cup which she hath filled fill to her double. How much she hath glorified herself, and lived deliciously, so much torment and sorrow give her: for she saith in her heart, I sit a queen, and am no widow, and shall see no sorrow. Therefore shall her plagues come in one day, death, and mourning, and famine; and she shall be utterly burned with fire: for strong is the Lord God who judgeth her." (Revelation 18:2-8)

We should extract ourselves from all of these cultural impurities, and pray for mercy – and REVIVAL. God may yet give us more time!

FROM THE FRONTLINES: CURANDERISMO

There is a form of ritual magick known to most along the border regions of the United States and in Mexico known as Curanderismo. It is considered "folk medicine." It employs a strange mixture of Catholic prayers, saints, candles, along with standard magick tools such as spells, potions, powders, ointments, and amulets.

One warm spring evening, our team traveled to a modest home outside the city to pray for a family. It was a Christian family. It was an Evangelical, Bible-believing, born-again family.

The year before, their 10-year-old son had taken ill. The doctors could do nothing. He was wasting away. The father's prayers weren't "working."

So, he resorted to what he knew – what he was raised with. He hired a Curandera (a woman who practices Curanderismo). He paid her a good sum to work a cure for their son.

She did, and their son recovered. It was a miracle!

But the father and mother were convicted and mortified. They knew they had gone beyond God's boundaries to get this "miracle."

The Curandera called them, expecting her next payment for her next "limpia" (cleansing). They gently explained to her that her services were no longer needed.

She was furious. She cursed them, threatened them. "You will regret this!" she cursed.

A few days later, they found a sacrificed animal on their back porch.

Within days, the beautiful 35-year-old mother was in a wheelchair, hands twisted into deformed claws, looking more like 85 than 35. The doctors could find nothing wrong with her.

Finally, they reached out to us for help.

We listened to their entire story. Then, we had the father renounce and repent of his unbiblical – however well-intentioned – pact with a Curandera. The wife and grandmother prayed as well.

We were all stunned as the mother's hands uncurled, her face untwisted, and she was, in minutes, 100% restored to health!

We were equally stunned when we watched their son suddenly twist and contort into the same disfigured shape with which his mother had been afflicted.

This is the first time I had witnessed a "jumper." It had been evicted from its host and went for the next vulnerable victim.

We had the father pray and take authority over his son, and we expelled the demon – at which point it began to take the grandmother. She too had been part of the pact. We continued to pray and get them to renounce every bit of their involvement until the final door was closed, and it had to go.

My prayer is that the family never again opened up the door to that demonic – though culturally acceptable – world.

My guess is – after they saw the additional price tag of the Curandera's working – they never did.

Prayer makes the Christian's armor bright; And Satan trembles when he sees the weakest saint upon his knees.

- William Cowper

12 ENCOUNTERS AND EXTRACTIONS

Now we move on to some specific encounters with the demonic world in the scriptures and extractions from those they infested.

First, let's look at the Word of God to see how Jesus dealt with them:

Just A Word

"When the evening was come, they brought unto him many that were possessed with devils: and he cast out the spirits with his word, and healed all that were sick." (Matthew 8:16)

All it took from Jesus was just a word from Him. It was the power of Jesus' word and nothing else that expelled these evil invaders.

I truly wish all such encounters were as simple for us: just a word. Honestly, I do not know why there is such a wide range between ease and difficulty in extracting demons. In my experience, there have been times a demon has left immediately. At times, it has taken hours; sometimes stretched out over days, and some broken up into sessions over the course of time. I believe that is often because the human body, mind, and soul can only take so much trauma. You have to remember – these people's bodies have been invaded by an alien entity of the real kind – not some extraterrestrial being, but an extra*dimensional* demon. It cannot be anything but horrible, invasive and destructive, no matter how hidden. And if it has been entrenched over a period of years, you can imagine that it will not let go without a fight, and the toll it takes on the human body and mind can be extreme. God in His mercy often gives time to recover between prayer extraction events.

Of course, there are always "Monday Morning Quarterbacks" on this issue – "Well, Jesus cast them out just like that. Why can't you?" Honestly, I don't know and believe me, I would like nothing more than for deliverance to be a quick, neat affair. And, as Jesus said, some only come out by prayer and fasting. I wish that they would just come out! (It always seems to be those who have never encountered a demon, or prayed for people who are infested with one, who offer the most criticism on this matter.)

Yes, I have seen demons immediately depart. And I have seen some ministers that seem to have more of an edge than I in that regard, and God bless them.

But it seems like, even though some extractions have been easy, many have been difficult, exhausting, and occasionally prolonged. It is, in my humble opinion, often a bit like surgery. Sometimes you can go in and do the surgery and the patient is on the way home that day. Some, however, require hospital stays and recovery. And occasionally, it requires more than one surgery, with time in between to recover.

I believe it is a mistake to grab hold of a "one size fits all" demon extraction method or plan. One of the first rules of engagement in war is that no battle plan survives the first field battle. We must be sensitive to the Holy Spirit and totally reliant on Him; and who is able to do such warfare? Only those who walk humbly and without preconceived ideas about "how it goes." Once you have boots on the ground, your only clear focus is that this thing is evil, it must go, and there is no negotiation. You know that Jesus' Name and the power of His Blood alone can win this battle; you will not stop until He prevails against the enemy!

So, whether we, like Him, can cast them out with a word, or whether it takes many – determine that it *will* be cast out!

A Mute Spirit

"As they went out, behold, they brought to Him a man, mute and demon-possessed. And when the demon was cast out, the mute spoke. And the multitudes marveled, saying, "'It was never seen like this in Israel!'" (Matthew 9:32-33)

According to this passage, his affliction was caused by a demon making him unable able to speak.

Again, one size does not fit all, and just because one thing is true, does not mean every similar situation is the same. Just because a demon caused his affliction, does not mean all illnesses and sicknesses are caused by demons or demonic infestation.

I do believe that all sickness, disease and death is a *result* of the fall and the sin that Adam and Eve brought into our world. God is the God of life, not death.

However, not all illnesses are directly caused by demons. Do not assume that they are, or you will hurt a lot of people in praying for them to have illnesses cast out and nothing happens. On the other hand, there is no question that some people are physically afflicted because they have been touched by demonic spirits. I do believe that Satan delights and revels in illness, sickness, and affliction. I also believe he delights in the world of mental illness. But as with physical affliction, just because some mental illnesses may be demonically caused, created or induced, does not mean they all are. I have met far too many amateur deliverance people who assume all mental illness is demonic and can be cast out. Tread very, very carefully, my friend. Some mental illnesses are the result of physical chemical issues: If you take some people off of medication, you may have opened the door for a violent incident or worse. Do I believe God can heal such things? Absolutely. But do not assume that mental illness is all about demons. There is simply too much at stake if you are wrong.

A Sign

"But if I cast out devils by the Spirit of God, then the kingdom of God is come unto you." (Matthew 12:28)

"But if I with the finger of God cast out devils, no doubt the kingdom of God is come upon you. (Luke 11:20)

Jesus used a specific phrase here, "The finger of God" which referred to both the writing of the ten commandments, and the defeat of the demonic occult powers of Pharaoh's magicians. (Exodus 8:19)

It is clear by this passage that one of the absolute signs that the Kingdom of God is in our midst is that demons get expelled. It is amazing to me that in this day, most churches and prayer meetings are shocked when such an event takes place! It should be an occurrence that doesn't make believers even bat an eye, it is merely an acknowledgment that God is at work and they simply go to work casting it out. When God's Spirit is present and the Kingdom rule has come to bear, of course the demonic presences in our midst, should they be there, will expose themselves, and by our insistence, go fleeing from the power of the Living God.

Unclean Spirit

"When the unclean spirit is gone out of a man, he walketh through dry places, seeking rest, and findeth none." (Matthew 12:43)

The word "unclean" here is "akathartos." It means without cleansing or the ability to be cleansed. Kathartos is where we get the word catharsis. When someone emotionally vents or just "lets it all hang out" we call that a "catharsis." The person feels better afterward because they have unburdened themselves, they have let out all the junk that was in them. It is no surprise that demons are "akathartos." They are spiritual garbage trucks that simply keep ingesting uncleanness and filth and sin, and have absolutely no way of being cleansed from it. When we feed on garbage, uncleanness, and sin, if demons attach themselves to our habits, they become "feeders" on our sins. It is no wonder that the more control we allow them to have through that feeding, the more unclean, ugly and filthy we feel. Once they are gone, we again become cleansable by the precious blood of Jesus.

This verse also shows that demons are restless, completely unable to find rest. They are obsessed with the need to inhabit human flesh. Without that, they cannot vicariously experience human things and human pleasures and human sins. When someone is demonized, they too feel that sense of restlessness – the inability to rest. Almost everyone I have known who has been delivered from demons has a new sense of peace – and the ability to sleep well - many for the first time in years.

Torn

"And there was in their synagogue a man with an unclean spirit; and he cried out, Saying, Let us alone; what have we to do with thee, thou Jesus of Nazareth? art thou come to destroy us? I know thee who thou art, the Holy One of God. And Jesus rebuked him, saying, Hold thy peace, and come out of him. And when the unclean spirit had torn him, and cried with a loud voice, he came out of him." (Mark 1:23-26)

It may seem self-evident, but it always stirs me to realize that one of the things that affirms the truth of all Jesus was, is that demons always recognized Him. "I know who you are, the Holy One of God!" Demons have constantly proclaimed – better than many Christians I might add – that Jesus is Lord. And this is what the scriptures say, that "every knee shall bow, and every tongue confess, that Jesus Christ is Lord, to the glory of God the Father." (Philippians 2:10-11)

Notice here too, that Jesus silenced them. I have seen far too many "deliverances" where the demons were fully engaged in arguing, screaming, growling and making a spectacle. Soldier, be very careful. You are not there to get information or be engaged in the many fascinating bits of intrigue the demons will surely try to entice you with. There are times that certain questions are necessary – but you must silence them and then demand in His Name - not listen and enquire. Jesus silenced them and prevented them from prolonging what had already been a terrible ordeal from the one who had been demonized.

The word "torn" is "sparasso" – convulsed with an epileptic seizure. It is not uncommon for the demon to try to physically injure the person when it leaves, as it is attempting with all its strength to claw and cling to the body they have inhabited. We must be prepared to make sure that the person does not become injured in the process of getting set free. These things do *not* want to leave. We need to provide safe people who can make sure the person is not further hurt while taking care not to be over-restraining or injurious in our zeal to see them set free.

The Tombs

"And when he was come out of the ship, immediately there met him out of the tombs a man with an unclean spirit who had his dwelling among the tombs; and no man could bind him, no, not with chains: Because that he had been often bound with fetters and chains, and the chains had been plucked asunder by him, and the fetters broken in pieces: neither could any man tame him. And always, night and day, he was in the mountains, and in the tombs, crying, and cutting himself with stones. But when he saw Jesus afar off, he ran and worshipped him, And cried with a loud voice, and said, What have I to do with thee, Jesus, thou Son of the most high God? I adjure thee by God, that thou torment me not. For he said unto him, Come out of the man, thou unclean spirit. And he asked him, What is thy name? And he answered, saying, My name is Legion: for we are many. And he besought him much that he would not send them away out of the country. Now there was there nigh unto the mountains a great herd of swine feeding. And all the devils besought him, saying, Send us into the swine, that we may enter into them. And forthwith Jesus gave them leave. And the unclean spirits went out, and entered into the swine: and the herd ran violently down a steep place into the sea, (they were about two thousand;) and were choked in the sea. And they that fed the swine fled, and told it in the city, and in the country. And they went out to see what it was that was done. And they come to Jesus, and see him that was possessed with the devil, and had the legion, sitting, and clothed, and in his right mind: and they were afraid." (Mark 5:2-15)

Can you imagine the horrible nightmare world this poor man lived in? Violent, untamed, in pain, crying. And no one could do a thing. This passage often brings me to tears. You can almost feel his anguish.

In all the years I have prayed for people, my reaction has always been the same. I feel a gut-wrenching pain, and tears come to my eyes because I feel the torment that person must be enduring under the hand of this wicked thing. It fortifies my determination to see them set free.

The agony of demonization can scarcely be described. It makes you want to do whatever is necessary to see the person set free.

When they saw Jesus coming, they ran straight to Him and worshipped Him. Does that seem strange to you? Worship is not just a sign of adoration and love, as we take it – it is utter surrender to the One who created all of us. That's why when people say, "Hey, I believe," - in some vague way concerning Jesus- I quote them James, who says plainly, "Even the demons believe and tremble." (James 2:19) Demons know better than most people that HE IS GOD. Every place Jesus went, they called out who and what He is.

Legion

The demons identified as "Legion." In the Roman military, that is approximately 6,100 troops. I cannot imagine the inner torment these things caused the man – the clamoring, the voices, the unrestrained evil!

We'll Go Anywhere

Once Jesus confronted the demons, they begged Him not to send them out away from the country – to the "dry places," as other scriptures indicate – but they were willing to go into *any* kind of a body. They picked the pigs feeding on the hillside. Jesus sent them there.

Even the pigs were so disgusted and overcome by their evil that they chose suicide by water rather than abide their presence! They killed themselves to get free of them.

The miracle came. The people in the town found the man "sitting, and clothed, and in his right mind." It was a miracle no one could have done but Jesus. I can't imagine the overwhelming joy and gratefulness this man, who was an object of rejection and fear for so long, must have felt for Jesus.

But if he was expecting everyone else to be happy, he was sadly disappointed. They were afraid. They were afraid of him before, but now they were afraid of him because they could not deny what God had done. So rather than rejoice and follow Jesus, they told Him to leave. (I wonder if a part of it was because they weren't supposed to be in the pig business in the first place?)

The area of spiritual warfare and demonic extraction should be something the church understands, works in and supports. Instead, I find most believers are just afraid of it like the people above.

I constantly remind my classes that if you are in Jesus, there is no reason to fear demons. They, in fact, fear Jesus in *you*. But I find so many just can't make that leap, and they choose instead to take an "out of sight, out of mind" position. That is what the demons count on, which is why they are so big on smoke and mirrors, terrifying growling, threats, and weird manifestations. Once you realize that's about all they have, then you can get over the fear and get to work.

Analysis of an Extraction

Let's look at a significant passage in Mark concerning a boy who was brought to Jesus to be delivered from a demon, and examine each part of it:

"Then one of the crowd answered and said, 'Teacher, I brought You my son, who has a mute spirit. And wherever it seizes him, it throws him down; he foams at the mouth, gnashes his teeth, and becomes rigid. So I spoke to Your disciples, that they should cast it out, but they could not.' He answered him and said, 'O faithless generation, how long shall I be with you? How long shall I bear with you? Bring him to Me.' Then they brought him to Him. And when he saw Him, immediately the spirit convulsed him, and he fell on the ground and wallowed, foaming at the mouth. So He asked his father, 'How long has this been happening to him?' And he said, 'From childhood. And often he has thrown him both into the fire and into the water to destroy him. But if You can do anything, have compassion on us and help us.' Jesus said to him, 'If you can believe, all things are possible to him who believes.' Immediately the father of the child cried out and said with tears, 'Lord, I believe; help my unbelief!'"

"When Jesus saw that the people came running together, He rebuked the unclean spirit, saying to it: 'Deaf and dumb spirit, I command you, come out of him and enter him no more!' Then the spirit cried out, convulsed him greatly, and came out of him. And he became as one dead, so that many said, 'He is dead.' But Jesus took him by the hand and lifted him up, and he arose. And when He had come into the house, His disciples asked Him privately, 'Why could we not cast it out?' So He said to them, 'This kind can come out by nothing but prayer and fasting.'" (Mark 9:17:29)

Destructive

"It throws him down; he foams at the mouth, gnashes his teeth, and becomes rigid." Why are demons so destructive? First, because they are inhabiting a foreign body not meant for them. As much as they "need" a body, a body is a mismatch and is just barely more comfortable than not having one. Second, they are quite insane. They act out all of their own destructiveness in injuring the body they inhabit. Third, when they are forced to come out, they often injure the body they are in. They often only come out ripping or tearing at their host. We must demand their disempowerment at this stage and not allow it to injure the person on its way out.

Since Childhood

I am struck – and extremely moved – by the fact that this boy was tormented since he was a child by this demon. He probably had very little childhood that had not been destroyed by this ugly thing. It is hard for us to grasp – but, scriptures will attest to it – children do get demonized. In fact, most of the scriptural accounts of demonization Jesus dealt with were in children.

How do children get demonized? This is where the "experts" get a little too expert for me. I think it can happen in a variety of ways. I think it can happen in utero; it can happen by injury. I found it of interest that several well-known occultists "found" their psychic powers after an injury or illness; Edgar Cayce, a world-renowned psychic was one of them. A parent who takes their child to a psychic, curandero, medicine man or other occult "healers" can open those doors, too.

Is it fair? No. Why should a child suffer? Is it right? No! It's a horrible spiritual violation. But don't spend too much time trying to analyze these events and "get a handle" on them. Our job is not to figure it out but to make sure the evil demon is dispatched. That is all.

Humiliation

The person who is demonized is already in a state of agony and humiliation. Notice when the boy started to manifest and the "people came running together" that Jesus immediately dealt with the demon and caused it to come out. His action prevented it from becoming a spectacle and further humiliating the son and His father. This speaks deeply to me, especially after seeing so many deliverances over the years that became circuses, crowd-watching events and Christian spectator activities. I have also seen deliverance "pile-on's" where everyone wants to get in on it. Shame on us! That poor soul is already suffering more than we can imagine; should we add to their humiliation and fear by surrounding them, shouting at them, making their awful torment the center of attention? God forbid. Do everything within your power to protect that person's dignity and deal with that demon in a setting that is away from prying eyes, accident-watchers and self-styled exorcists. Never, *ever* allow someone to be humiliated.

Unbelief

This particular incident is chronicled in both Mark 9 and Matthew 17. It helps to read both to get the full context because if you just read the one, you can lose the context and use it to tell people if they don't get the demon cast out right away it's just because of their unbelief. In fact, when Jesus was confronted by the father about the fact that his disciples couldn't cast out the demons, he was, according to the context of Matthew, surrounded by a crowd of people and questioning Pharisees. The Pharisees were always trying to trap him and constantly looking for validation of their criticism of him, even in his disciple's failures. It was to not just His disciples, but to them, he said, "You faithless generation." To the lot of them.

When you fast forward to Jesus' private conversation, he told them "Because of your little faith" – not that they had *no* faith, or they surely wouldn't have even attempted the extraction. He said that it was little, and their faith needed to grow like a mustard seed. "Howbeit," – or "besides," He said, "these kinds of demons only come out through prayer and fasting." I believe this speaks to two things: One, that there are specific kinds of demons that are not easily dislodged for numerous reasons, whether longevity, family entanglement or gross sin or some other thing we do not know. And two: It is not just a moment of fasting and prayer, but a disciplined spiritual life that is constantly seeking God with prayer and fasting, a life that is steeped in the power of God by deliberate intent that is fit to the task in more difficult extractions. So, we must live in such a way that we don't have to "prepare," as much as we stay prepared by these things.

Spirit of Infirmity – A Deeper Look

"And, behold, there was a woman which had a spirit of infirmity eighteen years, and was bowed together, and could in no way lift up herself. And when Jesus saw her, he called her to him, and said unto her, Woman, thou art loosed from thine infirmity. And he laid his hands on her: and immediately she was made straight, and glorified God." (Luke 13:11-13)

We need to be very careful not to casually or carelessly "diagnose" people. Our language and cultural understanding of things can automatically lead us to conclude that this woman had a demon since in our media age "spirit" "ghost" and "demon" are so interchangeable. But when Jesus cast out demons, he confronted them. Here, he merely spoke freedom to her by His Word. "He sent forth His Word and He healed them." I am not saying it may not have been demonically agitated, but there is neither contextual nor verbal evidence here that it was a demon. There was no expulsion evidenced, just instant healing. I say this because we are quick to call something a "spirit of infirmity" and attempt to treat it as a demon and cast it out as such, and I simply do not believe the scriptures here support that.

This is important only so that you will understand, once again, that "formula deliverance" is not a good idea, and is often based on ideas that the scriptures simply don't support. The word "spirit" used here seems to indicate more of a disposition mentally and physically created by illness - which does not *rule out* demonization - but the fact that there was no extraction leads me to conclude that the idea that a "spirit of infirmity" is a demon cannot be supported by this verse.

A demon extraction will almost always produce freedom from a number of things, often physical ailments. But because they can cause those things, does not mean that they are always the cause of illness. Be careful not to be too confident of your own wisdom in your attempts to diagnose and deliver people!

Keep Your Perspective

"And the seventy returned again with joy, saying, 'Lord, even the devils are subject unto us through thy name.' And he said unto them, 'I beheld Satan as lightning fall from heaven. Behold, I give unto you power to tread on serpents and scorpions, and over all the power of the enemy: and nothing shall by any means hurt you. Notwithstanding in this rejoice not, that the spirits are subject unto you; but rather rejoice, because your names are written in heaven.'" (Luke 10:17-20)

There is absolutely no room for arrogance or pride in this vital work. Jesus made it plain here that their joy was not to be because demons did what they said. It was to be in the fact that they were redeemed.

I recently encountered some young people whose church is nearly entirely built on "casting out demons." Having witnessed some of the chaotic messes they call deliverances in their congregation, I was very concerned when I heard some of them talk about how fun it was to cast out demons. If you're enjoying it, you're not really casting out demons. You're just being played by them. And if you are saying it's fun, your focus is totally off and wrong. Don't be thrilled that demons obey. Be thrilled only that you were redeemed and your names are written in the book of life!

So Many Children

I am struck, again, as I read through these accounts how many of the demonized were young people and children. As a result, it has stirred in me a deep desire to be as ready, as disciplined, as in prayer and close to Jesus as I can be, so that He might use me as He needs to see these precious young lives set free. Satan hates innocence, and he hates the young that have not yet been ruined by his ugly ways. It's time to sue him for custody of this generation and to seek to set all the little ones free that have been injured by his vile touch. God grant us all we need in this crucial hour!

Who Does God Choose?

"Now when Jesus was risen early the first day of the week, he appeared first to Mary Magdalene, out of whom he had cast seven devils." (Mark 16:9)

Those of us who have been delivered out of great darkness, and those who have been touched to the core by the demonic, often feel "less than" or "not like others." Be encouraged. It was to Mary Magdalene, one who experienced the depth of darkness and demonic infestation and was completely set free, that He first appeared. She was chosen for one of the most miraculous moments in history.

If God has so redeemed you, you are not less than, you are being prepared for great work in His Kingdom!

13 NEW TESTAMENT REFERENCES

Let's continue to look at the scriptures and spiritual warfare, demonization, and tools of victory over the enemy. I trust that you have not been discouraged so far, perhaps thinking that you were picking up a "how to" guide. It is indeed that, but unless we lay a scriptural foundation of "how to," then what we do is going to be hit and miss at best, dangerous and unscriptural at worst. And the victims of demonization cannot afford for us to be out and about on our own on this. Once we have thoroughly laid the foundation from the Word of God, we can hone our weapons and plan our strategies from there.

Swept Clean

"When an unclean spirit goes out of a man, he goes through dry places, seeking rest, and finds none. Then he says, 'I will return to my house from which I came.' And when he comes, he finds *it* empty, swept, garnished. Then he goes and takes with him seven other spirits more wicked than himself, and they enter and dwell there; and the last *state* of that man is worse than the first. So shall it also be with this wicked generation." (Matthew 12:43-45)

Let's look at this verse one part at a time and look at the original language.

The word "unclean spirit" is mentioned several times in scripture. To review, unclean is the Greek word *akathartos*. *Kathartos* is the root word from which we get "catharsis." It means a release or relief – the ability to get released from something. Again, when we think of someone having a catharsis, the picture is someone that vents their emotions. *Akathartos* is "without cleansing" - the inability to find relief, to be cleansed from something. An unclean spirit is a demon that binds all the nasty junk and uncleanness to the victim it inhabits. It is sheer torture to be so bound, so unable to find relief or release or healing or cleansing from sins and brokenness. Unclean spirits are some of the most horrible, perverted, filthy demons that there are.

- The words "seeking rest" -*anapausis* – means without motion.

Demons are frantic and driven. The only place they rest even a little is when they inhabit a human. That tells me that they once knew what it was like to have a body.

- "He finds it empty" - scholazo – means at leisure – devoted wholly to leisure – loitering – free from labor.

   This tells me that it is crucial that we keep our houses full. Satan and his demons seek to inhabit empty places, people that are wholly devoted to leisure and without any spiritual content.

   Remember that Satan and his demons are drawn to empty voids. That is why Yoga and transcendental meditation are so dangerous, as well as many new age/new spirituality techniques that teach you to close your eyes and "empty your mind of all thoughts." As believers, we are to fill our minds with the Word of God, not empty them. Our minds need to be filled with something – and if we do not fill it with truth and the Word of God, then the enemy will come and fill it with trash. And if we empty it completely, the enemy has free reign to move into our thoughts.

- He finds it "swept, and garnished" - kosmeo – means put in order, or cosmetically made to look good and clean. But it was still empty. It's not enough to go to church, sing a few songs, tithe, do a couple of good deeds. Those may be good, but they can also just be cosmetics masking a spiritually desolate soul.

- "Seven other spirits more wicked will dwell there" – means to settle there, to house permanently. Metaphorically, this speaks of spiritual powers coming to dwell, as God "dwells" in the temple. We are the temple of the Holy Spirit. Without Jesus, we can also be a temple for wicked spirits.

   There are, as with many of Jesus' parables, several different meanings: There is the plain meaning: this is what *can* happen spiritually, and the symbolic meaning, which Jesus makes plain in the last part of the verse, and is to be taken as the true context of the verse: He is talking about that generation. He is saying that He had come to "sweep the house clean." But if they did not fill the house with Himself, then all the demons Jesus daily had been casting out would return, and worse. And they surely did. It was a message to the house of Israel.

I urge a great deal of caution here. Many deliverance ministers scare people half to death by telling the person who has been delivered that if they stray or return to sin or fall in any way, that all the demons that have been cast out will immediately return with seven times the demons. Yes, it is important to fill our lives after we have been delivered, but you can't paste a "one size fits all" pronouncement over people based on this part of the teaching. If we took this to apply to all of us, then every time we sinned again, we would expect a truckload of demons. We need to help people receive grace and forgiveness if they fail, not fear and condemnation. This parable was not a diagnosis; it was a warning to Israel about what would happen if they rejected the Messiah.

Oppression

"How God anointed Jesus of Nazareth with the Holy Spirit and with power, who went about doing good and healing all who were oppressed by the devil, for God was with Him." (Acts 10:38)

The word "oppressed" means, "To exercise harsh control over someone." It is stating the obvious, but Satan's goal and the job of demons is to exercise harsh control over everyone and anyone they can, through disease, death, sorrow, depression, rage, drugs, alcohol, sexual issues and any other way they can. Those who have fallen under the control of these flesh sins and human maladies often find that the "puppetmaster" and his servants are nearby to attempt to use those things to control their lives. You don't need to be demonized to feel their effects. Every believer will at some time feel the harsh breath of the enemy when they are vulnerable, and even more so when they fail in some area: most often, the "harsh control" of condemnation. That is why it is essential that we teach believers when they fall or fail and sin, not to stay down but to immediately get up and be cleansed by the blood of Jesus and keep walking. More Christians have been derailed by condemnation than any other sin or issue. "If we confess our sins, he is faithful and just to forgive us our sins and to cleanse us from all unrighteousness." (1 John 1:9) Satan counts on us wallowing in our failure and guilt. He will lie and say, "God can't forgive you, you've already failed time and time again! How many times do you think he's going to keep forgiving you? The demons came back seven times stronger!"

It's good to know that Jesus gave us that answer, when Peter asked how many times he should forgive his brother. Jesus' reply: seventy times seven. That is a Hebrew term for infinitely; or, as many times as they ask. God will not ask of us what He will not do Himself. The greatest defeat to the oppression of condemnation is forgiveness and restoration.

You may fall, but always fall toward the cross! You are not defeated unless you quit!

The Demonized Fortune Teller

No matter where you go, if you are truly carrying out the work of the Lord, it will agitate and bring out demonic opposition. That is just a given. Paul and his crew were met by opposition in the most unassuming form:

"Now it happened, as we went to prayer, that a certain slave girl possessed with a spirit of divination met us, who brought her masters much profit by fortune-telling. This girl followed Paul and us, and cried out, saying, 'These men are the servants of the Most High God, who proclaim to us the way of salvation.' And this she did for many days." (Acts 16:16-18)

So, what's wrong with that? It was like having your own traveling fan club. Today there's probably a lot of us who would love to have groups of people going around while we minister telling people how awesome we are! And she was telling the truth, wasn't she? What was the issue? What was it that Paul discerned that caused him to turn and confront it?

"But Paul, greatly annoyed, turned and said to the spirit, 'I command you in the name of Jesus Christ to come out of her.' And he came out that very hour." (Acts 16:18)

As the expression goes, the devil is in the details. And he certainly was with this situation. For in fact, what this traveling fan was really saying was, according to the Greek, "They proclaim to us A way of salvation." That is a big difference from "THE way"! Satan is a master deceiver, but he always trips himself up in some way, for the truth is not in him.

This has been an extremely crucial scripture in this age we live in. Everyone claims to be "spiritual." Everyone claims to believe in Christ! But, the devil is in the details. Very often when talking with people about Jesus you will learn they believe in Jesus *and* Buddha, *and* Hinduism, etc. Or that they believe Jesus can save you, but so can believing in any other god or goddess.

One of the most consistent things I have heard in the decades of deliverance has been an unfolding of demonic theology; and it is also often spoken through the mouths of mediums and trance-channelers that purport to have the dead – or "ascended masters" – speak through them. That theology always includes: 1. The Bible is not the Word of God, 2. Hell isn't real, 3. All paths lead to God and 4. Jesus is just A way to God, one of many.

So when this young woman began proclaiming that they were showing A way to God, Paul finally got annoyed enough to put a stop to it. He knew it was a demon, for he knew Jesus was THE way to God, not one of many.

I encountered a similar situation some years ago that gave me a little understanding. We were doing a Halloween evangelism outreach at a park. After the band played, I began to share my testimony. Within just a few minutes, a middle-aged woman with a Bible came to the front and began to loudly yell scriptures from the book of Revelation. She sounded very spiritual. Then she began her own "preaching" which was nonsensical and clearly not from God. I attempted to overcome her yelling which became increasingly screeching and scary but to no avail. We continued as best we could, but she created so much confusion that we couldn't completely overcome the attack. She was a "Christian" by outward appearance but had been sent by the devil to disrupt the work of the Gospel. Here was a person who sounded profoundly spiritual and was quoting the Bible better than most believers. And here is where you need to understand that the devil and demons know the Bible better than most preachers. They work to bring a false religion and a false message into any true Gospel work they can.

In this age, it is supremely important that we understand this dangerous time we are in and learn to confront it. I have never seen such a time in which false religions are being adapted by the church in such subtle forms. Compromises are being made with other religions in the name of "unity," and more and more mixed messages of new age content are being repackaged as truth. Christlam, Hindu religion- based Yoga and meditation practices, and the practice of drawing prayer circles are becoming common within the church. We must know what the scriptures teach and stand on them. And we must recognize the subtle lies and confront them. The woman who followed Paul, demonized, probably sounded as good as any believer the church had at that point. But Paul had the discernment not just to discern the demon, but also to ferret out the lie it was proclaiming! May God give us such sharp discernment in this hour!

The spirit that controlled this girl was a spirit of divination, or a "python." Greek mythology has it that it is "… the name of the Pythian serpent or dragon that dwelt in the region of Pytho…was said to have guarded the oracle at Delphi and been slain by Apollo." It is interesting that in whatever culture Satan rears his ugly head, it nearly always manifests as a serpent – just like in the beginning.

Divination – soothsaying – which was this young lady's slave occupation – is to act as a seer, to prophesy, to utter spells, to divine the future, to rave through "inspiration."

I believe in prophecy more than I ever have because the Word of God is clear about prophets and prophecies being a necessary part of the church. But in this day of great deception, we have to be keenly discerning and careful. There has been so much undiscerned spiritual activity and manifestations that claim to be the Holy Spirit in the last few decades - much of which is plainly not from Him – that every prophet and every "word" and prophecy *must* be judged and discerned.

I remember many years ago, during the Watergate scandal surrounding president Richard Nixon that one of the most famous faith preachers – and the most revered – gave a prophecy that said, "Thus says the Lord, my servant Richard Nixon is innocent, and I will vindicate him, saith the Lord." Months later, Nixon was exposed and his presidency was ruined. He was NOT vindicated, and he was not innocent! That was the biggest false prophecy I had ever witnessed in my young faith at that point, and it was a great object lesson: Just because someone gives a prophecy, does not mean it is from God. We are obligated to discern, and to judge.

I believe in all the gifts of the Holy Spirit, and I am not a cessationist – I believe those gifts are current and more needed than at any time in church history.

But if this little incident in Acts tells us anything, it points to the fact that if there is a real, then Satan has made sure there is a counterfeit. He can counterfeit *all* of the gifts of the Holy Spirit!

Remember the Bank teller analogy I gave previously: You have to handle the *real* (the Word of God) enough that you recognize the false immediately. Why is so much deception coming into the church? Because believers are not trained to handle the real thing – God's Word – so well that a lie cannot slip past them. Satan is counting on this mass ignorance of God's Word in the church in the last days so that he can bring in all manner of lies and delusions, and eventually present the antichrist – who, unfortunately, I believe many Bible-ignorant believers would vote for if he ran for president. We need a generation of new disciples who are so filled with the Word of God that lies cannot survive in their midst.

I sincerely believe that one of the reasons there is so much deception in the western church today is because the churches have weakened the importance of the Word of God both in the pulpit and in personal devotions so much that all we get are just snippets to support affirmations, not fiery words to produce real disciples. If all you get daily and on Sundays is just a fragment of the Word, then your armor of discernment will be full of chinks and holes.

Determine now to fill yourself so completely with the Word of God and the Spirit of God that no lie will sneak by you.

The end of this particular story is that, thank God, this young woman was freed when Paul expelled the demon from her but also – and it's a good warning for us in warfare – "But when her masters saw that their hope of profit was gone, they seized Paul and Silas and dragged them into the marketplace to the authorities." (Acts 16:19)

Lesson One – most forms of occult divination and practices eventually come down to making a profit, whether it's psychic hotlines or bestselling books like *The Secret*.

Lesson Two – when you oppose these activities and get people out from them, be prepared for backlash and attack. It just comes with the territory. But it's absolutely worth it, to see people bound and in slavery to darkness find freedom in Jesus Christ!

Sons of Sceva

(Or, You Better Figure Out Who You Are Before They Do)

"Then some of the itinerant Jewish exorcists took it upon themselves to call the name of the Lord Jesus over those who had evil spirits, saying, 'We exorcise you by the Jesus whom Paul preaches.' Also, there were seven sons of Sceva, a Jewish chief priest, who did so. And the evil spirit answered and said, 'Jesus I know, and Paul I know; but who are you?' Then the man in whom the evil spirit was leaped on them, overpowered them, and prevailed against them, so that they fled out of that house naked and wounded. This became known both to all Jews and Greeks dwelling in Ephesus; and fear fell on them all, and the name of the Lord Jesus was magnified. And many who had believed came confessing and telling their deeds." (Acts 19:13-18)

There is so much to be learned through this portion of scripture. Let's look at the main lesson. You cannot borrow someone else's authority. "We exorcise you by the Jesus whom Paul preaches." That's almost like saying to a man with a gun, "I command you to put your gun down by the authority of a police officer I heard about." You've got *nothing*. Maybe you watched a few episodes of *Cops*. That doesn't make you a police officer, and no self-respecting criminal would pay any attention to you at all.

As with so much we have done in Evangelical/charismatic circles over the years, we tend to see something done and we try to imitate it, whether it is a loud preaching style, someone's prophetic utterances, or making people fall over. The same has happened in much of the deliverance movement. We see something done a certain way and assume it's like a tool you just pick up and use and it will work for you. But the tool of deliverance or demon extraction is a dangerous tool that in fact should only be wielded by those who understand the authority of Jesus and have learned to walk in it. Otherwise, it's like handing a toddler a chainsaw. Don't do deliverance ministry just because you saw someone else do it. In fact, don't do it unless God clearly calls you to it. And if you try to do it the way that these itinerant exorcists did, you can expect similar results. Every believer *can* do the work of casting out demons. But never *seek* to do it unless you are very sure God is calling you to do so!

We have a local church that is fairly far off the theological reservation, and they have built a reputation as a church that casts out demons. I think it's good to know if there are places or ministries that can legitimately deal with demons, but *this* place isn't it. This is a place that has built its services *around* demonic manifestations and "deliverances." I heard some of their youth talking about how awesome it was and how they got so excited about casting out demons. And I realized, these kids were in for a world of hurt. Remember: Jesus said *not* to rejoice that the devils were subject to us. A church that has as its main feature the activity of demons and the attention that is given to it, is a church that is being completely manipulated by those demons without knowing it.

You cannot borrow authority to do demon extractions. Just because your pastor does it, doesn't mean you automatically should. Your pastor, should God use him in that regard, has been equipped by anointing, calling and necessity for it. Just because the evangelist does it, doesn't mean you can or should. If you imitate deliverance ministers or ministries just because it seems fun and exciting, then you are in for a real shock.

I have never understood those who are excited, fascinated or drawn to demonic extractions. Anytime I hear someone say they love to do deliverances, I have to admit, they impress me as someone who has not ever done a real one. Anyone who has done real extractions will tell you – they are most often draining, nasty, ugly, often difficult, and never "fun."

These sons of Sceva learned that demons are a bit brighter than they were. The demons knew all about Jesus – and they knew about Paul, because (1) Paul carried the authority of Jesus, and (2) Paul had a habit of making them vacate their houses. But what did these men have? A wrong motive and presuming to borrow authority from someone else.

And trust me, demons know whether you have it or not. I read about one particularly drastic demonization, so severe that the person in charge ordered no one – not even another minister – to move or speak unless he told them to. One person – arrogantly wanting a "piece of the action" and with a closet full of sins – disobeyed and tried to cast the demon out, which resulted in the sudden recognition and exposure of his *lack* of authority, a humiliating reading of his hidden sins in front of everyone by the demon, and a sudden physical attack that left the man in the hospital for a month.

DO NOT PLAY GAMES WITH THIS. If you don't go in for the right reason and motive, and if you don't carry the true authority of Jesus Christ, the most hopeful outcome you might wish for is to lose your clothes and get scratched up a bit. Clear?

So how do you know if you have His authority? First and foremost, those that have it realize they don't have anything in themselves, that it is all *His* authority. Just as a police officer with a uniform, a badge, and a gun has been commissioned to enforce the law, He has commissioned us to carry out His Word and will. A police officer would be foolish to ever confront a crime or a criminal without those three very important symbols of his authority. Our uniform is His armor, our badge His shield of faith, and our weapon the Word of God. The devil knows whether you carry them or not. Make sure you do.

Even then, no badge and uniform is assigned without training. "Rookie" police officers are the ones most vulnerable, because even though they are right out of the academy, well…they are right out of the academy. The shield and uniform matter. The training matter. But the experience makes the officer a force to be contended with. He knows who he is, and he knows what to do.

In spiritual warfare, it is vital to know you carry His authority, are armed with his weapons, but don't act arrogantly because of it. Walk in humility and walk carefully. And it is good, if God should grant it, for you to learn the ropes from those who have already plowed the field.

The last thing we learn from this story is that when this failed exorcism happened, word got around, and "fear fell upon them all" and "the name of the Lord Jesus was magnified." Who has the power? Jesus has the power! Jewish itinerant exorcists were common in those days, and they had moderate success. But the only name these demons recognized as absolute was Jesus.

As ugly as these events are, it is always my prayer that it would not bring attention to the event but rather the one who dealt with it, the Lord Jesus Christ.

And as a result of this event, "many who had believed came confessing and telling their deeds."

Again, if Jesus does the delivering, it wakes people up, makes them realize the reality of spiritual warfare, the demonic and our need to be cleansed and ready – and more confession and deliverance can take place.

Are We Fellowshipping with Devils?

Part of walking in freedom and holiness is being willing to sever the ties with those things we formerly engaged in that were sinful and destructive. Paul wrote to Corinth very strong words on a multitude of issues. Part of the reason is that Corinth was a city very much surrounded by and steeped in wickedness. It was much like the San Francisco of its time – a port city, filled with idolatry, false gods and sexual debauchery of all kinds. It would be a tough work to get the church of Corinth in the right place. Paul addressed an issue relating to idolatry:

"What am I saying then? That an idol is anything, or what is offered to idols is anything? Rather, that the things which the Gentiles sacrifice they sacrifice to demons and not to God, and I do not want you to have fellowship with demons. You cannot drink the cup of the Lord and the cup of demons; you cannot partake of the Lord's table and of the table of demons." (1 Corinthians 10:19-21)

The word "demon" here speaks of a spirit that is inferior to God but superior to men in its strength. It's good to remember that so that we stay on God's side and don't get too haughty about ourselves.

Fellowship is the word koinonos. It is closely related to the same word for Christian fellowship. It is to be joined to, be in fellowship with, linked like a chain to.

I am thankful that Paul wasn't completely specific about the kinds of idolatry he spoke of here, but it is assumed based on his other writings that it had to do with meat sacrificed to idols. But he made it plain that we are not to do what idolaters do, and we are not to join in their activities. Don't partake in things dedicated to evil and demons.

How does that translate for us? I think it would do well for us to look at the movies, music, video games, books, etc. that we indulge in. Do they have an evil theme? Are they sexually stimulating? Are they grossly violent and anti-God? Are they filled with antichrist themes? Are they filled with occultism, witchcraft, and sorcery? Well, if so, why are you fellowshipping with it? In so doing, you are opening the door to demons and giving them permission to be there and to influence your life.

It is vital we do an honest and thorough housecleaning in this regard. I have been shocked how many believers would never let their child or teen watch an R-rated movie with sexual themes or occult themes, but they cling to their blood and gore movie collection like a pet god. Get rid of it all, and allow no door for demons to influence your house, your family and your walk with Jesus.

Condemnation and Snares

"And a servant of the Lord must not quarrel but be gentle to all, able to teach, patient, in humility correcting those who are in opposition, if God perhaps will grant them repentance, so that they may know the truth, and that they may come to their senses and escape the snare of the devil, having been taken captive by him to do his will." (2 Timothy 2:24-26)

In every church or meeting place, it seems like there is always someone who is argumentative, oppositional and divisive. I have been in ministry for many years, and I have seen it consistently – someone who is convinced of a certain position or doctrine, or doesn't like what the pastor teaches, and creates issues, argues during Bible studies, and brings division among the people.

Paul tells us that these people have been taken captive by the devil to do his will. What is that will? To disrupt, disturb and distract from the purposes of the Kingdom. Paul says God wants us to not argue back, but in humility correct them, with the hope they will repent and that truth can come to them, and they will wake up (come to their senses) and get out of the devil's trap.

I think it bears mentioning here that there are many, many issues we may not agree on. Mostly, the things churches and believers differ on are minor: Do you have to speak in tongues? Is Jesus coming back before, in the middle of, or the end of the tribulation? Do you have to be fully immersed to be truly baptized?

And frankly, I have seen believers nearly throttle each other over such issues.

In Bible school, it was kind of a way of life. We would stay up all night arguing with each other, each of us absolutely convinced we were right, and convinced that the other person was probably not even saved or was going to hell for disagreeing. It made for some very exciting – and sometimes near violent – Bible studies!

But after Bible school, I came to know that my obsession for arguing did not come from Him who called me, but from the evil one who wanted to ensnare me in the trap of being argumentative and divisive, proud and unyielding. I am thankful for that deliverance. Now, when I see such a divisive debate that is only hurting people, I try to take people aside and reason with them about just staying to the basics of our faith and not turning small doctrinal disagreements into deal-breakers worthy of disfellowshipping people.

One of the most divisive – and to me, satanic – arguments I have seen over my lifetime that has shredded more fellowships and friendships than I can count, is the debate over Arminian/Calvinist thought – Did God choose you and you have no choice, or is it our choice to be saved? I have seen believers almost come to physical blows over this. I do my best to reason with those who don't realize the devil is using them to break up fellowships and relationships by explaining to them that the church has been debating this for 2000 years, and has not come to an agreement. Why do they think they will win the argument? It's a demonic distraction!

Leadership and Authority

Although the scripture we will now look at has to do with the establishment of elders and deacons in the church, it is clear that it is relevant to any sort of Christian leadership position:

"...not a novice, lest being puffed up with pride he fall into the same condemnation as the devil. Moreover he must have a good testimony among those who are outside, lest he fall into reproach and the snare of the devil." (1 Timothy 3:6-7).

It has always been a dilemma for me as a youth pastor to see the incredible potential of so many young people, and to realize how easy it would be to just put them up front and let them lead. In fact, that seems to be the modern template for not just youth ministry but church leadership. I think we need to look very carefully at this verse. The word "novice" is "newly planted" or a new believer. Paul is warning us not to put new believers in leadership. It doesn't matter how talented they are, how gifted they are or how willing and eager they are. They need to be proved on the battlefield of the everyday Christian life of struggles, temptations, and trials first.

The reason is quite simple: If we put new believers in leadership, they get prideful. They may have the anointing of God, be very gifted, have the respect of others, have others who look up to them, and have the approval of the other leaders, but all of those things can swell their heads very quickly. In fact, the devil is looking for just such young and newly anointed leaders because they are such easy targets. All it takes is a bit of flattery, a few followers and a little sense of accomplishment and suddenly, you think you're something you're not. The devil will pull out all his tricks to exploit your personal weaknesses to trip you up and take you out of the fight right off of the starting line.

We need to make it clear to people – leadership isn't a privilege; it isn't power, it isn't prestige, it isn't being admired and loved and sought after, it is not an elevation and a first seat at the show. And God forgive the decades of the American church Evangelical media excess that has given young leaders that impression.

No, leadership is foot washing, it is toilet cleaning, it is fasting and heartbreak and rejection and stress and struggle and long nights and disappointment and tears and frustration and lack of support and misunderstanding and a host of other "non-perks." Ask Paul:

"For I think that God hath set forth us the apostles last, as it were appointed to death: for we are made a spectacle unto the world, and to angels, and to men. We are fools for Christ's sake, but ye are wise in Christ; we are weak, but ye are strong; ye are honourable, but we are despised. Even unto this present hour we both hunger, and thirst, and are naked, and are buffeted, and have no certain dwellingplace; and labour, working with our own hands: being reviled, we bless; being persecuted, we suffer it: being defamed, we intreat: we are made as the filth of the world, and are the offscouring of all things unto this day." (1 Corinthians 4:9-13)

"…in labours more abundant, in stripes above measure, in prisons more frequent, in deaths oft. Of the Jews five times received I forty stripes save one. Thrice was I beaten with rods, once was I stoned, thrice I suffered shipwreck, a night and a day I have been in the deep; in journeyings often, in perils of waters, in perils of robbers, in perils by mine own countrymen, in perils by the heathen, in perils in the city, in perils in the wilderness, in perils in the sea, in perils among false brethren; in weariness and painfulness, in watchings often, in hunger and thirst, in fastings often, in cold and nakedness. Beside those things that are without, that which cometh upon me daily, the care of all the churches." (2 Corinthians 11:23-28)

That is true leadership. And that is why it is crucial that leaders are not beginners, but need to be raised, discipled, battle-hardened. To not do so is to put them in peril of failure before even finding their place. It is worth waiting for!

Demons Believe

I live in a town that has more religious people per square inch than any town I've ever seen. Everyone is a "Christian." Everyone believes in God and Jesus. And most of them don't have even the slightest idea what it means to belong to Jesus and be a true believer. They believe in God like I might believe we have a president. It just states a fact, it doesn't mean in any fashion that I know the president personally.

It is important to stress to people that being a believer is not acknowledging some degree of facts, more or less, as to the existence of God or Jesus. Being a believer is surrender of your entire life to the One who died on the cross.

So, in fact, it is *not* enough to just "believe." James tells us why:

"You believe that there is one God. You do well. Even the demons believe—and tremble!" (James 2:19)

Even demons believe in Jesus, yes, they do. And every one of them will spend an eternity in hell.

Believing in Jesus is a complete and total giving of your life to Jesus.

Seducing Spirits

"Now the Spirit speaketh expressly, that in the latter times some shall depart from the faith, giving heed to seducing spirits, and doctrines of devils; speaking lies in hypocrisy; having their conscience seared with a hot iron…" (1 Timothy 4:1-2)

We need to understand that most people don't just jump right onto the deception bandwagon. They are seduced into lies, just as the Adversary seduced Eve. If Satan stepped up in red underwear with a pitchfork and a tail, we'd ignore the obvious attempt. But it is more often what my friend Johanna Michaelsen termed, *The Beautiful Side of Evil* in her book by that same name. (I recommend this book wholeheartedly to anyone wanting to understand the subtle seduction of the "light side" of the occult. I also recommend *The Light That Was Dark* by Warren B.Smith.) Evil is most effective when clothed in religious or holy garb, disguised as an angel of light.

The word "seducing" also means impostor spirits. They are posing as if they were from God, and they are actually demons. Many times, over the years, I have met people that started out well but somehow accepted some odd twist of scripture, or some slight mistranslation of the plain meaning of the Word of God, and in so doing opened themselves up to an impostor religious spirit that eventually turned their teachings into cult teachings and false doctrines. Do not be of those who depart from the faith. Don't listen to seducing spirits. Test everything with the Word of God. "Prove all things; hold fast that which is good." (1 Thessalonians 5:21)

Miracle Devils

"And I saw three unclean spirits like frogs coming out of the mouth of the dragon, out of the mouth of the beast, and out of the mouth of the false prophet. For they are spirits of demons, performing signs, which go out to the kings of the earth and of the whole world, to gather them to the battle of that great day of God Almighty." (Revelation 16:13-14)

"And then shall that Wicked be revealed, whom the Lord shall consume with the spirit of his mouth, and shall destroy with the brightness of his coming: even him, whose coming is after the working of Satan with all power and signs and lying wonders." (2 Thessalonians 2:8-9)

Most Christians are shocked when I tell them that Satan can heal. "I thought only God could heal!" Well, true healing only comes from Jesus. But in the world of the occult, New Age and New Spirituality, it is common to see "psychic healers" and "psychic healing" as well as other types of occult healing, such as Reiki. And people get "healed." In fact, what happens is that the same Satan that afflicts people with illness can make that infirmity or demonic illness leave if it will bring glory to the occult healer or lead people further into occult bondage.

The scriptures are clear that those who practice the occult can, in fact, make things happen – from levitating things to false healings, to manifesting all manner of strangeness. The sad thing is - and I know because I used to practice these things - they think it is their own gift making it happen, their psychic or occultic powers at work. The truth is, all they are doing is inviting invisible demons to take their wishes, curses, workings or commands, and make them happen – if they can. It is all a way to bring attention to the occult and away from Jesus Christ who alone is the source of true miracles.

Christians should be particularly aware, because we are starting to see more and more strange, supernatural manifestations in the church, and not all of them are from God. Not at all. We must test these things, knowing that not every supernatural thing is of God. There is a precedent for this, of course, when Moses confronted the Egyptian magicians who were perfectly capable of doing supernatural things. And of course, Moses' serpent/staff ate the little serpents that they manifested, because God's power is not a counterfeit, and if there is a confrontation, Satan and his counterfeits are always exposed for what they are.

We should be aware that as we get closer to the return of Jesus we *will* see more demonic miracles and "signs and lying wonders" that are sent to deceive people, and this *will* get into the church. So how do you discern? I will go into that question in more detail in the next chapter, but this may help a little:

1. Always ask, "What is the purpose of this?" If it doesn't directly lead to glorifying Jesus, or if it leads people into glorifying or becoming focused or obsessed with the "miracle" or "manifestation," then I would be very careful.
2. Be cautious of any "supernatural" thing that requires a specific method, or any kind of device, object, or physical manipulation to make it "work." There is a difference between true miracles from God and things that border on the metaphysical. We need to discern the difference so that we aren't caught up in the wrong things.
3. Don't be afraid to test these things. That doesn't make you a doubter; it makes you wise. I was actually able to examine some "gemstones" that had manifested in a church. They turned out to be cubic zirconium and junk jewelry. God's not cheap, so if he's going to do this, he's not going to bargain shop at Kmart. Later it was learned that the gemstones came from someone who had them "appear" in her mouth. It was fraudulent. Love Jesus enough to not just accept anything that comes along, because there will be counterfeits, and we need to protect His Name in our midst.
4. If it doesn't feel right, you need to listen to the voice of the Holy Spirit and stay away from it.

These are just a few things that will help to keep us safe from error in these treacherous times.

"Discernment is not a matter of simply telling the difference between right and wrong; rather, it is telling the difference between right and almost right."

- Charles Spurgeon

14 DISCERNMENT

"To another the working of miracles; to another prophecy; to another discerning of spirits; to another diverse kinds of tongues; to another the interpretation of tongues:" (1 Corinthians 12:10)

Discerning of spirits, or discernment, is a much-discussed "gift" or manifestation of the Holy Spirit through believers.

The scriptures do not give a lot of information about this gift, so we must first look at the words used in this passage, then try to shed light on its various meanings and applications.

Discerning – diakrisis – means a judicial estimation; to separate thoroughly; decide; hesitate; discriminate; determine.

Spirits – pneuma – means a spirit, i.e. human, a mental disposition, an angel or demon.

These words allow for the discerning of matters concerning both human spirits *and* angelic/demonic spirits.

Many people narrow the definition of discernment to the ability to tell what kind of demon is at work in a situation. That can certainly fit this verse, but there is more.

Many more people narrow the definition of discernment to pertain to someone who can tell when something or someone is in error scripturally, and that can certainly be part of it as well, but more closely is defined as a teaching/exhortation/correction office.

I have seen abuses on both sides. I have met those who "discern demons" and then diagnose a person with everything from a demon of fingernail biting to a "Jezebel spirit."

On the other side, I have known those who set themselves up as "watchmen" (and God knows we need them!) but then proceed to nitpick every small detail of a church, ministry or doctrinal difference for any divergence at all.

Don't misunderstand me. There has never been an age when true watchmen and true discernment are more needed. But when we scream "heretic!" and "apostate!" over small differences on things like speaking in tongues, the timing of the rapture, Arminian vs. Calvinist, etc. then I am concerned that it is not the gift of discernment working through us but the spirit of criticism.

And when I say "spirit," I am not saying "demon." It is human spirit. Discerning of the human spirit is really a major part of discerning that we need to grasp.

I find true discerning of spirits to be very rare these days.

So, what is it? How does it work? Is it a static gift or can it be developed? Here are a few insights that I trust will help us understand this crucial gift a little better:

1. Discernment is not just being able to point out doctrinal errors, i.e. "discernment ministries." That is not discernment of spirits per se, but is more being an exhorter of Biblical truth and using the scriptures to confront crooked and erroneous teachings. And that is sorely needed in this time of dilution of the Word of God. But it is not discernment per se.
2. Discerning of spirits is both a manifestation of the Holy Spirit *and* a weapon and tool that can be developed:

"But strong meat belongs to them that are of full age, even those who by reason of use have their senses exercised to discern both good and evil." (Hebrews 5:14)

"For the word of God is quick, and powerful, and sharper than any two-edged sword, piercing even to the dividing asunder of soul and spirit, and of the joints and marrow, and is a discerner of the thoughts and intents of the heart." (Hebrews 4:12)

How do you sharpen your discernment? By eating a steady diet of the strong meat of the Word of God.
By reason of use our senses are exercised to discern both good and evil.

The word "senses" – *aistheterio* – means perception.

"By reason of use" – *hexis* – means a power or habit acquired by exercise.

Because discerning is both a knowing and a sense, it can be very troubling when it first begins to work.

You may be in a gathering, and someone catches your attention and suddenly you feel sick to your stomach. That can be discernment.

I once had a meeting with a father about some issues with his child, and what started as a calm meeting quickly escalated as the father began to exert his dominance over church spiritual authority and make it plain that he was calling the shots. I calmly explained why that was not so, but as he talked, I felt something hit my stomach so hard it nearly took my breath away. I realized something vile and destructive was at work, and though his words were relatively calm, what was working through them was terribly demonic. That was discernment.

Or you may be talking to a believer as they are expressing their thoughts on some spiritual matter and an internal alarm goes off that says, "Something is wrong with what they are saying. Something is off about it." That is discernment!

One of the difficulties is that you often sense something, but you have nothing concrete to go on at first. Listen to it nevertheless. Many times, you will feel something is wrong before you understand why. Ask God to give you clear understanding and revelation of what it is about.

I once had a conversation with one of my spiritual mothers, a prophetic truth-teller with razor-sharp discernment. I had been troubled by some things I was "picking up" in some situations I was involved in. "Don't you ever wish you could turn off this discernment thing for a while?" I asked, and she laughed. "Oh son, that is *never* going to happen," she replied. And it hasn't!
  3. Just because you discern something, doesn't mean you have to confront it. You may just be asked by God to pray for that person

or to keep a watchful eye on a situation. One time, God spoke to me and said, "I do not show you these things about others so you can criticize people, but so you can pray for them."
4. Even though discerning is a perceptual gift, it is *not* some kind of psychic guesswork. Although there are times you may sense something is wrong, don't "guess" about what it is. Discernment is not guesswork. It is sometimes a specific knowing of someone's intent or knowing their spirit or doctrine is seriously off, or they carry a demonic influence that is affecting their lives and that of others. If it's not clear right away, wait. Pray. God will show you what the alarm is about.

"I don't like that man. I don't know why, there's just something about him that gives me the creeps!" Be careful; that is not necessarily discernment either, it might just be a personality clash. Don't spiritualize your own issues and conflicts with people.

Having said that, there *may* be times where you get a bad sense about someone or something. That *could* be discerning. But don't speak of it to others; pray and ask God the truth of it before you say anything or tell anyone.

5. Learn to know the difference between demonic spirits and human spirits.

Too many people are ready to "diagnose" and cast demons out without even the simplest discerning of what other things may be causing trouble for someone. I think it is very important not to act until you have ruled out everything else as causal to their condition.

Consider:

- Schizophrenia can mimic both "possession" and supernatural strength that may be associated with the kind of demonic strength a demonized person may have, which may lead to a false conclusion that they are "possessed."

- Some drugs can create what seems to be "supernatural strength" in a person, which can lead to a false conclusion that they are demonized.

- Some people can be complete deceivers and have *no* outward evidence of demon control!

All of this should sober us, and make it very plain that discerning is not a guessing game nor something to be desired lightly, but is a serious, crucial tool in both protecting God's flock as well as getting people set free from real demonic control.

All of this should make us seek God for the real thing, and be willing to be responsible for carrying and wielding that weighty weapon of our warfare.

Father, we ask that you would help us to walk in the truth in these matters, and to walk in the real discerning of spirits. Help us to do that hard work of digging into Your Word so our senses can be disciplined, sharpened and ready for the battle we are engaged in. And help us to wield that mighty weapon, not as a bludgeon to hurt people, but as a surgeon's implement, to divide between soul and spirit, ferret out demons from every pocket they are hiding in and cause them to flee. Help us to use this sword to bring clarity to situations where the enemy is seeking a foothold or seeking to deceive or seduce. Make us humble servants who know that we ourselves have no "gift" but rather we are the vessel of the Holy Spirit – who IS the gift – and who works in and through us as we yield to You completely. In Jesus' Name.

Gregory R Reid

There is no such thing as spiritual blessing without corresponding fierceness of attack. That is the law of the battle.

- Amy Carmichael

Gregory R Reid

15 NIGHT TERRORS

Nearly every believer I have known in my life – and many nonbelievers as well – have had the following experience: They are half awake, half asleep, or more often in a dream and slowly a feeling of terror and dread overcomes them, a darkness and a sense of evil begins to seep into their dreams, and they are screaming to try to wake up. They wake up halfway, trying to scream but something is choking them or sitting on their chest and they are unable to move.

There are variations of this, of course. And there are just nightmares, which all feel evil and terrible and foreboding, and often cause us to wake up yelling and in a cold sweat. That's different.

This other thing is – well, supernatural. And it is one of the most well-documented phenomena in church history.

Of course, today, scientists blithely dismiss it with an "it's a chemical this, combined with a neurotransmitted blah blah blah." Which is really just whistling in the dark at something you cannot explain and is terrifying if it's not scientifically explainable.

I will share a bit of my own story here. As a child, my earliest memories were of astral projecting. That is where you actually leave your body and go somewhere else. I didn't know what was happening except that I saw myself above my body and was being carried by an unseen force, taken out of the window and through the neighborhood and other places. Then I was taken back and slammed into my body with a loud whirring and horrible noise, feeling like I was surrounded by a horrible evil presence. I would try to scream for my mom and dad, but no sound would come out of my mouth. When it departed, I would run upstairs and get in my parents' bed and stay there till morning. They had no idea what was happening to me and I couldn't tell them about it.

I was too young to know what was happening. I only learned in my teenage occult studying years what it was. It was called "astral projection" – leaving your body. It is an actual occult practice. I didn't learn it from a book. I had no control over it whatsoever.

Only after I came to Jesus and renounced all my occult practices did I understand that this "astral projection" was demonically forced on me as a child.

In the occult, I was constantly surrounded by "things." Even as a child, I felt them and sometimes saw things. From about age 9 to 15, I studied and began to practice the occult, and I "assumed" those things were my spirit guides. So I did not fight them. I just ignored them as much as possible, except for one particular "guide" which spoke to me through the Ouija board.

The moment I renounced the occult and all of its workings, these "spirit guides" that had been with me since childhood turned on me. Shortly after I had given up everything of the occult, I awoke at three in the morning with the similar "choking" paralyzing experience I had felt when I had left my body as a child. I just lay there in fear, groaning, trying to scream, nothing coming out. All I knew to do was to say "Jesus help me" over and over in my mind. Suddenly I heard what sounded like a loud clap of thunder, and I was fully awake and staring into the face of the most nasty, hideous, half-human half-mutilated-flesh demon you could ever imagine. I said, "Who are you?" and it told me its name. "What do you want from me?" I said, terrified and trembling. It threatened to destroy me. I just said, "Jesus, help me please, help me, help me!" and I slowly watched it fade away.

Absolutely shaken to the core, I told one of my new Christian friends about it, wondering if he was going to tell me I was crazy. "It's just a demon," he said casually. "Just rebuke them in the Name of Jesus and they'll go away. "Really?" I replied, kind of excited about that possibility.

Some time passed, and then once again, I half-woke from a terrible evil presence in a dream to some ugly thing trying to suffocate me. I couldn't speak. I prayed in my mind, "Jesus, help!" Suddenly I could speak, and I pointed at it and said, "Get out of here in the Name of Jesus Christ!" I recall a look of shock on its face as it just vanished. That was the night I began to understand my authority in Jesus Christ.

Similar incidents continued on and off for years. Through them, I began to understand just how real our enemy was. My rejection of scientific "explanations" is because I have fought these things face to face, and I know what causes many of these "night terrors" that so many others experience.

I was not surprised to learn years later of how well documented this phenomenon is in church history. In fact, there are classifications of some of these demons, in particular, "incubus" and "succubus," the names given to demons that sought sexual interaction with females or males. And yes, that is a real phenomenon as well.

Again, remember that demons seek to take a human body in order to act out their own sinful, insane and blasphemous ways through a physical vehicle very much like they may have once had. They are feeders that attempt to find vulnerable humans and find an open door to them. Night attacks like this are just one of the various ways they seek to terrorize – and sometimes gain entrance – to us.

How to Deal with Attacks

If you are faced with such a night attack, what do you do?

1. Call on Jesus' Name immediately, even if you can only do so in your mind or attempt to say it through the paralyzation.

2. GET UP. Turn on the light. Don't go back to bed right away or you may have to do this again.

3. Get the Bible – preferably the book of Psalms – and read it out loud. They *hate* the Word of God, and they really hate hearing it. So read it, out loud, and they will flee. Keep reading till you can go back to sleep.

4. Every night, pray and ask Jesus to cover you and send His angels to protect your sleep. I always quote this verse out loud: "I will both lay me down in peace, and sleep: for thou, Lord, only makes me dwell in safety." (Psalm 4:8) I read this two ways: That He will only make me dwell in safe places, and that He alone is the one who can make it safe. I think both are correct, and with this verse, I seal the

   night with His Word as a safeguard against attack.

5. If you have a terrible/frightening dream, remember, it's usually just a dream. But if there is a demonic attack with it, then put on your armor and hit them hard with the Word of God. If you have a seductive or sexual dream that is evil, deal with the evil thing that brought it and don't fall under condemnation. We can't control our dreams and we are not held accountable for things in our dreams, only for the content of our minds and hearts in our waking moments.

These attacks, I have found, most often occur when a person is tired, overworked, has fallen out of time in the Word and prayer, or is emotionally vulnerable. Stay rested, guard your heart, and stay Word-ready. And remember – if you're being attacked, that's not necessarily a bad thing. It means you got the enemy's attention. Only worry when he's not worried about you!

To discern spirits we must dwell with Him who is holy, and He will give the revelation and unveil the mask of Satanic power on all lines.

- Smith Wigglesworth

16 DOORS OF ENTRANCE – BASICS

Just how do demons gain influence, entrance, and control?

Scripturally, some of the answers are obvious. The demonized woman Paul confronted rather likely was invaded when she called on the Pythonic divination spirit to work through her – although we do not know if there may have been a prior open door.

Some demons appear to be, if not attached to, then the resident cause of afflictions: The person with a deaf/mute spirit, for example.

While we touch on this, let me caution you with the utmost severity: Do not make the mistake of assuming that because someone may have a "deaf" spirit, therefore all deaf people's deafness is caused by a demon. That is inaccurate, unscriptural, and hurtful. Never assume a person has a particular demon because they have a particular affliction, sin or problem. That kind of cut-and-paste, one-size-fits-all, connect the dots deliverance is simply dangerous.

We also have the demoniac of the Gadarenes. We don't know why he became demonized. We don't know how the doors were opened. We only know where he ended up, and how he was left.

Here is where we must nail down another very crucial rule of warfare: **How a person became demonized is not as important as just getting them set free.**

And while Jesus did ask for a name once, He did not ask how or when they got there. (He only asked one father how long his child had been afflicted.)

But no two situations are alike. Don't be bound to a "formula" for deliverance. The only "formula" is obedience to God in the moment.

So while it may not *always* be necessary to ascertain how a demon entered a person, it may at times help us to understand the doors that allowed them legal right to be there, which often gives us the knowledge to pray specific prayers to close specific doors of entrance.

Again, there is no "formula for deliverance."

At times, we have prayed for the extraction of a demon, and we could not even engage the person's will in order to find out how or if they had opened a door.

At others, through discernment and a few Holy Spirit led questions, God gave some specific details of doors that were opened that, when the person repented and closed those doors in prayer, they were immediately set free.

And all scenarios in between!

As we will expose some specific details and doors of entrance in the next few chapters, please keep in mind:

1. None of this is a diagnosis. Be extremely cautious of methods, manuals and definitive formulas for how demons work, how they got there or what they do. And beware curiosity: it will trap you in their traps. These guides are simply that – guides - not set-in-cement, push button, failsafe, "works every time" techniques.
2. There is a great deal we do not know. (Nor do we necessarily need to know.) Demonization – though there are surely some things we do know about how it happens – can sometimes be like spiritual Russian roulette. Some people who have been demonized seem to have done nothing at all to warrant the invasion. I have also seen people come to Christ who did horrible, demonic things and yet went through no "deliverance" at all except salvation! God knows why. I can only trust him for what I do not know, and use His word and wisdom and what I do know to navigate the treacherous minefield of demonic invasion.

The Battlefield

Let's go over the lay of the battlefield again. It sits on property that has been ceded and deeded to the devil until Jesus' return will inaugurate His Lordship over the entire globe when the Kingdoms of this world will become the Kingdoms of our Lord, and of His Christ, and He shall reign forever. (Revelation 11:15) Jesus, in fact, declared that Satan had been driven out from his legal place – expelled! – by Jesus' death and resurrection. (John 12:31)

So, if he's been expelled – then from what? Why is he still acting like a conquering king?

It is because he has deceived the whole world into his lies. He has taken the lie of Eden, that man can be his own god, and spread it over nations and histories and generations, and he has limitless energy in his quest to have the entire world under his control.

Like the story of the prisoners of war who did not know that their captors had already been defeated until they were given the information the enemy had tried so hard to keep from them, the world lies in darkness and despair. Satan works to keep them from hearing the truth – that Jesus defeated him. Satan knows he has lost. So all he can do now is lie, and deceive, kill and destroy, and keep as many people as he can in his demon-run prison from discovering the truth – Jesus has already defeated them all!

That is why our role is so crucial. We must carry the message. We must unlock the doors to the prisons and proclaim, "The war is over! Jesus is here to set you free."

So, we see the battlefield yet to be taken – lost people wandering aimlessly, being lured into places and to people and given things that are all under the control of a vast army of demons who seek one thing only – to inhabit humans. They are like invisible vampires, seeking for the slightest breach, a tear in the soul, a rip in the mind, a fracture of the heart in order to insert their demonic finger and rip open that wound or sin in an attempt to feed off of their sin, grief, and brokenness.

A blood-bought soldier of Jesus, entering that battlefield, will send demons flying, scattering, or hanging on for dear life to their victims, doing everything in their power to silence the believer's voice and to keep their victims from Jesus – and from freedom.

That is the battle we enter. And we are here to rout the enemy and take prisoners out of darkness into the Kingdom of God. To the battle!

FROM THE FRONTLINES: PARTY CREW

A few years ago, a young lady in our youth group brought a young man to a concert outreach we were doing. He had a heartbreaking life, and at a young age found himself on the streets and part of a "party crew." I learned a lot in a short time. There were 50-100 kids – some as young as 13 – who were part of this crew. They lived in treehouses, parks, and people's back yards. Drugs, drinking, survival, and sex were their pursuits. They gave each other a fragmented sense of "family" in a world that had given them nothing but rejection, abuse, and abandonment. They gave each other a sense of belonging. All of that kept them together.

That, and their "party crew" identity.

Jesse came to our outreach and found himself weeping in the arms of one of our youth leaders who had preached hard that night, warning, "I don't want to go to one of your funerals because you were high and got killed in an accident. You should be high on God!"

Jesse gave his life to Jesus that night, and we were overjoyed. I signed the Bible we gave him so he could remember the night he was saved.

But the pull of the Crew was too much. Within weeks, he was back into the party life.

Just weeks later, he and three of his other Crew members – driving high – were instantly killed in a car wreck.

We stood outside that night by the wooden cross the kids had hastily put in the ground at the makeshift memorial site where the accident took place. I was moved and heartbroken to hear the words of the "crew" as they expressed their terrible grief and loss, a plea from one to stop using drugs, jokes about smoking pot with their friends and St. Peter, and everything in-between.

As I focused on the cross, which was covered in names and sentiments done with felt tip pens, I was taken completely off guard by the satanic pentagram that someone had drawn on it. Spiritually angry, I quietly walked up to the cross, poured anointing oil on it, and quietly rebuked the demons that bound these kids. I stepped back into the crowd and felt a dark presence next to me. The young man carrying that presence shuddered. Something in him recognized Someone in me, and I realized he had put the pentagram there.

Within days it was back to business as usual. In fact, on the day one of the kids was cremated, the parents invited all the kids over to their house – where all the drugs and drinking continued all night.

That is a stronghold. I learned later that the name of this party crew was "The Cult of Dionysus" and was a literal satanic group that was dedicated to the Greek god of drunkenness and debauchery. As I said, if you call them, they will come. And they certainly did.

I learned that this "crew" was established by adult devil worshippers who had committed their coven to the pursuit of drugs, drinking, darkness, and death.

And it had just taken three of its young members who had no idea what demons drove them. They would not be the last. Within a short period of time, there would be two more deaths associated with kids in this crew.

Satan has set up an entire world around drugs, drinking, sex and partying in order to attract – and demonize – and kill – our kids. It is time for believers to start praying in earnest for the destruction of this stronghold in this generation, and for an outpouring of the Spirit of God to set them free.

The liberty of the man of the world is liberty to commit evil without restraint; the liberty of a child of God is to walk in holiness without hindrance.

- Charles Spurgeon

17 SPECIFIC DOORS OF ENTRANCE PART ONE

THE THREEFOLD CORD:

SUBSTANCE ABUSE, THE OCCULT, AND SEXUAL SINS

"And if one prevail against him, two shall withstand him; and a threefold cord is not quickly broken." (Ecclesiastes 4:12)

This verse in Ecclesiastes is referring to the vulnerability of a person who is alone, and the strength of a person when they have someone to help them – or more than one person.

There is an underlying spiritual principle here that I believe also applies to the demonic realm. The strength of an army is not in one soldier alone, but in, as they say, "an army of one" – many acting in consort. It applies to the demonic army as well. It is difficult for the demons at best, since each is ruled by others who are also ambitious and pernicious in their own destructive ways. But they do obey orders from those higher up and as this verse suggests, there is strength in numbers. A spiritual stronghold - a demonic influence that seems impenetrable and makes it difficult to bring freedom to a person – is sometimes comprised of a cluster of demons acting as a "threefold-cord" that is hard to break.

In all the years of praying for people for deliverance, I have seen one particular stronghold – a "threefold cord" – that appears to be consistent, difficult, and is both personal and generational. That is the three-fold cord of:

-Drug and/or alcohol bondage

-Occult/new age/false religion practices or lineage

-Sexual sins and bondages

When we pray for people, it is sometimes necessary to discern the root causes of the demonic influence. Almost every time, those who struggle with one of these issues also struggle with the other two, if not personally, then connected and rooted in their family background.

The above practices - as well as the corresponding principalities and demons behind them – combine to create a stronghold. People who have a history of alcoholism, often have a history of family sexual abuse, and/or occult practices. People who are addicted to sex or pornography often had that door opened through drug or alcohol use which lowered their resistance. People who practiced the occult, or had an occult/false religion lineage, often also struggle with drugs and alcohol and/or sexual bondages.

The idea of generational occultism/false religions, drug/alcohol abuse and sexual sins and problems is a hard concept to grasp. But the scriptures say:

"The Lord is longsuffering, and of great mercy, forgiving iniquity and transgression, and by no means clearing the guilty, visiting the iniquity of the fathers upon the children unto the third and fourth generation." (Numbers 14:18)

The consequences of sin are passed from generation to generation. Only Christ can undo the generational damage that sin does.

When you are counseling someone who is being demonically harassed or worse on one of the above issues, it is worth digging a little to see if the other two "cords" may be attached as well. Once they are exposed and renounced in prayer, their power is loosened and the person can more readily get free.

"But that isn't fair for a child to suffer for something they didn't do!" Of course, it isn't "fair." Satan isn't "fair." He never plays fair. But Adam gave him blood rights to us. Only the blood of Jesus can break it.

I personally came from two lines of generational alcohol abuse and occult/false religion lineages. Those things were there even in my earliest remembrances. Demons manifested to me as young as I can recall. Did I ask for it? No. But my parents were not believers at the time, and they had no way of preventing the generational spiritual damage they themselves were afflicted with from passing on to me.

When parents do not cut off these generational strongholds and spiritual ties by coming to Christ, then the children are open game. Not all will inherit the sins in exact ways, but they often suffer in related ways, i.e., alcoholic or drug-abusing parents providing an environment for the "second cord" of sexual abuse or confusion to come into the children's lives.

Perhaps this story will help you understand this principle. When I was 31, my mother called me and told me that my insurance policy had come to term and I could either reinvest it or get the cash for it. I was shocked. "What insurance policy?" I asked. "We took out a policy on you when you were born; you didn't know that?" I certainly didn't! And I was thrilled to find out!

They had taken out that contract for me when I was born. I had no idea about it until all those years later.

In the same way, when parents don't walk with Jesus, they are in effect putting their children under the contract of the garden - under the curse of sin because of disobedience. A child doesn't need to know that to be subject to it, and as soon as sin gives birth in the child, they die spiritually until regenerated by the blood of Jesus through forgiveness of sins. Just as I had no idea I was under a contract but it was there regardless because my parents signed the papers *for* me – children are subject to the contract of sin and death if the parents do not cancel the contract through Jesus Christ. If they do not, and a person comes to Christ, then it is up to that person to claim their freedom and cancel that contract at the Cross. I would love to say it all just "goes away" at that moment, but Satan is a legalist, and you have to sometimes go to court and bring the papers and show him that he has no more legal right to you, or your children, or your loved ones. He'd just as soon not have you know that anyone took out a policy on you!

Now let's look at some of the doors of entrance that may give way to demonic influence. Again, just doing some of these things may not cause demonization, but people who suffer from demonization almost always can trace their condition back to one or more of these open doors.

Occult Doors

"Many of those also who used occult arts brought their books together and burned them before all men; and they counted up the price of them, and found it to be fifty thousand pieces of silver." (Acts 19:19)

The early believers recognized the danger and seriousness of occult practices and occult items, and so they burned them, as if to indicate that this was not just a danger but a poison which they needed to be completely cleansed of, not just spiritually but physically. The following are some of those items that the enemy consistently uses to make people open to demonization.

Ouija Board

The Ouija Board was developed as an American household "game" by investors, including a William Fuld, who sold it through the Kennard Novelty Company. Fuld became the sole investor and marketed it around the world. He died falling off a ladder at the building the Ouija Board had told him to build. Eventually, it was sold to Parker Brothers, which sold it to Hasbro. It was a wildly popular game, did not work for most, and ended up in attics across America. In recent years, it has been repackaged by Hasbro as, among other things, glow in the dark editions, and pretty pastel colored ones to attract young girls. In addition, there is an "angel board" produced by another company, to seduce ignorant churchgoers and unsuspecting New Agers into thinking that they are actually talking to God's angels!

We have prayed with so many people who were under horrible oppression that had completely forgotten that they had an Ouija Board somewhere in their house. (Usually in the attic!) Great relief was found in getting rid of it. And yes, I recommend burning it. That way there's no chance of anyone else getting hold of it. And despite all the rumors to the contrary, they do not fly around the room when you try to burn them and they do not show up again days after throwing it in the trash. It's pressboard. It burns quite nicely. I am not saying there may not be some kind of reaction when you do it, but please remember – 99% of everything Satan and his demons do externally is smoke and mirrors to try to terrify people. Don't be put off by his tricks, no matter how scary they may appear.

The idea behind the Ouija Board has an unknown history, some tracing it back to ancient China. It is just a revision and variation of the ancient "Ob" – "water bottle" divination. In modern times, both poet William Keats and Alcoholics Anonymous founder Bill Wilson were devotees. Wilson even had a "spook room" where they did regular Ouija sessions. (Unfortunately, he was also part of the government LSD program along with "Doors of

Perception" *Brave New World* author Aldous Huxley.) (http://en.wikipedia.org/wiki/Bill_W.)

The movie *The Exorcist* was based on a true story, not of a girl but of a boy who used an Ouija Board to talk to a deceased relative, and it opened the door to the drastic full possession which the movie portrayed.

The Ouija Board is an extraordinarily dangerous game, and even some people involved in the occult – especially white magick, Wicca and New Age – will tell you to avoid it because it is evil. If those who are doing the occult think it's dangerous you should pay attention!

The Ouija Board is one of the surest and quickest ways to open demonic doors and invite demonization. It is important that a person repent of any involvement with it, and if they have an Ouija Board, to get rid of it as soon as possible. If a family member or parent or anyone else practiced it, then it's important to renounce the practice and pray and ask Jesus to cut its influence off from you.

Curanderismo

Curanderismo is a practice most well-known in Mexico and in Hispanic culture. It is a mix of Catholicism, candles, and "folk magick." It involves a mix of Christian spirituality, saints, candles designed for different "workings," potions, powders, prayers to saints, lotions, and other paraphernalia designed to do "limpias" (cleansing). It also – although this is denied by some practitioners – may involve spells and curses against enemies for those who pay the Curandero or Curandera to do a "working."

Whatever others may call it, biblically it is still the occult, and it is witchcraft. Its roots go back to the Aztecs. I work and live in a predominantly Hispanic city and culture, and it is almost standard practice to have to pray for people for the renunciation and rejection of Curanderismo practices in their families – either direct or extended. In addition, many have had recollections of being ill as children and having a strange person (usually an older woman) come in, light candles, and rub an egg all over their body, either to "read" the sickness (divination) or get rid of it. It is ancient occult witchcraft, and a prayer of renunciation and rebuking of any demonic influence from that practice needs to be done, and a severing of the influences from generation to generation.

Astrology

Yes, that fun and cute little thing in the paper or on the net that tells you according to the stars what your future is supposed to be, what "sign" you are based on your birthdate. It is forbidden by God:

"You are wearied in the multitude of your counsels; Let now the astrologers, the stargazers, and the monthly prognosticators stand up and save you from what shall come upon you." (Isaiah 47:13)

Renounce any involvement in it.

New Age/New Spirituality

This is a very broad term, but includes a wide variety of practices including reincarnation, crystal magick, chakras, transcendental and other forms of meditation, angelology, psychics, ascended masters, alien teachings, etc. The core beliefs revolve around all paths leading to God, that everyone has the Christ spirit and the "divine within," and spiritual experiences are highly sought after.

The scriptures are very clear on reincarnation:

"And as it is appointed unto men once to die, but after this the judgment." (Hebrews 9:27)

Also clear is Jesus being the only way of salvation:

"Jesus saith unto him, I am the way, the truth, and the life: no man cometh unto the Father, but by me." (John 14:6)

"Neither is there salvation in any other: for there is none other name under heaven given among men, whereby we must be saved." (Acts 4:12)

When the core beliefs of new age/new spirituality are removed, one sees easily what the "source" of the teachings are. Renounce it all, cut the demonic ties to it and be free. Receive the truth of the above truths in scripture without reservation, and you will be delivered from the lies.

Wicca/Witchcraft

The practice of modern Wicca, witchcraft, or "white magick" are all part of the same ancient worship of pagan gods and goddesses. Modern Wicca is a much more sanitized version of real witchcraft, which makes it even more spiritually dangerous. It is harder for people involved in this practice to see that the source is really from the devil. Satan promotes anything that turns people away from the Creator of the universe and Jesus Christ - and on to false gods and goddesses. Wicca provides a "gentle" version of real witchcraft to seduce people who would outright reject Satanism or black magick.

What is the difference between Wicca, witchcraft and white and black magick?

Wicca is a bit of a modern invention, more attuned to ecology and Greenpeace, women's causes and new age spirituality than hexes, curses, or any harm to animals. Of course, there are always exceptions. But the goddess/god worship is the main destructive feature of Wicca, as they open themselves to the real demonic forces behind the façade of human gods and goddesses.

Witchcraft is a universal practice of spellwork, dealing with the underworld and "otherworld," which goes by different names in different cultures: Voudon, Santeria, Brujeria, Palo Mayombe, etc. I know Wiccans would protest to high heaven about them being considered a "harmful" religion, as their modern motto is "Do what you will and harm none." Even at that level, however, opening up doors to what God forbids creates a dark and unpredictable, confusing and lost world.

But in other cultures, "Wicca" is considered not even real. If you want to understand real witchcraft, one needs to go into the interior of Mexico, where witchcraft is deadly, or to Haiti, where Voudon (voodoo) is a bloody and curse-filled religion at best. Haiti is known as the island that is 98% Catholic and 100% Voodoo. Like the Old Testament nation of Israel, people often profess faith in God yet call on dark and deadly pagan gods to actually "get things done."

Any form of witchcraft whatsoever – be it mild Wicca or deadly witchcraft

– needs to be renounced, cleansed and broken.

The damage of witchcraft within families from generation to generation tends to be strong and profound, with a lot of tiny tendrils wrapping around the family and personality. Patience in the Word of God, prayer and fellowship and a diligent cutting off of these tendrils will bring God's promised freedom.

Psychic Workings

If you've been to a psychic, had your fortune told, or your palm read, or Tarot cards done for you, then it is an open door to the demonic.

I have talked to people who believe that they were born with psychic powers. I do not doubt that, but it is important that they see that it was not a gift from God but rather a product of a breach in their spirit that allowed a familiar spirit to give them information that they could not humanly have. Once that psychic ability is renounced and broken, they are no longer able to intuit as they did before. It can leave an empty place in them. God needs to fill that with His Spirit. It is good to know that the real thing belongs to God! Two of the gifts of the Spirit – the word of knowledge and the word of prophecy – are what God really intended for us to walk in. The difference is – "psychic power" is a counterfeit, something a person thought was *their* gift, *their* abilities. But what the Spirit gives are *His* gifts working through us, and *His* alone.

Occult Books, Movies, Video Games

Books and movies with occult themes such as *Harry Potter*, vampire themes like *Twilight* and numerous others are open doors to the occult world and demonic influence. Again, it doesn't mean that if you have read them or seen them or played games that had those themes that you are "demonized." In fact, the main danger of these things is that they change your worldview into an antichristian one. Occult books and movies have done a great deal to mold the thinking and religious bent of an entire generation. I am not surprised to find that one generation down from the worldwide obsession with *Harry Potter*, vampire and zombie media that we are beginning to enter the first post-Christian generation in America. We need to connect the dots.

Though you may think these things are harmless because they are fiction, they are occultic and need to be renounced.

The newest trend, in fact, is teen "supernatural romance" books, which often include sexual relations with vampires, werewolves, and the "undead." If you remember what I wrote about demons who seek sexual contact with humans, you will understand how much trouble this generation is in spiritually.

Occult Music

Music is one of the most powerful means for demonic influence, and as we get closer to Jesus' return, we see how Satan is becoming more blatant in the antichrist themes of bands and songs. From the comparatively harmless songs of a young man named Elvis who brought "rebellious rock and roll" to the world, to the drugged out, occult-themed bands of the sixties and seventies, to the Satanic rock bands of the '80s, we have now reached a new level of occultic influence in music. It's an age in which none of this shocks or is warned against. The music is simply ingested without filters. We never forget anything we've ever heard. Though we may not "recall" it consciously, we take it all in subconsciously, and the messages of anti-Jesus, drunkenness, drugs, sexual abandonment and violence are filling up a generation like filthy water in a well that is being consumed without any concern for its effects. Demonic and antichrist music unquestionably opens doors to the demonic realm. Famous artists now blatantly display upside down crosses, pentagrams, sing of the vilest of satanic themes, and no one bats an eye. We just keep making them richer by buying their products.

Occult Jewelry, Art and Paraphernalia

Occult Jewelry, amulets, art pieces, artwork, and a number of other items are "touch points" for the demonic. Some disagree with me, saying that demons don't "possess" objects. They may not "possess" them, but they are drawn to them, and they do "tag" them. The demonic world is a vast network spiritually. Demons "mark" their territory like dogs. And items that are devoted to the occult are considered theirs, so when a human obtains them, the demons are able to bring oppression through the objects. I don't know how that works. But it does. There have been many occasions where we have been praying for someone's deliverance and we were getting nowhere. Then we would pray and ask God to reveal what was hindering the person's release. Suddenly they would recall some piece of jewelry or another object that had occult meaning or ties. Once it was destroyed, they were free.

Occultists and people who practice magick know that this works. It is called "sympathetic magick." They can do a working on an object, give it to someone and wait for its effects to kick in. Some people might think, "But it doesn't work if you don't believe in it!" Nonsense. That's like saying electricity doesn't work if you don't believe in it. Try disbelieving in electricity while you put your finger in a light socket.

How does it work? Remember a primary principle when dealing in the demonic realm: If you call them, they will come. If it's been dedicated to the occult world, it will draw the demonic inhabitants of that world.

There was a reason that those who did blood sacrifices in the Bible always returned to the same spots – the "high places." The Bible says that the blood is the life. (Deuteronomy 12:23) The wicked spilling of innocent blood draws demons like flies. They are drawn to places of spilled blood, violence, sexual debauchery, etc.

In individual cities, you can see territorial demons set up. Drug areas are in one spot, gangs take another place, adult bookstores and strip joints another. Demons are quite territorial. When sinful man opens the door to the workings of the flesh, the enemy comes to govern. Cities that are New Age centers - like Santa Fe and Sedona - have demonic governance because people "worked the doors" of forbidden occultism until they swung wide open.

In the same way, God was very clear to the children of Israel – not just to *not* practice what the nations practiced, but to not take the objects of their worship, no matter how valuable. They were **accursed things**:

"And you, by all means abstain from the accursed things, lest you become accursed when you take of the accursed things, and make the camp of Israel a curse, and trouble it." (Joshua 6:18)

If we have "an accursed thing" – something related to the occult, the demonic or sexually perverted etc., whether it is music, videos, games, jewelry, art or other objects, then we will be spiritually powerless to walk like we should. Hear the Word of the Lord:

"There is an accursed thing in the midst of thee, O Israel: thou canst not stand before thine enemies, until ye take away the accursed thing from among you." (Joshua 7:13b)

Having or possessing pornography is governed by the same principle.

The things dedicated to the wicked one, either blatantly or subtly by occult meaning and purposes, is a stumbling block to us. It will subject us to demonic attacks and influences, and short-circuit our ability to fight spiritually. "Even if I didn't know it was wrong?" Even if. Especially if, in fact. I don't know how many people I have prayed for that had come under horrible oppression for some reason, and when we did a house search, we found some item that had occultic meaning that they knew nothing about. Once it was gone, so was the oppression. It's just like that.

Séances, Divination and Necromancy

Whether through a formal séance or an Ouija board, attempting to speak to a dead loved one gets the automatic attention – and often swift response - from a lying familiar spirit who will come to try to imitate the departed loved one. Again, do not talk to the dead, or even seek to.

People attempting to talk to the dead are as old as man's beginnings. From the very first, God laid down the law on it:

"And when they say to you, 'Seek those who are mediums and wizards, who whisper and mutter,' should not a people seek their God? Should they seek the dead on behalf of the living?" (Isaiah 8:19)

"Regard not them that have familiar spirits, neither seek after wizards, to be defiled by them: I am the Lord your God." (Leviticus 19:31)

Sorry, Potter fans!

"There shall not be found among you anyone who makes his son or his daughter pass through the fire, or one who practices witchcraft, or a soothsayer, or one who interprets omens, or a sorcerer, or one who conjures spells, or a medium, or a spiritist, or one who calls up the dead. For all who do these things are an abomination to the Lord, and because of these abominations the Lord your God drives them out from before you." (Deuteronomy 18:10-12, NKJV)

It should be perfectly clear by these verses that God forbids using occult means to tell the future (including psychics, tea leaves, palm reading, Tarot cards, astrology, etc.) and especially necromancy – talking to the dead.

Before I go into this, I realize that many people have occasional "talks" with our departed parents or loved ones in our grief – by that I mean, we are not trying to actually communicate with them, nor do they respond (gratefully.) It is simply a phantom pain reaction to the enormous grief of not having them there ever again in this life to talk with. I don't think this is necromancy – it is just working through grief. And obviously, if something answers, rebuke it! (Putting these verbal thoughts to prayer would be even better. "Lord, I miss ___ so much! Please comfort me in my grief…")

But beyond that, we are not, under any circumstance to attempt to actually communicate with the dead.

My own fascination with – and attempts at – communicating with the dead were a direct result of my following an Episcopal Priest named Bishop Pike. (I began to read occult books at the age of 8 or 9 or so, and his story compelled me spiritually to know more.) Pike was right along Jeanne Dixon, Edgar Cayce and Paramahansa Yogananda as my spiritual role models. Pike had found a medium to talk to his "son" who had committed suicide. Grief – and a spiraling list of apostate teachings and activities – drove him to contact his "son." His "son" answered, telling Pike he was alright, that there was no hell, and confirming all of Bishop Pike's apostate beliefs. Shortly afterward, Pike and his wife went to the Israeli desert in search of the "historic Jesus." Pike wandered off, got lost, fell and died, going to a Christless eternity unless he cried out for the real Jesus at the last minute. (And I hope he did.)

That is a perfect example of what necromancy and the occult leads to. God forbids it because God knows people are not, in fact, talking to the dead, but rather to demons who wish their destruction. Pike began with grief as a child through losing his mother; became an agnostic attorney; went to seminary; began to fight for abortion and gay rights; denied the virgin birth, hell and the Trinity; became a chain smoker and an alcoholic. By that time, he was ripe for the devil's ultimate deception. Pike reported "poltergeist" phenomena after his son's suicide, then pursued communication through famed psychic Arthur Ford, which was televised. From there, the step into eternal darkness was swift and final.

As a Pike devotee, reading of his tragic death made me reconsider talking to the dead! After all, why would his "son" lead him to that horrible end?

Another of my role models was the late Jeanne Dixon, who accurately "predicted" the assassination of John Kennedy. It immediately put her in a place of international fame and recognition. She claimed to be a Christian and to love God, and I followed her teachings right up until she had a vision of a serpent that came into her bedroom, curled around her, looked into her eyes, and showed her a vision of Antichrist arising out of Egypt. I wasn't yet a Christian, but I did remember something about a snake in the garden of Eden in Sunday School class as a boy. I knew it wasn't a *good* thing. I began to reconsider her "divination" too.

After being powerfully saved, I abandoned it all.

Divination and necromancy are absolutely forbidden by God.

A diviner was said to be possessed by the "baalath ob." She was called the "mistress of the pythonic spirit" or "she who spoke out of her belly." It was also called the "obidiah," and in the New Testament, it was the same sort of pythonic spirit that spoke through the young woman who was harassing Paul.

From Genesis in the garden to Paul and the woman with the "python spirit," to Jeanne Dixon and her "serpent revelation," little has really changed, especially people's gullibility and vulnerability to being seduced by the occult. The devil may be able to paint himself up with makeup to trap people, but he's still just a snake!

Astral Projection

The occult teaches that the "soul" resides in the solar plexus right beneath the ribcage, and that we are "tethered" to our body via a "silver cord." Even occultists will tell you how dangerous leaving your body – otherwise known as astral projection – is. They warn of the danger of that "silver cord" being severed while out of body, your soul being cut off, and you die. According to his wife, rock musician Jim Morrison was doing just that when he died.

Occult knowledge is full of twisted half-truths and destructive lies. But I believe the spirit, in fact, does reside in the center of us. Consider Jesus' words: "He that believes on me, as the scripture has said, out of his belly shall flow rivers of living water." (John 7:38) The word belly is "koilia" – the hollow, matrix, heart, upper belly. That is where our spirit resides. It explains to me why almost every time people are demonically attacked, the attack centers on their upper stomach area. It also explains why often, in demon extractions, a person feels their "guts" are being ripped out.

Astral projection is an extremely dangerous thing precisely because the demons are attempting to dislodge a person enough to allow them to come in the door and co-reside with them.

Our spirit does not reside in our brain, memory, or flesh. It is right in the center of us.

This became clear and important to me when speaking to a friend about his mother in law who had slipped into severe Alzheimer's. "She doesn't remember me," he explained. "She doesn't remember her husband, grandkids, or anyone else. But if I talk to her about Jesus, she can talk about him all day. She *knows* who He is!" What a comfort! Her mind no longer functioned, but her spirit was alive and well!

That is why true salvation is not just an emotional experience or accepting head facts. It's surrender of our spirit to God. Being born again is giving our spirit to Jesus to be saved, having our old man die, and to be born again in Christ. It may involve your mind and your emotions, but is much deeper than that. It is the surrender of the all of who we are. Salvation seals our spirit to Christ and closes every door to any familiar or demonic spirit that would seek to harm us.

Familiar Spirits

The Bible mentions those who have a "familiar spirit" several times. What exactly is a familiar spirit? From what I have studied scripturally, known observationally and confirmed in spiritual battle, a familiar spirit is:

1. A demon that seeks to speak through a medium, Ouija board or other means.

2. An "information demon." Familiars follow a person, memorize their actions, words, speech, experiences, history etc. Then when an unwitting person seeks to talk to that person after they die, a familiar spirit can nearly perfectly imitate that dead loved one. A "medium" will talk in the same vocabulary, tone and with the *knowledge* only that person would know, thus deceiving the loved one into thinking it's their departed loved one. Why? To gain entrance; to open a door; to seek possession.

We must get something absolutely clear: To be absent from the body is to be present with the Lord. (2 Corinthians 5:8) When you die, the elevator goes up or down. You don't stay and haunt your family. That's a deception.

Everything you see on TV about ghost busters, ghost hunting etc. is a lie. The "ghosts" they pursue are not dead people. They are demons seeking a way to invade human flesh and take them over, or delude people into seeking occult things.

I know this may fly in the face of your traditions and maybe personal experience, but the Bible makes it perfectly clear that when we die, we are not here anymore. We're with Jesus or separated from Him elsewhere. And there is no scriptural recognition of "ghosts," only familiars.

So, if a deceased loved one appears to you or starts to talk to you, rebuke them in the Name of Jesus. It's not who you think it is. It is a demon, a familiar spirit.

Today, they do not call it divination but "trance channeling." Channelers claim to let the "departed" speak through them. Many claim that the "ascended masters" are talking through them. ("The ascended masters" is an old occult teaching about souls who have reincarnated many times and gone on to be "gods" elsewhere.) The Bible calls them principalities. (Or it may just be a demon with a spiritual Napoleon complex.)

Oprah Winfrey once heavily promoted a book/DVD called *The Secret*. Fitting in perfectly with Ms. Winfrey's post-Christian new spirituality views, *The Secret*, written by Rhonda Byrne, is a collection of occult ideas as old as Babel. It has been repackaged and reworded to make people receive it more easily. Even many Christians fell for it.

The Secret is based on the "law of attraction." The teaching is that you attract from the "universe" what you put out in either negative or positive energy, thoughts, etc.

All of this originates from Hermes Trismegistus, one of the fathers of occult/magick writings and practices. From him came the phrase, "As above, so below." That phrase is considered the key to *all* magick. It alludes to the belief that we are all divine, that man and God are equal. The universe is the same as God in this teaching, which is why Ms. Winfrey often speaks of praying to "the universe." It teaches that God is the same as man, and man the same as God.

But the actual basis for the book/DVD *The Secret* is really the "trance-channeled" messages from "The Abraham Group," a group of "Ascended Masters" (demons) that took over and spoke through medium/trance channeler Esther Hicks, as documented by her and her husband Jerry.

Ms. Hicks had read the book *Seth Speaks*, which is about a "trance channeled" being that called itself "Seth." Hicks sought that experience. The result became the source material for the world-renowned book *The Secret*, seen as so harmless by everyone, including many Christians who have unknowingly adapted its principles without knowing it is the doctrine of demons.

So, if you are a believer and you have this book or DVD, throw it out, renounce it and repent of it. It's the voices of demons through God-forbidden mediumship.

One last note about The Abraham Group's vessel, Esther Hicks. When she was first taken over, the question was asked about what was the best way to grow in her "spirituality." My Christian yoga-practicing friends better take careful notice of the demon's reply:

"Sit in a quiet room in loose clothing and *focus on your breathing.*" That is precisely what Yoga teaches. More on Yoga later.

The Voices of Lies

Inevitably, the voices of "departed loved ones" and "ascended masters" are uniform in their theology:

1. Jesus was just a man who had the "Christ spirit."
2. The Bible is not the Word of God, all religious books have equal truth.
3. There is no hell.
4. All paths lead to God.
5. We are ALL God.
6. Jesus did not die for your sins.
7. Jesus is not God.
8. We are reincarnated many times.
9. There are no "last days."
10. "The Christ" will return as an enlightened self-realized human to save the world and bring peace.
11. There is no judgment.
12. Everyone goes to heaven.

Sadly, these very doctrines of demons are beginning to be taught within the "emergent church." They are unwittingly aiding and abetting the demons in their "last days" push to deceive mankind.

Two Bible Incidents and A Warning

"But what about the witch of Endor? She called up Samuel. Doesn't that prove it's ok, and that there are ghosts?" (1 Samuel 28:7)

A couple of things. First, Saul had been abandoned by God. Second, not everyone agrees it was Samuel. Third, if it was Samuel, he didn't claim he was wandering the earth but rather disturbed from his rest. Fourth, he came to pronounce final judgment on Saul. I believe God allowed it to do just that, and to make it clear that the "medium" didn't do it. (She was terrified and shocked when it actually happened.) Does this sound like it was okay to do this? Saul did a forbidden thing, and it was answered by judgment. God allowed this once and approves calling up the dead *never*.

An interesting aside is that "Endor" means "The fountain of the circle." Circles and triangles are historically used for occult purposes. This doesn't prove that is why it was so named, but it is possible it was why she chose to be there.

"But what about when Jesus was talking to Moses and Elijah? Doesn't that prove we can at least communicate with departed saints?" No. Jesus had an open door to heaven. When this incident happened, (Matthew 17:1-9), Jesus was transfigured. When Peter tried to interject himself by asking if Jesus wanted them to build them a little shelter, God spoke in the midst of this glorious meeting of Jesus and Moses and Elijah and said, "Listen to my Son!" In other words, no, you *can't* be part of this meeting! Keep your attention on Jesus! So, beware of those who say they can talk to the dead saints because Jesus did. He's God, they aren't. Whoever they are communicating with, they're not from God.

I am concerned because I have heard a number of self-professed prophets and teachers claiming they went to heaven and spent this amount of time with Paul, two days with Moses, etc. This is a deception. *We are not allowed to talk to the dead - period!*

Remember that fortune telling, the Ouija, palm reading, tea leaf reading, Tarot cards, astrology, numerology, and any other effort to "predict the future" are forbidden by God. Remember that there are no ghosts:

"We are confident, I say, and willing rather to be absent from the body and to be present with the Lord." (2 Corinthians 5:8)

If anything claims to be a departed loved one, it is a familiar spirit – a demon.

Remember that there is no such thing as reincarnation:

"And it is appointed unto man once to die, but after this the judgment." (Hebrews 9:27)

The occult world is dependent on the teachings of divination, necromancy and reincarnation. Be armed with the truth so you may help others be free from these lies.

Drug Abuse

It should go without saying – but unfortunately, we are at a time when it must be said: Any drug taken for any other than medicinal purposes is an open door to the demonic.

I have fought this battle for generations, having been saved during the hippie era. "But the Bible says all the herbs of the earth are for our use!" people would say, proving that people's ability to justify their sins knows no creative bounds. God made sharks, too. Good luck swimming with them!

We need to get down to the Biblical and historical nitty-gritty on this issue. Remember, the word sorcerers in the Bible is *pharmakeus* – the same root word that we get the word pharmacy from. Anyone familiar with the occult, magick and sorcery understands that drug use is common, and in that world, drugs are considered useful and even necessary to open up the door to the "other side." In nearly all cultures, those that practiced sorcery and magick also used drugs – peyote for the native Americans, Absinthe for the literary and artistic set, and toxic fumes from springs for the Greeks and Romans whose "seers" inhaled them to see their visions and receive their "prophecies."

The fact that the root word for sorcery is pharmakia really needs little further explanation. People are fooling themselves if they think that "casual" drug use is harmless. It always opens doors to the demonic world.

Prescription Drug Addiction

There is little question that addiction to pain killers, etc., brings with it a stronghold of the enemy. What may be medicinally helpful in the short-term need can over time easily become a destructive bondage that requires not just detox but at times breaking off of demonic "feeders" as well.

Alcohol Abuse and Binge Drinking

Those who cannot stop drinking are unquestionably physically, emotionally and psychologically dependent on alcohol. But there is also a very strong demonic component that digs in after a long period of time that makes the person unable to be free without strong prayer for deliverance.

Party Spirit

Those who cannot stop participating in drug/drinking parties no matter how they seek to be free are under demonic bondage. (See "Party Crew" story.)

There is a "party spirit" so to speak – a demonic strongman behind much of the drinking and drug partying that is taking thousands to their eternal death, especially our youth. Prayer is often needed for deliverance from this ugly bondage.

Sexual Sins

Now we come to one of the most controversial and crucial areas of open doors to demonic influence – that of sexual sins.

Before we tackle specific sins and their effects – and there is not enough space to tackle more than a few of major concern – we need to set forth the foundational understanding of sex in its spiritual context. Much has been written about the mechanics of sex, the dynamics of sex, the emotional and psychological implications of sex, even the morality of sex, but there is little written on the spiritual element, and it is to this, and through this, we will bring understanding and truth that will help set people free. For without addressing those dynamics, concerns and connections, many people will stay bound – even as believers – for years without freedom. I pray with all of my heart we can change that in this hour of great sexual promiscuity and wickedness.

A Few Myths

1. Myth: Sex is just a physical act. You can have sex without feeling love and it really doesn't matter or affect you very much.

Fact: Sex with a person is never just a physical act. It entwines you – whether you "feel" it or not.

"What? Do you not know that he who is joined to a harlot (porne) is one body? For two, saith he, shall be one flesh." (1 Corinthians 6:16)

Now quite obviously, it is not here referring to some transmogrifying act in which two bodies literally become one monstrous body. So we must infer that a much larger meaning is here, which, in fact, is borne out in experience in real lives.

Sex is never "just sex." You are joined with another person psychologically, emotionally, mentally and spiritually.

The implications of "being one" are that all the walls are down in that sexual act, every door open and every barrier removed that separates two people into two people. It is designed to be a profoundly spiritual act.

When the Word said, "What God has joined together, let no man rend asunder," it's not just a good line to end a wedding with. It speaks to the sacred bond that God intended for one man and one woman for life. The sex act in a godly marriage unites two as one, with each other and with God:

"For this cause a man shall leave his father and mother and be joined unto his wife and the two shall be one flesh. This is a great mystery; but I speak of Christ and the church." (Ephesians 5:31-32)

The sexual union in marriage is a shadow picture of Jesus and our bond with Him. Any other context lessens it, degrades it, and in other contexts like "gay marriage," mocks it.

God created sex for procreation, for pleasure, and to reflect the spiritual union of God and His people. That is why the scriptures speak frequently of idolatry as adultery against God. There is a spiritual element to sexuality we do not comprehend that is sacred, fragile, and to be guarded at all costs.

So sex is never "just sex."

All honest people will admit that having sex, and then severing that tie, is like sticking two pieces of flypaper together and then ripping them apart.

That's how *God* sees it. And, that's how it really is.

When the spiritual dynamic of sex is removed or ignored, then all that's left is the pleasure, and the psychological, emotional bond. In a godly context, sex is meant to be a gift that opens your heart to your spouse and to God. In an ungodly context, sex becomes the object, the drug, the goal on which you hope at some point to build a life, a marriage, a family.

It is no coincidence that for many church youth, their drop-off point from God corresponds precisely with their loss of virginity. The sudden central focus of sex – its passion, pleasure, intensity, and desire for more – causes their flesh to suddenly clash and be in contradiction to God's Word about waiting until marriage. And that conflict can cause them to simply erase God from their priorities, their lives, and their beliefs. Tell me sex has no spiritual component!

When God spoke for us to run from fornication, wait until marriage, not commit adultery, avoid uncleanness of the flesh and spirit, not commit homosexual acts and not have sex with animals, it is because He knows the great cost of disobedience and the heartache and spiritual damage it will cause.

What we were given as "one" person was meant to be given to one other person in marriage for life (barring death and remarriage) and to be one *only* with that one person.

Every time you give yourself away to another person, you give away part of yourself – you and the other person have imprinted and changed and absorbed part of the other person. Every time, you lose part of yourself and bleed in the parting.

Once that boundary is crossed, it often leads to more encounters, with each encounter leaving more damage and emotional and spiritual fragmentation. I believe this fragmentation and such a way of life this creates is profound, and only Jesus can bring healing and restoration. And He can and will.

STD's

But there is a deeper reality we really need to grasp. If sexual contact with another is in fact not just physical but spiritual union, then if the person you have sex with is demonized, then those demons will have access to you now as well. Sexual union outside of marriage – fornication – is one of the quickest ways to demonization there is. Sexually Transmitted Demons. We must make it very clear that if you have a sexual union with someone who is demonized, that demon now has access into your own life. Every single demonic influence which that person has will now influence you. They now have instant access into your world. Why? Because you gave them the right to. You have to pray through these former unions and ask Jesus to deliver you from any demonic tie or bondage that may have entered your life as a result of that union.

I have prayed with many people who became demonized after a sexual relationship with someone who was involved in the occult or other demonic activities. After we prayed and broke those spiritual bonds and ties, they were able to be delivered.

2. Myth: Sexual fantasies are harmless.

Fact: Sexual fantasies are spiritually dangerous. This is why the scriptures tell us to be "Casting down imaginations, and every high thing that exalteth itself against the knowledge of God, and bringing into captivity every thought to the obedience of Christ." (2 Corinthians 10:5)

In the world of magick and witchcraft, nothing is more important and key to working magick than the imagination. While creative thinking is a gift from God, we are walking on dangerous ground when we try to employ our imagination in wrong ways. For example, one of the techniques now taught as young as kindergarten age is "creative visualization" or "finding your imaginary friend." Those techniques easily break down the fragile, God-given barriers that keep demonic spirits from breaching ours.

When you engage in sexual fantasies about another person, you are doing two things: One, you are violating another person's sovereign will and choice, and two, you are giving legal power for demons not just to have a foothold in your mind, but to empower demons to harass and try to influence and violate the person you are fantasizing about.

This became very clear to me a number of years ago when I was counseling a young person who was being barraged and overwhelmed by sexual thoughts about one of the other youth group kids – someone they had no attraction to at all. We prayed, and it stopped. I was not surprised to learn later that it was the *other* person that had initiated the sexual fantasies!

Your mind was designed for Jesus to reign. Keep it clean!

Any sexual activity outside of marriage has the potential of opening you up to demonic influence.

I will deal with this later in the section on prayers for deliverance, but it is important to go through your own sexual history and pray, asking God to cleanse you and to sever any spiritual connection (some call it a "soul tie") to the other person. I have talked to so many people that, even though married, struggle years later with sexual and romantic thoughts about someone they had been sexually involved with years previously. They felt guilty and tormented by those thoughts. But when we went through the prayer to sever those emotional, psychological and spiritual ties, the person was delivered from those thoughts once for all.

Homosexuality

As of this writing, homosexuality has become a white-hot issue culturally. It has gone, theologically, from being a clear sin issue to a social phenomenon, a psychological conundrum, and a moral landmine.

The big debate in the last few decades concerning homosexuality has been: Is it a result of nature or nurture?

First, the "born this way" theory as yet has yielded no credible science. I do think the "nurture" theories - that circumstances, family and parental relations and other early age sexual events and exposure contribute greatly to homosexual development - are valid explanations for much of a person's homosexual feelings and leanings, regardless of how gay advocates seek to ridicule and discard that position. The fact that a huge number of gay men report childhood/preteen molestation, and many lesbians report that they had been sexually abused or raped, validates at least in part the thought that gays aren't born, but rather suffer the results of significant childhood pain and misdirection sexually.

I will not debate the issue, even though people are screaming for debate, and change of law, and rewriting of Holy Scripture. God's Word does not change because society wants it to. The Word of God is clear – sexual acts between men and men, or women and women, are forbidden. God calls it sin.

One of Satan's successful campaigns in this era has been to rewrite our language – homosexual is "gay," homosexual acts and desires are a "lifestyle" – opposing the sin is "hate speech."

In order to bring freedom to people, we need to stay scriptural in our language, our understanding and our prayers. In this brief section on open doors, I will try to approach homosexuality in just that manner.

1. Sex between two people of the same sex - God calls sin. (Leviticus 18:22, 1 Corinthians 6:9-10, Romans 1:26-27)

2. God never refers to "gays" or "homosexuals" as an all-consuming thing which involves soul, body, way of life, friends, sexual acts etc. God, in fact, does not see "homosexuals" or "lesbians." He sees broken, sin-bound people who are trapped and robbed of His perfect will: marriage, children, family. (Excluding those called to be single.)

God created man and woman for each other. All of history, nearly 2000 years of church history and Biblical truth from Genesis to Revelation attest to that truth. (It's only been in the last 50 "enlightened" years that liberal theologians have tried to alter these truths.) Then, sin entered into the human race, and men and women without God left every good thing God planned in search of forbidden, destructive things – murder, lust, drunkenness, fornication, theft, adultery, child abuse, slavery, pornography, bestiality, homosexuality, greed, rage, war.

Homosexual acts are just *one* of the manifestations of sin and the brokenness it brings. It is an *act* done - not a description of a person created to do so. No one was created by God for homosexual acts. It is a product of sin and brokenness. And as with all other sin acts, it carries consequences. The consequences of repeated indulgence of any sin are entrenchment, addiction, bondage, and a demonic stronghold. You become a slave to that which you indulge:

"Verily, verily, I say unto you, whosoever committeth sin is the servant of sin." (John 8:34)

This is not a debate about love. We do not truly love those bound in homosexual sin if we paint that life as anything but what it actually is – a painful, life-robbing, satanic trap. And frankly, I believe most gay people, if they are wholly honest with themselves, would admit that they would do almost anything not to have been saddled with this painful bondage and isolating wound.

Remember that the person and the sin are separate things. But a sin can, in time, mold a person's character, and then create an identity based around that sin. God only sees the person infected by sin's deadly disease. And this particular sin and activity are powerfully transforming and addicting.

None of this is a judgment. It is a spiritual and scriptural observation.

From a spiritual warfare perspective, the "gay life" and gay world are permeated with demonic structure, underpinnings and networking like few other arenas. Like the "party spirit" stronghold I spoke of, the principalities that rule it fight their victims tooth and nail to keep them bound and prevent their escape.

When a person makes the decision to extract themselves from the gay culture and cease to engage in homosexual acts, the battle begins. Old friends may call and attack you for trying to change or cajole you into returning. Fears and loneliness may come in like a flood. It is so crucial to be around solid, supporting believers during this struggle.

"Why is it so hard to get out?" one says. That's not the question. The right question is, "How do I break the grip of this awful bondage and walk with Jesus?" It is not easy. It is as difficult as drug addiction, drunkenness or any other sin-entrenchment. I do not believe God promises no struggle, or a guarantee of marriage – though I certainly know many friends who broke the chains of homosexual enslavement and are married – yes, happily – with kids. You will be tempted, yes. Anyone with *any* sin addiction will have to stay close to Jesus to overcome temptation. In fact, a homosexual lust temptation is no different than a heterosexual one. Lust is lust. Both are sin.

God does promise overcoming power. But you have to make a 100% decision that returning to that way of life is not an option. Even if you slip. Even if you fall 100 times.

Over the course of many years, I have come to understand that there is often a demonic component to both the development of, and the perpetuation of, homosexual feelings and acts.

And yes, there is a difference between "playing doctor" and the kind of entrenched developed homosexual desire that creates a stronghold. One person I counseled with described an awful presence that intruded in a dream as a young boy, transformed him into a "girl," and allowed another "male" to sexually violate him. He was eleven years old. He awoke scared, ashamed, and overcome with an alien desire that soon bore fruit in uncontrollable imagery, pornographic addiction, and homosexual longing and lust. That became the genesis of a long struggle with homosexual desires and acts. In addition, older men picked up on his "wounding" and started him on a horrible cycle of molestation at the hands of predators.

To me, it was clear that the very genesis of his struggle was a demonically created and influenced lie through a demonic dream that allowed them to use his body as a vehicle for their own lusts. Deliverance, shutting the original doors and recognizing the lies he had believed brought him great freedom.

In another situation, I was contacted via a hotline by a young high school student who sought counseling about his feelings of being a woman trapped in a man's body. We met at a local coffee shop, and he poured out his life story.

As he spoke, I was absolutely stunned as the atmosphere at our table began to change, and I watched his face "overlayed" with a completely foreign image that mutated his entire face into that of a sensual older woman. It stayed on him for most of the rest of our visit, fading just before we parted ways. There was no question in my mind that his perceptions of his "wrong gender" were not his, but the result of a spiritual interloper, an invader seeking to set up residence in his confusion.

I am not saying gays and lesbians are "possessed." But I do believe that the genesis of the struggle and transformation into a way of life that is steeped in depression, loneliness, emptiness, promiscuity, substance abuse, violence, and often suicide is rooted in demonic influences. People are not born this way. It does not happen just by birth.

What if a person did not open the door, did not seek it? Again, there are an astonishing number of gay people who report molestation or rape as a child or young teen. Remember the earlier discussion of "transference through sexual contact?" It is like the seeds of destruction of personhood are passed from the predator to the child.

Unfortunately, gay activists have portrayed such a positive (and false) picture of the gay life, that many men, rather than speak of their abuse, speak of their gratefulness to the older boy/man who initiated them and helped them "come out." What a horrible lie.

When a person's first sexual contact is a violation, it creates inroads and intrusions for demonic influences to begin working within that hurt and wounding.

But what about all the men who are molested and didn't turn out gay? The seeds of destruction planted by sexual violation often take a different turn, resulting in self-destructive behavior, isolation, broken relationships, and substance abuse.

I believe that in seeking to set people free from homosexual bondage, it is necessary to go in prayer to shut the original open doors and prayer for deliverance from any demonic influence that seeks to keep the person in bondage. On occasion, it may necessitate an extraction of a sexually predatory demon.

It is difficult for those who are on the outside to comprehend the depth of pain and struggle those afflicted with homosexual desires face. Tread with mercy, love, compassion, grace, and the anointing of discernment and the healing power of God.

Adultery

Adultery is an open door to the adversary, and without God's help, immediate repentance, forgiveness, and reconciliation – as well as closing every door – the danger remains that a demon which delights in breaking up homes and destroying families will get a foothold and seek to create another adulterous situation as soon as possible. If the stronghold remains, the person may end up becoming what is often referred to as a "serial adulterer." The person must acknowledge and forsake their sin completely. On occasion, there may also be a demonic component to adulterous impulses, especially if they are compulsively repeated. We won't call this "the devil made me do it." We'll call it "the devil helped me do it." Prayer for deliverance and for cutting of spiritual/emotional ties to the other person(s) may be necessary. Prayer for the protection of the children is needed as well, as they often "take on" the guilt and fear of growing up and doing the same thing their parent did. Satan would love to seek a secondary open door in that way.

Pedophilia

Pedophilia is sexual lust for an underage teenager or child. Although sexual acts with a minor are of this writing still against the law, I believe the lowering of the "age of consent" is not far off. Just as gay activists positioned themselves as a persecuted minority with civil rights issues, eventually overturning marriage laws and changing the course of a nation, so pedophiles are working hard to normalize their lusts. They have for years worked through the organizations of "The Renee Guyon Society," whose motto is "sex before eight or it's too late" and "NAMBLA," the North American Man-Boy Love Association. Even as of this writing they are seeking to have their "condition" removed from the diagnostic manuals as a "mental illness," and are pushing instead to have themselves called "MAPS" – "minor-attracted people."

Let me make it plain: sex with an underage child is a crime and a great sin. I am sorry to throw cold water on my contemporaries who like to say, "All sin is the same." This one is not. Jesus said, "Then said he unto the disciples, It is impossible but that offences will come: but woe unto him, through whom they come! It were better for him that a millstone were hanged about his neck, and be cast into the sea, than that he should offend one of these little ones." (Luke 17:1-2)

I also want to make it clear that I am *not* saying child abusers can't be saved, forgiven and set free. They absolutely can.

But we have to understand that this is an extraordinarily damaging sin, and the demons behind it are pernicious, predatory and devastating. A child is innocent, trusting, and mostly intact. Predators destroy their trust and shatter their whole being.

It is a myth, by the way, that most boys who are sexually abused become abusers. Very few do. Most molested kids – especially boys - just become self-destructive, isolated and tormented by fear - and fear of becoming "the monster" that destroyed them. The devil delights in the condemnation and fear he brings to victims of predators. (For more insight, please see my book, *The Color of Pain* from Lighthouse Trails Publications.)

The predatory abuse of children is demonic acting out at its deepest level.

A person so bound must make a 1000% turn away from their sin and be willing to go through a real extraction of this ugly demonic ruiner of children, if necessary.

Pornography

Pornography is unquestionably one of the most sinister weapons in Satan's arsenal for the destruction of families, individuals, and Christians.

Before the Internet, pornography was hard to find, difficult to make and a shame to possess. Kids had to steal it from their fathers or borrow it from their friends. History tells of archeologists, when uncovering ancient Canaanite sites, came out physically ill from seeing the horrible pornographic depictions they found. So it is nothing new. But it is definitely demonic and destructive. Child pornography was legal on the streets of Hollywood until the mid-1970s. And although it has become illegal in most countries, because of the internet it is flourishing and becoming more violent and horrible than it ever was before, defining the meaning of evil at a new level.

This "baptism of filth," as David Wilkerson termed it, has blanketed the world, families and even Christian ministers. It is still "shameful" enough to remain a horrible secret for many, especially believers. (That is why it is so important to find a trusted person to confess to and receive prayer so that God can break Satan's snares of secrecy and condemnation and shame.)

Now that pornography is accessible with the click of a mouse or the quick use of a smart phone, the demonic world of pornography is now feeding on millions of people.

And I believe feeding is the correct description. As previously stated, I believe that demons once knew what it was to have a body. In those bodies they indulged in filthy and perverted practices beyond anything previously known, which was partly the cause for the annihilation of the race of Noah's time.

They still desire these ungodly practices. They are full of lust but they have no body to act it out with. The only way they can act those lusts out is vicariously – by attaching themselves to humans who will either carry out the lustful acts or by trapping them in the pit of pornography. Pornography is a great evil.

That is not meant to bring condemnation on anyone, because there is already so much guilt attached to pornographic addiction. My intent here is to suggest that (1) pornography was a specifically created evil that was meant to destroy lives and families and to violate the sanctity of sex and marriage, and (2) a person struggling with this addiction and sin may not just be struggling with the mental, emotional and sin elements of it, but there may also be a demonic component.

If that is true, then I believe it may be necessary to receive prayer with people you trust for any demonic attachment that is feeding off of the pornography addiction. It is an intense enough struggle without the demonic element, so it is well worth not just renouncing it, but having solid prayer to close the doors so nothing is able to feed off of this very painful struggle.

Let me conclude by reiterating that not all open doors mean that a person is demonized. But there is surely a kingdom and forces that delight in the destruction of humans and will push every door open they possibly can to keep a person in slavery. Jesus has come to break every chain.

Aggressive Christianity is the world's greatest need.

- A.B. Simpson

Gregory R Reid

18 SPECIFIC DOORS OF ENTRANCE PART TWO: FALSE RELIGIONS

False religions can be a major open door to demonic bondage. The spirit of deception is most able to mislead the multitudes cloaked in the guise of spirituality, sacred texts and "holy" activity in false religions. The following are some of the strongest false religions that require absolute renunciation of all their beliefs, and a breaking of the mental strongholds and lies learned. At times, it may require extraction of a demon from some area in a person's life.

Islam

Islam is a religion begun by a young tribesman who went into a cave and was "visited" by one he believed was the angel Gabriel. What was spoken to him was recorded and was the beginning of Qur'an. Islam is a religion filled with bondage, judgment, fear, no grace, and no certainty of God's love at all. The Qur'an is a "progressive" book which is initially friendly toward the "people of the book" (the Jews) but progresses into heavy taxes demanded of Jews and Christians and even violence and beheadings for unbelievers. Islam is a terribly fearful way of life. There is no personal relationship with Allah; there is no certainty of paradise. Even Mohammed said he had no assurance he himself would be in paradise.

Allah is not the same God of the Jews and the Christians, despite the ignorant proclamations of many Christians. Even Muslims know Allah is not the same God as the Christians and Jews. They do not believe Jesus is God the Son. They do not believe Jesus died on the cross, but rather Judas took his place at the last minute. It is another gospel. As to the visitation from Gabriel, Paul says in Galatians 1:8:

"But even if we, or an angel from heaven, preach any other gospel to you than what we have preached to you, let him be accursed."

Jesus came to set Muslims free from the curse of bondage, legalism and a loveless religion to have a relationship with the Living God who offers salvation, forgiveness and certainty of salvation and God's love through Jesus.

Even now, Jesus (or Isa, as Muslims call Him) is revealing Himself in person and in dreams to Muslims all over the world and turning them to salvation through His death and resurrection. At the same time, I have heard multiple accounts of Muslims experiencing deliverance from demonic forces when they receive Jesus. Islam must be renounced, and we must be prepared to help them through deliverance if necessary.

Hinduism

Hinduism is an extraordinarily dark religion. It contains over 320 million gods, many of which are depicted as hideous and demonic. (Because in reality, they *are* demonic!)

Few religions open such a pure door into the demonic underworld as does Hinduism, without the practitioners knowing it. The philosophy behind it – reincarnation, Karma, attaining "nirvana" through multiple reincarnations - is unbiblical. You even have to be careful about talking to Hindus about "eternal life," because they don't want that. To them that would just be an endless cycle of reincarnation until they reach the cessation of individuality through becoming part of the oneness – "a raindrop falling into the ocean' - Nirvana.

Hinduism, Yoga, transcendental, and other forms of meditation have taken an even more subtle approach in the Western world. Yoga is promoted – even among Christians – as spiritually harmless, a physically helpful exercise, or just nothing more than "wellness" and meditation techniques. But hiding behind the practice of Yoga are strong demonic influences.

Every yoga pose is a prayer to a Hindu god or goddess. Hinduism teaches that the goal of Yoga is to open up seven "chakras" to eventually allow the "Kundalini" spirit (a serpent god - sound familiar?) which they believe is dormant at the base of the spine, to "uncurl" through the chakras and explode out of the crown of your head. Then you become "self-realized" – one with the "divine." That is the true end goal of Yoga.

Harmless? Hardly!

Experiencing the Kundalini is serious and damaging, and often requires extraction. And they are not easy or painless ones.

You may have heard the expression, "mantra." Most people don't even know what that is. They think it just means a phrase you repeat a lot. But a "mantra" is, in fact, a name of a Hindu god that you are given when practicing Yoga, and you are to repeat the name of that god or goddess over and over to help you connect to the "divine within." Hindus greet each other with the phrase, "Namaste." It means "the god in me recognizes the god in you."

You have heard of the phrase, "what comes around, goes around"? It's based on Hinduism. It means whatever you do in this life, good or bad, you will reap in your next incarnation.

Hinduism created a "caste" system in which the poorest are literally left to fend for themselves. The "untouchable" caste are those who are believed to be born to poverty because that is their karma earned through past lives. People under the Hindu caste system are bound to worship and feed a cow while a starving person who is an "untouchable" is allowed to die of starvation. In Hindu thought, it is a kindness, because they will hopefully reincarnate into a better station in life.

The poor are allowed to starve, while the "Brahmin" caste is elevated and revered, in the belief that they have reincarnated enough to earn that privilege.

For centuries, there was a practice known as sati (it still happens in some areas) where the widow of a deceased husband was cremated alive on the funeral pyre of her husband, since she had ceased to have value.

Some of the harshest persecution of Christians in India today comes at the hands of Hindu priests and practitioners.

Belief in reincarnation is a doctrine of demons (1 Timothy 4:1) and requires renunciation for those who believe it. The scriptures say, "It is appointed unto a man once to die and after this, the judgment." (Hebrews 9:27) There is no reincarnation. This is the only life we have in which to choose Jesus!

I recommend for those wanting to understand the deep-seated demonic nature of Hinduism to read *Things as They Are – Mission Work in Southern India*, a collection of "boots on the ground" newsletters from missionary Amy Wilson-Carmichael of Dohnavur, India. They chronicle her mission work to rescue boys and girls as young as five from the horrors of Hindu temple prostitution, as well as stories of bringing Brahmin caste family members to Jesus – only to return the next day and find that they had been so badly tortured and abused that they had lost their minds. The real face of Hinduism in practice is not benevolent but is in fact ruled over by the demonic spirits of hell that seek to "kill, steal and destroy."

Every ounce of Hinduism must be renounced in prayer by those who practiced or studied it – including renunciation of, and abandoning of, all Yogic practices, "Christian" or not.

Buddhism

Buddhism also teaches the "divine within." And even though Buddha allegedly told people not to worship him, they did, which is idolatry. There are many practices of magick and calling on "spirits" in Buddhism. It is a thoroughly unbiblical false religion and has to be renounced to be free from its influences.

We do not have the "divine within." We are made in the image and likeness of God, but the sin nature entered us, we sinned, and we died. When we come to Jesus, we are not given the "divine within," as if we can attain godhood as these religions teach. There is only one God and His Son Jesus Christ. We are to be imitators of Christ. We are *not* Christ. People without God are not children of God. Jesus said to the Pharisees, "You are of your father the devil, and the lusts of your father you will do." (John 8:44) Only when we come to Jesus and are born again, do we become "sons of God," adopted, heirs of Christ. The teaching that we are divine is a lie.

Jehovah's Witnesses

The Jehovah's Witnesses are a false religion which teaches "another gospel." It teaches that Jesus was not God the son, that there is no hell, and that only 144,000 will ever go to heaven. Their founder, Charles Taze Russell, gave four prophecies concerning the exact dates of Jesus' return, the resurrection of the saints and the judgment, all four of which came and went without fulfillment. The Bible is very clear that anyone that says things like this - and they do not come to pass - is a false prophet (Deuteronomy 18:22) and they need to be rejected. Much bondage and fear come to those who are under this false religion, and when a person comes to the true Jesus out of the Jehovah's Witnesses, all these things need to be renounced and forsaken.

Mormonism

One of the most potent false religions is Mormonism. Joseph Smith, its founder, was a Mason who claimed to have been visited by the "angel" Moroni, who showed him golden tablets which he read with a "seer stone" (divination) placed in a hat and from that he "interpreted" them from their original "reformed Egyptian" language.

From that came *The Book of Mormon*, which is not the Word of God, but what Paul called "another Gospel":

"But though we, or an angel from heaven, preach any other gospel unto you than that which we have preached unto you, let him be accursed." (Galatians 1:8.)

The Book of Mormon is filled with Biblical sounding terms and phraseology. But if you have a scintilla of discernment, you know from the first page that this is clearly not from God.

The doctrine of Mormonism reduces Jesus to merely **a** god among many gods. The Mormon creed is, "As man is, God once was. As God is, so man will become." It teaches that Jesus was *our* savior, just as we will go on to be gods with a god family and be a savior to other worlds. It teaches that Jesus and Lucifer were spirit brothers and that God asked Jesus and Lucifer which one would save the earth; Jesus said yes, Lucifer said no, and that is why Jesus is our Savior instead of Lucifer. Mormonism teaches that Jesus was created, not the creator. (Cf. John 1:1-2) The Mormon doctrine taught that blacks were an inferior race for many years, until 1978 when the ruling Mormon body declared that they had received a revelation that reversed that doctrine. (See note on false prophets under Jehovah's Witnesses. Also, read Malachi 3:6: "For I am the Lord, I do not change; Therefore you are not consumed, O sons of Jacob.")

The appeal of Mormonism for many is that, unlike most Evangelical churches, Mormons take care of their members – from cradle to grave. We could and should learn from that. The Evangelical church is losing more members to Mormonism than any other religion, and I believe that is the primary reason. When our churches - which, unfortunately, often do not care for the needs of their members and can too often be unconcerned and unloving – fail to be the true church, then the Mormon church is more than willing to pick up the pieces and take them in.

Nevertheless, it is a cult. Regardless of how they may try to posture themselves as just another Christian denomination, it is an unbiblical cult – another Gospel. And as with all cults and false religions, prayer is needed for Mormons who have come to Christ or who have Mormon bloodlines, for shutting doors, renunciation and shattering the power of the spirit of deception and false religious lies.

Scientology

Scientology is a non-Christian mind control cult. Many famous celebrities are members, including Tom Cruise, Kirstie Alley and John Travolta. It comes across as a scientific self-improvement system, but it is far from that. It has established clinics, schools, and even drug rehab centers.

But even if you discount the coercive, cult-like atmosphere of Scientology, what is really behind it?

Its founder, L. Ron Hubbard, was the assistant to satanic High Priest Jack Parsons in the late 1940's - early 1950's. Jack Parsons was the founder of the Agape Lodge in Pasadena, California, and he was a direct disciple of world infamous Satanist Aleister Crowley. Parsons created the solid fuel rocket for our space program and was a brilliant scientist. He was very well respected. They still refer to the Jet Propulsion Laboratory as "Jack Parson's Lab." (Coincidentally, it is only open to the public for tours one night of the year – Halloween.) Parsons dedicated his satanic lodge publicly with the help of the mayor of Pasadena and other notable people such as actor John Carradine, who read a poem for the inauguration.

Parsons blew himself up in a black magick experiment in the early 1950s.

But before he did, his assistant High Priest, L. Ron Hubbard, allegedly took a significant amount of money, moved to Florida, bought a boat and started to tell friends that he was going to start his own religion and make a million dollars.

Thus, Scientology was born.

Scientology is a combination of self-help, science fiction stories, strong-arm membership tactics, and indoctrination, secrecy and anti-Biblical teachings.

Anyone ensnared in the web of Scientology will need prayer for the back of this demonic spirit of error to be broken. They will need solid Bible study and immersion, and spiritual deprogramming to break the lies which are at the root of the doctrines of Scientology.

Masonry

Masonry or Freemasonry is an extremely occultic secret lodge that requires secret oaths, which the Bible forbids:

"Again, ye have heard that it hath been said by them of old time, Thou shalt not forswear thyself, but shalt perform unto the Lord thine oaths: But I say unto you, Swear not at all; neither by heaven; for it is God's throne: Nor by the earth; for it is his footstool: neither by Jerusalem; for it is the city of the great King." (Matthew 5:33-35)

Masonry accepts all religions as equally valid and is filled with occult religious symbols of the most ancient and sophisticated kind, including the Pentagram – which is used for the women's lodge, the Eastern Star. It also makes use of the Baphomet - the satanic goat.

Many innocent people are pulled in by invitation to the Masonic order, being told it is a Christian organization, or a charitable group, or some other lure. But it is not Christian at all, though it uses Christian symbols on occasion.

Perhaps you didn't know this before. Now you do. And now you are responsible to obey God in truth and renounce your affiliation and membership with this occultic organization if you have one. No Christian should have anything to do with Masonry.

One of my spiritual mothers in her 80's told me how she had joined the Eastern Star when she was younger. Then one day, while looking at her Lodge ring, God spoke to her: "Why would you belong to anything that says there is any other way to Me except through my Son Jesus?"

She immediately got rid of the ring and never went back.

Prayers of renunciation are important to break this bondage of the occult world of Freemasonry.

For further reading on cults and world religions, I highly recommend the book, *Reaching a Lost World*, which is part of the Intensive Discipleship Course series by my good friend Vinnie Carafano. It is a heavily footnoted volume covering major belief systems and filled with fascinating firsthand accounts from the mission field.

Till sin be bitter, Christ will not be sweet.

- Thomas Watson

Gregory R Reid

19 SPECIFIC DOORS OF ENTRANCE PART THREE SINS OF THE HEART

It is so easy for us to think of demonic influence as only happening to dirty sinners and unclean people and liars and thieves and pornography addicts and drunks.

We could not be more wrong.

In fact, much demonic bondage, and the hardest to get people delivered from is not seen at all. They are the result of unresolved sins of the heart. They are sins that eat at the fabric of Christian character, keep people in bondage all their lives, flourish in church, and are some of Satan's favorite sins – because the demons that are assigned to these messy issues can just sit back and feast on the evil and the brokenness and the wicked thoughts and intentions of believers who never deal with their own hearts. In fact, it allows them to use people as vessels to spread gossip, slander, hatred, unforgiveness, and a host of other things.

Some of these sins of the heart are sins that we simply adopted or adapted to as a result of wounding – rejection, anger, neglect, abandonment. We allow the unresolved feelings to grow in the dark until they begin to become a stronghold, and then they begin to control our behavior, our words and eventually our actions. A person can become demonized if they persist in these things without seeing them for what they are and getting set free from them. Let's look at some of these heart issues.

Unforgiveness

How many people have you heard say, "I'll forgive, but I won't ever forget." (Maybe you've said it yourself.) God doesn't ask you to forget things, because you really can't. Only God can do that. But many times when a person says this, they have already signaled that they haven't really forgiven.

Jesus had many things to say about forgiveness. He made it an absolute priority in His teachings. He said if we did not forgive, we would not be forgiven:

"For if you forgive men their trespasses, your heavenly Father will also forgive you. But if you do not forgive men their trespasses, neither will your Father forgive your trespasses." (Matthew 6:14-15)

Jesus told a parable about a man who owed a lot of money:

"Therefore the kingdom of heaven is like a certain king who wanted to settle accounts with his servants. And when he had begun to settle accounts, one was brought to him who owed him ten thousand talents. But as he was not able to pay, his master commanded that he be sold, with his wife and children and all that he had, and that payment be made. The servant therefore fell down before him, saying, 'Master, have patience with me, and I will pay you all.' Then the master of that servant was moved with compassion, released him, and forgave him the debt. But that servant went out and found one of his fellow servants who owed him a hundred denarii; and he laid hands on him and took him by the throat, saying, 'Pay me what you owe!' So his fellow servant fell down at his feet and begged him, saying, 'Have patience with me, and I will pay you all.' And he would not, but went and threw him into prison till he should pay the debt. He begged his debtor to forgive him, and he did. But then he went and throttled a man who owed him mere pennies. When the man who was owed much found out, it says he put the other man in prison until he had paid every penny." (Matthew 18:23-30)

Among the many lessons in this, one that often gets missed is that when you do not forgive, you are cast into "prison" – spiritually, emotionally, and even healthwise.

Unforgiveness can be deeply hidden and run the gamut from very early childhood hurts to last week's offense from a church member or co-worker. We know we are taught to forgive, and we're also wrongly taught that we're not supposed to feel negative things. So many times, we just take the injury in, ignore the hurt, and put it away in the dark. But in the dark, it grows and festers. And when it does, demons can get a foothold, then a stronghold.

Demons love unforgiveness. It's their own private sewer swimming pool.

Hidden unforgiveness manifests in many ways – brittle responses, sarcastic communication, cynicism, mistreatment of others, and Pharisaical judgment of others.

Whatever is hidden can become fertile ground for demons to gain a foothold.

Left hidden and undealt with, unforgiveness can manifest as health problems, cold love, and mechanical religion.

Unforgiveness can easily become a family curse and stronghold. Often, unresolved unforgiveness over an injury results in passing on identical injuries to children, and so the damage continues and the demon cesspool remains intact from generation to generation.

Between one extreme of holding on to unforgiveness and the other of being expected to just stuff it all inside and suffer injuries, is there a way to healing and deliverance? Most certainly. It is in learning that when we are injured, we need to immediately take it to God, and have it out with Him. The Psalms are full of David's heart-wrenching agony over being hurt, rejected, forgotten. He poured it out to *God*. And in doing so, He found God's healing love.

Often when I have had to bring a deep injury before God, it required extensive prayer time with a Bible, a notebook, and an open heart before God. We have to bring the injury to Him and tell Him exactly how we feel about it. The Bible says to *be* angry, but do not sin; don't let the sun go down on your wrath. (Ephesians 4:26) If you seethe over the hurt overnight, Satan begins to create an emotional stronghold. Deal with it right away; tell Him how angry, how hurt, how wronged you feel! Then take it to the foot of the cross, ask for His healing, and forgive the one who injured you.

Forgiveness, it must be understood, is not a feeling. It means to "give forth." It is giving it back to God, and handing it back to the person, as if to say, "I will not let this bind me. I let this person go and put them in God's hands." It will make you feel utterly powerless at first. You may find out how much you *really* wish to exact revenge at that moment when you have to say the words, "Jesus, I forgive ____." But it does not matter how you feel; it is about obedience. And when you forgive out of obedience, freedom comes.

But what about the next day, if the hurt comes back? Forgive again, and again, and again, whether you feel it or not. And one day soon, that hurt will be completely healed.

Sometimes we don't want to forgive because in holding on to it, we feel we will somehow be getting back at the other person. But the person usually does not care, or isn't even thinking about it, or doesn't know. And as the saying goes, unforgiveness is like drinking poison hoping the other person dies from it. The only one who will suffer is you.

It is important to note here too that for those who have been sexually abused, forgiving someone does not require you to ever be in a place where that person can violate you again. Forgiveness does not mean you even must see them again. It is vital that you not put yourself back into harm's way.

What about forgiving yourself? Yes, that is also necessary, lest it leads to self-despising. All unforgiveness, whether toward others or yourself, opens doors for lies and satanic poison to warp and control and contort your God-given character. Take each unforgiveness - new or old - to God, and verbally forgive out loud each person you have held unforgiveness for. Then pray and ask Jesus to cleanse you from the demonic cesspool of anger, rage, cynicism, cold love, or any other thing that the enemy has sown into you through the open door of unforgiveness.

Bitterness

"Pursue peace with all people, and holiness, without which no one will see the Lord: looking carefully lest anyone fall short of the grace of God; lest any root of bitterness springing up cause trouble, and by this many become defiled." (Hebrews 12:14-15)

One of the most insidious, acidic and poisonous demonic inroads into a person's heart is bitterness. Bitterness can be the result of unresolved injury, hurt and unforgiveness. It can also come from just not believing in God's goodness, but instead believing that you are wrongfully treated, mistreated, passed by or left out of the good things of life and that God doesn't really care.

For the demonic world, bitterness becomes a two-for-one bargain. The above scripture tells us that once a root of bitterness is allowed to grow, it defiles many. Bitterness poisons the person, and in turn, poisons those who are exposed to it.

So many churches are crippled by people who carry the root of bitterness. Bitterness in a person clouds every circumstance, makes every person an enemy, brings distrust of everyone and brings into its circle as many people as possible to *share* that bitter poison with. We ourselves become defiled when we listen to the voice of bitterness, consider its claims, and then receive as truth its perceptions. We will then become carriers of the virus of bitterness and begin to embitter others as well. Before long, we have not just a root but a full-grown tree. This is how many churches are torn apart.

Here is something I believe will help you. Life deals all of us heavy blows. Jesus said the rain falls on the just and the unjust. Life can embitter you if you let it.

A story is told in the Old Testament about the prophet Moses and the people of Israel:

"Now when they came to Marah, they could not drink the waters of Marah, for they were bitter. Therefore, the name of it was called Marah. And the people complained against Moses, saying, 'What shall we drink?' So, he cried out to the Lord, and the Lord showed him a tree. When he cast it into the waters, the waters were made sweet. There He made a statute and an ordinance for them, and there He tested them." (Exodus 15:23-25)

Jesus died on a tree for our salvation and our healing. That cross is the tree we can cast into any bitter waters of our lives, and it will become sweet.

The missionary Amy Carmichael once told a story of an offense that had injured her deeply. As she brooded over it, the Lord told her, "See in it a chance to die." I know this is not a popular thought in an age of "I have rights" and "I deserve the best," but when we received Jesus, we gave our rights up to Him. Paul said, "I have been crucified with Christ." (Galatians 2:20) If that is so, and if Jesus told us to pick up our cross and follow Him, then life is not about what is fair but rather how to be obedient to His Will regardless of what is fair, knowing that He is the rewarder of those who love Him. God is interested in conforming us into the image of Jesus. If He was crucified, then we should "Let this mind be in you, which was also in Christ Jesus; who, being in the form of God, thought it not robbery to be equal with God: but made himself of no reputation, and took upon him the form of a servant, and was made in the likeness of men: and being found in fashion as a man, he humbled himself, and became obedient unto death, even the death of the cross. (Philippians 2:5-8.)

In other words, rather than drink the bitter waters, see in things a chance to die to our own bitter reactions, our self-defense, our "what about my rights" thinking. Cast the cross of His grace and love into those bitter waters, and let them become sweet, pure and life-giving. If we do not, the bitter waters will, again, become a swimming cesspool for demons, who will not only seek to torment us but use us to embitter others. May God set us free from this demonic bondage!

I urge you if that root is in you, and even if it has grown beyond that, stop right now and ask Jesus to deal with it. Jesus wants to lay the axe to the root. (Luke 3:9). Let Him cut this diseased and demon-infested tree out of your life.

"Father, in the Name of Jesus, I bring before you my bitterness. I have been hurt, and I need healing. I have kept resentments, anger, unforgiveness and many other poisoned emotions and thoughts in my heart and mind, and worse, I have poisoned others. O God, hear the cry of my heart! I surrender every hurt, every slight, every offense to you and ask You to heal me; I surrender this bitter tree to you and ask you to lay the axe to the root of it and make sure it is completely gone. Help me to keep my commitment to give this to you, and as King David said, "Set a watch at my lips." (Psalm 141:3) Keep me from ever spreading poison again. In Jesus' Name, amen."

Self-Pity

Many of these heart-bondages are symbiotic and evil siblings. Bitterness, unforgiveness, jealousy and self-pity often go hand in hand and feed off of each other. It is the "threefold cord" principle at work again. Self-pity is a particularly ugly sin because it blinds the person to their need to be delivered from it. If someone is corrected for indulging in self-pity, that person may see the one who pointed it out as the enemy. I know we all have those moments. But it can become a demonic stronghold when we let self-pity feed, fester and create dark and terrible portraits of other people and the future. Self-pity is a faith-killer.

King Saul was a poster boy for self-pity. David was the ascendant star in Israel, and Saul let it fester in his heart. His actions became increasingly angry and ungodly:

"That all of you have conspired against me, and there is none that shows me that my son has made a league with the son of Jesse, and there is none of you that is sorry for me, or shows to me that my son hath stirred up my servant against me, to lie in wait, as at this day?" (1 Samuel 22:8)

A sadder scripture is hard to find; a King once so promising, so full of blessing from God, now, through his own lack of repentance and love, has become a whimpering paranoid. I often think of this when I am tending toward that self-pity sin, and it scares me out of it. Do I want all that God has done for me and everything others have seen God do for me, reduced to a portrait of weakness and selfish, childish reactions? Oh, this is a hard one, friends, but demons hide behind self-pity very expertly.

Deliverance from self-pity will require you to look yourself in the mirror and say, "That's enough. Dry your tears, give this to God, stop talking to others about how bad you have it, and get back in the fight!" And oh, this will hurt! But God has to hurt self-pity to death. When He does, the feeding ground of destructive thoughts and emotions will dry up, and the very oppressive demons that encouraged and nurtured much of your self-pity for their own vampiric life-killing needs will be forced to let go. Rebuke them and their every thought. Tell God your hurts! He knows. He cares. Don't let the devil put a "curse God and die" thought on you, or a Saul spirit that seeks support for your desire to just have people feel sorry for you. Be delivered of this undignified and humiliating demonic bondage, child of God!

Rage

"Be angry and sin not. Do not let the sun go down on your wrath." (Ephesians 4:26)

Anger is not a sin. God has anger. And God expresses anger. We are made in His image and likeness. Anger is not evil in itself. In fact, there is a time for anger. Paul, for example, said, "Who is weak and I am not weak? Who is offended and I do not burn with indignation?" (2 Corinthians 11:29 NKJV) Jesus was very angry when he overturned the money changers in the temple. There is a time for it.

But there is another kind of anger, and that is anger that is not expressed before God, that grows and builds and becomes rage. "The wrath of man does not work the righteousness of God." (James 1:20)

The fact is, human anger, if allowed to fester and be uncontrolled, becomes a demonic stronghold. How many men have you heard who beat their wives, and then say, "Honey, I don't know what came over me. I'll never do that again." But they do it again because something does begin to overcome them. Or women who angrily berate, castrate and humiliate their husbands and boys in an almost out-of-control way, then say, "I am so sorry, I love you so much, I don't know why I do those things!" They do them because they have let anger fester, and eventually demons begin to feed off of that unresolved anger and create rage.

I am not saying rage is all demonic. But I have sometimes seen people overtaken by rage whose eyes change, voices alter and are clearly being used by a demonic spirit. That is the stronghold of rage.

The way to avoid this, of course, is to do what the scriptures tell us. Yes, be angry. But don't let that anger go unresolved until the next day. Take it to God, get it out of your heart and let it go. Clear the channel. Clean out the pool of the debris and dirt of angry thoughts and intents. Allow the Holy Spirit to wash you clean. The demons will have nothing to feed off of for breakfast.

I think the gang world is a good example of anger becoming rage and then a stronghold. Most rap music is fueled by the poisonous drug of rage. You can literally see people's personalities change when they listen to rap music as they ingest a steady stream of verbal satanic themes about killing, raping, drugs, abusing women, etc. It feeds the rage. Much of rap music is demonically designed to perpetuate a culture that is filled with murder, sexual violence and fatherless and abused children. God deliver us from such rage. And as part of your own deliverance, you may need to get rid of *any* of your music that feeds this type of primal ungodly anger no matter what the genre, including satanic death metal.

Pride

Pride is one of the highest sins on God's charts. You probably were told that all sins are equal. They are not. Proverbs says, "These six things doth the Lord hate: yea, seven are an abomination unto him: a proud look, a lying tongue, and hands that shed innocent blood, a heart that deviseth wicked imaginations, feet that be swift in running to mischief, a false witness that speaketh lies, and he that soweth discord among brethren." (Proverbs 6:16-19)

It should make us tremble that pride is listed first. "God resists the proud and gives grace to the humble." (1 Peter 5:5) Satan was full of pride. "I will" was his defiant word of pride, and it cost him everything.

Church-going religious people and Christians are especially vulnerable to pride, and are quick to justify it. Pride hiding behind religious righteousness is especially pernicious to God.

Ask God to demolish the stronghold of pride in your life, even if you must be humbled to the dust. Satan reigns in the house of pride. You cannot allow pride to be the open invitation to demonic thoughts and influences that want to take up residence and use you as a destructive – and Christ-dishonoring – vessel.

Again, I am very reluctant to place people, especially young people, too soon into leadership for this reason. Paul spoke of this when he spoke of ordaining into leadership, saying:

"Not a novice, lest being lifted up with pride he fall into the condemnation of the devil. Moreover, he must have a good report of them which are without; lest he fall into reproach and the snare of the devil." (1 Timothy 3:6-7)

I have seen far too many people get elevated into ministries before they were ready, watched it go to their heads and created arrogant spiritual monsters. God deliver us from unbroken pride, lest it be our downfall and makes us the laughingstock of demons.

Self-Righteousness

Jesus spoke directly and forcefully to those in the religious community who were guilty of straining at a gnat and swallowing a camel, who made big parades of their giving, who lauded how much they had done for God, and who imposed on people rules that they themselves didn't keep. Jesus called them whitewashed tombs. They used to paint caves with white paint so that if people were walking at night, they would know not to go into a cave so painted because death was within. That is self-righteousness; looking good and religious on the outside, but full of death on the inside. Satan loves death.

Self-righteousness is a church destroyer and a destroyer of the grace of God in people's lives. God forbid, in our understanding of true holiness and the need to walk with Him in holiness, that we should become blinded vessels of arrogant self-righteousness who cannot see our own sins – who strain at a gnat and swallow a camel and are quick to point out sins in others. When we become blinded to our own sins and appoint ourselves the judge and jury over people who sin and fail, then we are firmly in the enemy's grip. Only complete repentance and being broken will destroy that stronghold in our hearts.

Gossip and Division

Gossip and Division are demonic twins as well. They work together to do their destructive work. Division pulls the switches, and gossip and slander do the murder, spiritual mayhem and ruining of lives.

There is a reason Solomon lists "those that sow seeds of discord among the brethren" as one of the top things God hates. (Proverbs 6:16-19)

Division is the puppet master of gossip. It plants the seeds, fuels the fire of gossip, then stands back, hiding, enjoying the chaos and heartbreak that results. More churches are destroyed by gossip gone wild - which allows division to step in - than anything I have ever witnessed – even more than adultery, robbery or heresy.

We must treat gossip as the filthy, destructive and demonic evil that it is. No more "I'm just telling you this so you can pray" nonsense. Gossip is gossip. It must be dealt with each time, every time, and I call on every believer to confront it when it is starting. When someone wants to pass on some little tidbit, remind the person that "love covers a multitude of sins," and tell them you don't want to hear it.

I remember a funny little story my spiritual mother told about a man who was trying to pass on wicked gossip to a Dutch friend about someone who allegedly did something terrible. The Dutch friend's reply was, "Vass you dere?" That should be right on our lips when gossipy friends try to pass on their "prayer concerns." "Vass you dere?" Did you see it? Were you present? Did you talk to the other parties involved? If not, **keep your mouth shut.** The word slanderer in 2 Timothy 3:3 is "diabolos." Devil. Stop being a little devil. Just stop it!

Another heartbreaking story was told – I do not know the source – about a good church-going Christian man and his wife and two children who were wonderful believers and loved by the whole church.

One day the man had a business lunch with a female associate at the local diner. It was a short business transaction.

The church gossip saw them and began spreading the rumor that he was cheating on his wife.

By the time he and his wife and children heard about it, it had already ruined them in the church without them knowing. They were shredded. They simply left, locked their doors, and never returned to church again.

A couple of years later, the woman who started the rumor was overwhelmed with guilt and conviction. She went to the man's door, not knowing if he would even talk to her. "I am so very sorry about what I started," she said remorsefully. Can you forgive me? How can I make it right?"

The man looked at her for a brief time, and said, "We do forgive you. Please stay here a moment."

He went and retrieved a pillow – and a knife. He stepped outside on a very windy day, ripped the pillow open and scattered the feathers to the four winds. "Can you retrieve all those feathers?" he asked. "No," she replied sadly. "Then neither can you retrieve all the hurtful rumors and things that have been said about us."

Do you understand? Gossip is acid, it is corrosive, it is mean, and it is ungodly. And you cannot undo the damage it does. So just stop, and ask God to deliver you from the ugly demon who sits on your head and pours vomit into your conscious mind for you to pass on to others. JUST STOP.

Jesus prayed, "That they all may be one; as You, Father, are in me, and I in You, that they also may be one in us: that the world may believe that you have sent me. "(John 17:21) Unity is very important to God. The scriptures are clear that sin-created gossip and division are ungodly and destructive.

There is a *false* unity. There is a move and drive spiritually right now to cobble together all religions and all churches under a "one world, one religion" antichrist agenda. But that is a unity only accomplished by discarding the validity and integrity of the Word of God and basic tenets of the faith. That is demonic unity. True unity must be founded in Biblical truth.

So now as we speak of division, let's broaden it to include the fracturing of families and churches. Divorce = division = shattered lives and shattered children. Child abuse creates division in the heart of the child which creates a fragmented and wounded soul. Alcoholism and drug use create division which creates perpetual pain, destruction and passing on of fractured hearts from generation to generation.

In church, gossip = misunderstanding, secrecy, mistrust, miscommunication, factions and the undoing of families and an entire church.

Gossip and division are powerful, demonically fueled strongholds and weapons of crass destruction.

If you are a perpetuator of these things, seek forgiveness, and ask Jesus to set you free. "Set a guard, O Lord, over my mouth; Keep watch over the door of my lips." (Psalm 141:3 NKJV)

Evidence of a Divisive Spirit Stronghold

- Constantly questioning the motives, integrity, competency or authority of others.

- Never giving anyone the benefit of the doubt.

- Never going to a person directly with your concerns, injuries, and offenses.

- Gathering to yourself a "posse" whom you have poisoned with your offenses, which they take on as their offenses as well, and who now (1) go to your defense, and (2) take your offense to a new group of people.

- Refusing to be corrected or go to the person directly according to scripture.

Spiritualizing their offenses, i.e., the pastor isn't right with God, that person is demonized, they won't listen to reason, they are a Jezebel, or an Ahab, etc.

- Carrying the dual traits of arrogance and self-pity.

Only a complete application of Matthew 18:15-17 will break the demonic back of this ugly stronghold:

"Moreover if your brother sins against you, go and tell him his fault between you and him alone. If he hears you, you have gained your brother."

Between you and THEM. So much heartbreak and so many broken relationships would be avoided if we just followed this one simple command: If you have an issue with someone, go to THEM! Knowing how crucial this is, I no longer talk with someone *about* someone unless they have gone to them first. Pastors, if we did that, much of the gossip and division in the church would just stop.

Critical Spirit

While I do not believe in ignoring issues, sins, or things needing correction, I learned long ago that before I ever take the mantle of Corrector in Chief and Anointed Cherubim in charge of pointing out people's faults, sins, and failures, God hands me a huge mirror and demands that I stand before it and examine myself brutally and completely. For our failure to do so is surely the cause of more murder-by-Christian than any other thing in the church.

A critical spirit has no mirror, no ability for self-examination. It can only hide behind a phony and unsubstantiated, "I know I'm not perfect, but…" before shredding everyone in their field of vision or circle of influence with a constant barrage of nitpicking, petty, acid comments, negative words and cynical responses.

If I've just identified you, you need deliverance because demons feed on all of those things. Anyone who has ever heard a demon speak knows that, while love, joy, kindness, truth, and gentleness are the language of heaven, then criticism, mockery, cynicism, and constant negative belittling is the language of these demons from hell. Be set free!

While all of these sins of the heart can be vehicles for the enemy to use and can lead to strongholds - if not checked and repented of – they can possibly lead to demonization. At the root, however, they are simply sins of the heart. And they, like every sin, must be repented of and forsaken. Only then can you ensure you will not be enslaved by your sin, used of the enemy and robbed of your full walk with Jesus. Claim victory over every one of them!

How can you pull down strongholds of Satan if you don't even have the strength to turn off your TV?

– Leonard Ravenhill

Gregory R Reid

20 LEVELS AND SYMPTOMS OF DEMONIC INFLUENCE

I want to repeat that I am in no way suggesting that demons cause all the sins and problems in the world or in our lives. Quite the contrary. All they do is push the ball down the hill that we already set in motion by our own sins. I am not a believer in the old "the devil made me do it" excuse. In fact, the scriptures are very clear in Galatians 5:19-21 where Paul lists the works of the flesh, that we allow our own flesh to create issues, including witchcraft!

However, demons are always seeking the open door. These are some of the levels of influence they gain, from the least to the strongest.

Level One - Thoughts, Impressions, and Dreams

Many times, I've counseled with young believers who were mortified when they found themselves suddenly barraged with filthy, hateful, sinful, despairing or even suicidal thoughts. Usually, and most often, this occurs when making a renewed commitment to pray, or to read the Word.

This is a typical demonic attack. First, come the horrible thoughts; then comes the condemnation, the thoughts of, "What kind of Christian are you? You hypocrite! You'll never be able to serve God!"

Most would agree that those accusations were from the devil, right? But then they say, "But Satan can't put thoughts in a Christian's head!"

If he put in the condemnation, which very few Christians would deny he does, don't you think he can put in the bad thoughts as well? It's a win/win situation for him. And even if you discover and rebuke the demonic thoughts of condemnation, they bank on you not making the logical connection: If the second thoughts of condemnation weren't yours, why do you think the first ugly thoughts were yours?

Demons know our vulnerabilities. And while they cannot read our minds, they see our actions and read our emotions. It's easy for them to design the demonic thoughts and whisper them to us. All they do is put the ball in play. If we take the bait and own the thought and let it stay and gestate and grow, then they have a toe-hold of bondage in our minds.

Do not assume that all thoughts originated with you!

So, what do you do when these thoughts come? Get your scriptures out. Recite them out loud. Psalms is very good for this. It will pass!

Again, you can't keep the birds from flying over your head, but you can keep them from making a nest in your hair.

This understanding of spiritual attacks on the believer is especially crucial regarding attacks of sexual thoughts, lusts, and sexual fantasies. We are sexual creations. And we are inundated with sexually suggestive and blatant images, conversations, media and input everywhere we turn. So it is very easy – especially in young people – for demons to initiate all manner of ungodly thoughts. This is a monumental battle. Youth and even children are being subjected to these demonic influences almost routinely. The schools and educational system - which has in many ways replaced God and become God in our society – forces kids to use the internet. Parents are overwhelmed, busy, tired and under attack everywhere. Keeping an eye on what their kids watch is getting very difficult. Even if a parent does monitor things at home, they have little control over what their kids are exposed to in school – or at their friends' houses - unless their kids tell them. One of our high school students came home one day very upset. His substitute teacher told the class that he was going out for a while, and they were free to open their notebook computers and look at all the pornography they wanted to so long as they didn't get caught or get him in trouble. Our student was mortified as he watched many of the other students do exactly that. Satan is using visual uncleanness as one of the most effective tools to keep kids in bondage and guilt, and Christian kids under condemnation.

Even if a young person does not deliberately view or pursue such material, they are still surrounded by it through music, movies, television, and friends. The rule and the tool remain the same – do not assume if you are being hit by perverted or unclean images that you are initiating them. It takes very little for something to cross our eyes, then for demonic influence to add to it and try to make us pursue it. The command is to *draw nigh to God*, and then to *resist the devil*. The tool is the Word of God. The minute something crosses your mind, stop. Rebuke it. Don't let it "nest." You can't control the first thought. But you can stop the rest. Keep your mind clean. Repent if you somehow failed and let it nest. Stop yourself from taking the next step, either in fantasy and sexual indulgence or in acting on another person because of a created fantasy. The battle for the mind in this age is fierce in a time of unfettered pornography and unrestrained – and encouraged – sexual activity. "Giving no place to the devil." (Ephesians 4:27) Stop him dead in his tracks!

Dreams

Dreams are also an area that demons often attempt to influence. As we have already covered in the chapter on night terrors, we can be especially vulnerable in our sleep.

Dreams are usually: (1) From God. (2) Us acting out or trying to work out our waking problems in our sleep. (3) Something we ate before bed (nonsense dreams). Or (4) Demonically initiated dreams.

You can usually tell the demonic ones: They are filled with terror, are sexually immoral, or contain dark, ugly things or activities.

The same principle applies here: Do not assume it is just "your" dream. Believers will sometimes have a dream that starts out normal, then becomes ugly, perverted, or terrifying, and then just demonic. One young person told me of having a dream in which a beautiful girl was attempting to seduce him, and he was feeling overwhelmed by lust. Just as she put her arms around him, he said, "Jesus help me!" and suddenly she became a hideous, long-fingered, twisted finger-nailed demon screaming at him, tearing at his face – then left his dream. It sought to use his youthful vulnerability to get a foothold in his life and hurt him spiritually. He learned how to pray before he went to bed and read scriptures to protect his sleep.

The night belongs to God. Take it back from the enemy. It is your right and heritage and His promise and blessing!

If you get attacked in your dreams, wake up, rebuke it, read some verses, go back to sleep. Kick out any lingering condemnation. We cannot control our dreams. There is no condemnation for what we cannot control. Just ask Jesus to cleanse your heart and mind from these demonic intrusions. Then let it go.

On the other hand, if you are feeding your mind on pornography, sexual fantasies or violent images, games or movies, those dreams will more than likely happen. The enemy wants to use them to get that foothold in you. Stop it at the source!

Level Two - Oppression

In the discussion about Christians and demons, the standard response is, "You can be oppressed, not possessed!" Leaving that treacherous and divisive argument aside for just one moment, just what is "oppression"? How does it manifest? What is the purpose the enemy designed it for?

Oppression can include but is not limited to:

- Bad, unexpected headaches
- Confusion
- Disorientation and inability to focus on scripture and things of God
- Overwhelming doubt
- Unreasonable and obsessive fears
- Irrational and disconnected or out-of-character demonic or sinful thoughts
- Unexpected discouragement leading to despair
- Persistent thoughts of giving up

It is not uncommon for a believer to be inundated by oppression for days before they recognize it is an attack. Sometimes that recognition only comes when a praying friend or loved one recognizes it and calls it out. Usually, all it takes is a prayer, rebuking of the enemy, some worship and a little time in the Word to break its back. It will begin to dissipate and lose its power or sometimes instantly stops. We have to recognize it for what it is and who is behind it and hit it head-on. Remind the enemy through God's Word that we are more than conquerors through Him that loved us. (Romans 8:37)

Level Three - Stronghold

A stronghold is an area in our lives where Satan has gotten a real foothold. "Stronghold" has several definitions from *The Strong's Concordance*:

- a protected place where the members of a military group stay and can defend themselves against attacks
- fortress
- a major center or area of predominance

In spiritual warfare, a stronghold is a place that the enemy has set up. It is a fortress, a place they can defend against attack or dislodging. Jesus said:

"No one can enter a strong man's house and plunder his goods, unless he first binds the strong man. And then he will plunder his house." (Mark 3:27)

A stronghold, in the context of spiritual warfare, is an area in someone's life where they have allowed demons to gain entrance over a period of time. The demons establish territory in a person's life and set up an outpost from where they can operate in an increasingly aggressive manner. A stronghold can be established, for example, when compulsive, repeat sin has made a bridge for a demon to cross the line from outside of a person and into their mind, emotions, and will. It may begin to affect them physically. The line has been crossed from outside influence to staking a claim and setting up a field of operations internally due to disobedience and sin. Compulsive, uncontrollable sin behavior may be an indication that a stronghold has been established.

Level Four - Conscious Demonization

Conscious demonization is when a person is aware that something has gotten hold of them and has begun to take control and act out of them. They may be flooded with violent, perverted or ungodly thoughts they know are not coming from them. They may find themselves suddenly saying demonic things or physically being manipulated in a way they know is not them. It may seem as if a separate personality and entity shove them aside when an episode happens. (This is the best and most effective time to get prayer for expulsion and extraction.)

Level Five - Perfect Possession

This is when a person is completely or nearly completely taken over by a demon or demons. It is rare but it does happen, and when it does, it is vital you handle it with the utmost seriousness and preparedness.

Indicators

These are just a few symptoms that might be indicators of some level of demonic influence and varying levels of that influence:

- Unexplained and repeated headaches that are not medically related
- Obsessive thoughts of evil or sin
- Compulsive sins
- Constant nightmares of an occult/demonic nature
- Overwhelming attraction to certain sins/addictions
- Addiction to violent/slasher or occult video games/movies/music
- Being drawn to people or social groups that are carriers of occult spirits, i.e., New Agers, Wiccans, gay groups, party groups, white supremacists, etc.
- Gradual or sudden aversion to church, Christians, the Bible, God, Jesus
- Withdrawal from others, especially believers
- Uncontrolled foul language (not Tourette's)
- Darkness in the eyes, eye color changes or eye shape changes
- Trancing out
- Blasphemy, loss of bodily functions

Those that are concerned that they have come under a demonic influence need to trace it back to the source and beginning, the point of entrance, and immediately seek prayer.

Ten Doors of Entrance:

Areas Demanding Guarding and Protecting

The following can act as a personal "checklist" to make sure you are staying on track and not allowing the enemy to have any doors open into your life. I recommend going over them and asking God to deal with any area where you have compromised or left the doors open for spiritual attack.

Are there any open doors in your:

Mind	What you think., what you read, what you imagine.
Body	What you do with the Temple of God.
Ears	What you hear and listen to.
Feet	Where you go.
Heart	Who and what you love – your affections.
Eyes	What you see and put before your eyes.
Soul	What rules your emotional life.
Mouth	What you say.
Spirit	What controls the very center of your being.
Hands	What you touch and put your hands to.

FROM THE FRONTLINES: DOUBLE JEOPARDY

Some years ago, I was not in a good place spiritually and had gotten my foot caught in some sin traps. I had hidden them very well. I didn't want to be where I was, but I was, well…trapped.

Nevertheless, I was asked to counsel someone at my office, a Christian who was very bound and tormented by crippling sins.

The counseling time went well, and I gave the best Biblical advice I could under my compromised condition. I knew I was on dangerous ground. As I always did, I asked if I could pray for them. "Please," they replied.

The minute I laid my hands on their shoulder, they went into 100% manifestation. My first thought was, "But they are a Christian, they confessed the Lord Jesus! They *can't* be doing this!" My second thought was that I was in great danger even attempting an extraction given my spiritual condition.

Before I had a chance to think about my theological and personal dilemma, the person convulsed and was thrown onto the ground, and I watched in horror as, on their backs, their body began to unnaturally arch until the person was a complete half circle, pivoted on their tiptoes and their head, teeth bared, snarling and cursing and speaking in a demonic language.

I was neither expecting nor prepared for this, and there was no one to help. Nevertheless, I attempted an extraction. I felt I was making progress until I commanded it to leave one more time and it began laughing at me. "You can't make us go! You are doing the same sins they are!"

I cannot describe the complete naked exposure of the truth about my sins that I felt at that moment. They knew they had me, and so did I. I was one of the seven sons of Sceva, and they dismissed me because my unconfessed sins took my authority away in that moment. (Remember – none of us are sinless – but *never* enter an extraction with unconfessed sins.) I felt punched in the gut. And even though I tried to complete the extraction, it would not go. I was forced to a draw, and I prayed until God mercifully restored the person to themselves, and I referred them to someone who hopefully was able to do what I could not. I suffered a great deal from that failure, but it was also one of the things that made me get my life back in order with God.

Nearly ten years later, I found myself in the midst of another very formidable extraction, but, after some time, I could tell it was quickly losing ground. Just as we reached the final clash and expulsion, a familiar laugh and glare confronted me. "Remember meeeeee? Ten years ago?" it cackled. I knew in an instant it was my nemesis from years before. "Yes, I do," I replied with confidence and authority. "But this time, I *do* have the authority to make you go, and you *will* go right now in the Name of Jesus!" It cursed me, screamed, and left.

I cannot prove that it was the same demon. But the important thing to remember is that they recognize God's deliverers, and they know whether we are fully armed or not. They know if we have hidden sins that we have not brought to the cross. Their goal is to keep us from stepping into their domain and taking prisoners from their vile grip. They will try to keep you from the battle, trip you so you cannot fight, or expose you when you are not operating under the authority that comes from a clean heart. They will fight you with personal accusations that will keep you from fighting if you do not close every door.

Get clean, get right, and get on with the battle. The only defeat is in quitting. The only victory comes in claiming the precious blood of Jesus for your cleansing, and the authority of His Name to make them go.

I am deeply thankful to God that he gave me a second chance to battle, and to win.

My main ambition in life is to be on the devil's most wanted list.

- Leonard Ravenhill

Gregory R Reid

21 RULES OF ENGAGEMENT

Spiritual warfare and demon extraction is not a hit-and-miss game.

In fact, I have often been frustrated and grieved when I've seen "pile-on" deliverances in which everyone takes a turn at the wheel to see if they can make something happen. "Are you a lying spirit?" "You're a spirit of confusion!" And on it goes.

The problem is, they're *all* lying spirits. And confusion is their primary weapon to avoid discovery. So they love to get unclear and undisciplined "deliverance" teams taking turns and stirring things up.

No, deliverance is exact and exacting. It's not shadowboxing, and it's not guesswork.

So just as in physical warfare, you need rules of engagement – ground rules.

These are some helpful ones.

1. Even the best battle plan rarely survives the first skirmish.

War is fluid. When you are doing a deliverance or engaging the enemy, you may have a neat little outline that you read somewhere that may go something like this:

    A. Bind the strongman

    B. Loose the angels

    C. Get the person to confess their sins

    D. Plead the blood

    E. Remind Satan that he is defeated

Now, each of those may be helpful at different points and are certainly true. But when you actually enter the arena of battle, everything changes. You are literally fighting in two dimensions, and everything happens quickly and startlingly. Your senses are painfully heightened. You will fight confusion, things may be appearing and swirling, temperatures may fall or rise, horrible ungodly thoughts may fill your mind, and a host of other unexpected events.

Does that surprise you? It shouldn't. In a physical war, the combination of danger, fear, adrenaline, bullets flying, screaming, etc. may completely shred the clean battle plan you may have gone in with. You have to adapt to the immediate needs of the moment and the changing strategy of the enemy.

Extractions are not always tidy and quick. Be prepared, be rested, be fluid and nimble, be willing to have the Holy Spirit give you specific orders on the fly. This enemy is much smarter and much nimbler than you are in your flesh, but not more than the Holy Spirit. Do nothing more and nothing less than what HE says, and you will be able to rout the enemy soundly and completely.

2. Work on your weaknesses.

Spiritual warfare is not a one-time event, but a lifetime career. Preparation is everything, and daily, constant vigilance is the posture of the true soldier.

Therefore, you must ask God to help you work on your weaknesses. Satan will look for every little chink in your armor, and when the battle is hot, he will stick his dagger in that spot and try to take you out.

So commit to going before God - right now – and have Him shed light on your weaknesses. Are you angry? Do you struggle with a hidden addiction? Are you spiritually lazy and Wordless? Do you hold grudges, have unforgiveness? Do you struggle with lust, pornography, self-pity?

Go before God with a thorough list of your weaknesses, struggles, and sins. (Yes, write them. You can throw them out when you're done.) Be brutally honest. Tell God where you are weak and struggling. Then, listen. Let Him put the searchlight on any hidden thing or area you were not aware of. Ask Him for cleansing, strengthening, scriptures and strategies for victory over these areas. Then let Him begin to work on these areas.

This isn't about grace vs. works. It's about "laying aside every weight and the sin that so easily besets us." (Hebrews 12:1) Spiritual warfare training requires bootcamp-brutal training and discipline. Athletes require brutal training regimens. This isn't about working to obtain your salvation. It is what Paul talked about when he said he would turn the boxing gloves on himself and nearly beat his own eyes out so that he would not be disqualified - (adokimos) – *benched*:

"Therefore I run thus: not with uncertainty. Thus I fight: not as one who beats the air. But I discipline my body and bring it into subjection, lest, when I have preached to others, I myself should become disqualified." (1 Corinthians 9:26-27)

This is an arena, and it is a battle. And if you're in, be in to win in the name of Jesus, and be willing to be thoroughly equipped and trained to battle well.

Haven't you ever watched a battle scene in a movie, or a hand-to-hand fight and said, "Well, that will never be me. Still…I wish…" Well, if you want the spiritual equivalent of that mastery, then you have to go to it, work on your weaknesses and get rid of all the things that are weighing you down and keeping you from reaching your fighting trim.

The enemy is sly, lithe, deliberate, stealthy and cruel. He knows his strategy and your weaknesses. It's time to step up and surprise him by closing the doors to sin, dropping the weights and repairing your armor. "Nor give place to the devil." (Ephesians 4:27)

3. Have a single, unambiguous aim.

When you engage in spiritual warfare, especially if you are engaging in deliverance, you have to have one single goal, without any cloudiness: To see the person delivered. If you are unclear, or unsure, or do not know what you are going to do once you engage the enemy, then it's best not to. Just like in Vietnam, we did not have clear and unambiguous goal. We kept changing the goals and the battle rules. On the other hand, in WWII we had one goal in Europe: Defeat Hitler and Mussolini. We focused, and we defeated them. In spiritual warfare, you have to engage the battle with a certainty that you are going to dislodge the enemy and not be distracted by anything that may happen in the course of the prayer. The enemy is good at smoke and mirrors; stay absolutely focused no matter what.

4. Pursuit.

If you are going to take spiritual warfare seriously, then you come to accept that the normal posture of a believer is battle mode, with battle gear, and battle ready. More than that, you realize that the entire world lies under the slavery of the Wicked One and the only ones that have any power to stop the Evil One and set his captives free are fully armored believers who know who their God is and know the authority that their Savior, Jesus Messiah, gave to them to destroy the works of the devil. That is what Jesus came to do; and the scripture says, as He is, so are we in this world. (1 John 4:17)

Therefore, our posture must be neither passive resistance to a world of sin nor a "circle the wagons" strategy that is just about "holding on to what we've got." No; we need to be in hot pursuit of the enemy. In any war, when it's retreat and circle the wagons on a consistent basis, you have already lost. At some point, you have to rout the enemy by pursuing him – deliberately, aggressively, and without relenting. Satan is our enemy. He is not going to let go of territory without a fight. **It is time for believers to stop bemoaning and start dethroning.**

In order to do that, God has to break our "retreat and build a fortress" strategy; you know, just keep having church, meetings, etc. and hope the enemy won't come over the walls. If we do that, we will fail to realize that because of our inactivity, he is *already* over the wall, sowing apathy, fear, compromise, division and careless ease.

The way to break through this is to go out beyond the walls. God has been teaching us how to go out into the public arena and offer prayer to people wherever we go. People do not expect this. Some will reject the message, some will get angry, but some will hear, and we have an opportunity to speak to them of a loving Savior and the need to give their lives to Him. Satan hates that. When you do this, you're treading on his turf. Good! I say with the blessed evangelist CT Studd:

> Some want to live within the sound of church or chapel bell
>
> I want to run a rescue shop within a yard of hell.

5. Maintenance of morale

One of the most crucial factors in a war is making sure your troops don't lose heart or feel the weight of war so much that they are struggling to keep the will to win. That's why the army supplied movies, USO events, etc. War is brutal and ugly, and it can make you reach a point of despair. The military would try to do all it could to remind the troops that there is life for them to look forward to once the war is won.

Spiritual warfare is the same – and the deeper you go into it, the more you understand this. It is easy to be discouraged by the fight, the losses, the struggles, the attacks. As someone once said, "Fatigue makes cowards of us all." Just like Nehemiah and those that rebuilt the walls of Jerusalem, they were constantly being threatened, mocked, distracted. They were told to keep their swords at their sides at all times except when they bathed and slept. With us, we have to keep that sword by our side even as we sleep.

That is why it is all the more important that we encourage those in battle with us, our ministry teams, our pastors, our elders, and those who are engaging the enemy on a daily basis.

Those who have walked with me understand that true spiritual warfare often entails vicious attacks, both satanic and people related. We are aware of the constant need to maintain spiritual morale, to lift each other up, to remind each other that Jesus has the ultimate victory.

These are the things we must commit to do and encourage each other to do if we are to remain vital and strong in the fight:

-Keep a consistent prayer and Word life. This is not optional. Those who have no ability to do this need to stay clear of the fight.

-Pray for everyone that you are near, and who are near you, especially ministry people, on a consistent basis. We have to watch each other's backs.

-Check up on each other frequently to make sure no one is injured, hurting, discouraged or falling down.

-Take the Sabbath seriously. I don't care what day you take. But take it you must. This commandment is a necessity for spiritual survival. If it is so, just for the average believer, how much more so for those who feel the heat of the battle and the hot breath of the enemy on their necks on a daily basis? You must rest, you must recharge, you must replenish your physical, emotional and spiritual strength every week for one day. To neglect this is to put yourself in danger, as well as those around you.

-Take time to laugh, to have fun, to do something that has nothing to do with spiritual warfare. After all, even though we know the war is life and death, if you are constantly covered in the scent of war and death, it will eventually start to seep into your pores and come out through your talk, your walk and your outlook. Jesus is still Lord – no matter how serious the battle. And if in an earthly army there are scheduled times off, how much more do *we* need it? It is good to take times where we just enjoy the company of family, of friends, free of war talk and war stories. Just enjoy all the good things God has given you. Rejoice in the Lord always. Take time to enjoy a sunset, watch the birds and listen to the laughter of your children or grandchildren. It reminds us what we are fighting for. It also reminds us that one day, all the warfare will be finished and heaven will be free of all the tears and agony and battle of this life.

If you put some of these safeguards in place to keep up your morale, you will be a soldier ready for any battle.

6. Cooperation

This is crucial in any army. All parts must be working together as seamlessly as possible. Whether in a ministry team or in an actual working deliverance team, it is imperative that everyone is in sync and following protocol and chain of command. It can't be ten people all with different agendas and goals. It has to be ten people bringing their varied callings and giftings and working toward that "one unambiguous aim."

7. SNS/WCP

This was a well-known acronym during World War II: **Situation Normal Suspended/Wartime Conditions Prevail.** It was the understanding that because of the gravity of the war, people had to act accordingly. They would have to do without, they would have to cut back, they would have to support the war effort, even sacrifice family members to the military. It was the realization that the world – and indeed our country – was being threatened by an evil malignancy and if we did not stop it, it would eventually take away all we had. So, we adapted. We understood that life as we had known it needed to be adjusted, we needed to tighten our belts and accept that normal life was temporarily suspended until the war was over. It brought a sense of unity and purpose to our nation to know that. Wartime conditions prevailed until the end of the war.

We as believers are at war. And of course, there are different types of warfare. *All* must have and wear the armor at all times.

But as the scriptures tell us, not everyone actually goes to the battlefield. In the Old Testament, there were those who fought on the battlefield and those who "stayed with the supplies":

"For who will heed you in this matter? But as his part is who goes down to the battle, so shall his part be who stays by the supplies; they shall share alike." (1 Samuel 30:24)

There is a sense in which we must all do warfare. But when it comes to hands-on warfare, some "stay with the supplies." Like stateside families during WWII, some helped with war bonds, some with rubber and metal drives, some became "Rosie the Riveters" or did other things to support the war effort from home. The reward was the same.

In the same way, some will pray warfare prayers; some will fight with their armor to keep themselves strong, some will pray for those who are doing field battle in ministry. All have a part. But trust me, not everyone is called to do the blood and mud battling. I would never want anyone to do some of the things I have had to do and see the things I have had to see.

Frankly, it used to bother me. I worked as a law enforcement trainer on occult crimes for over twenty years, and I saw my fill of crime scene photos, autopsy photos, and death scenes. I had to read horrible literature, and I had to be exposed to vile demonic fights the likes of which have left their scars to this day. I would try to make believers aware of how real and how ugly this war was, in the hopes of recruiting them to do something somehow. Mostly, there were no takers. Only now do I really understand; they didn't need to see all I did or be exposed to it. For most, it is better to "stay with the supplies." (Just send a check, please!) I was able to forgive those who said, "You're glorifying the devil," to understand those who said, "You scare me!" and to pray for those who couldn't take hearing the full story, and yet were able to say, "You have our prayers and our support." Since then, I have been able to have dinner with church friends without sending them into an alternate universe with my war stories. And I save my battle stories for specific times needed, and for those who also have seen the fight up close and personal. None of this makes me better. I am simply a warrior by calling, and that is what I understand, know, live, breathe, sleep and do. I cannot and must not expect everyone to share that calling.

Yes, Jesus said, "In My Name you will cast out devils." And if you are a believer and walk with him, you likely will, and you must be prepared for it. That is the reason for this book. But full-time? No. That's a rare call indeed, and frankly, I wouldn't wish it on anyone.

Regardless, every believer must have the understanding and mentality to know that we are indeed at war, and our battle with the enemy on whatever level – whether for our own walk, for our family, for those who do not know Jesus, or for those bound by sin and wounds – that battle is never finished in this life. Wartime conditions for the believer prevail from the time we come to Jesus until we go Home. Only then does the war end. Until then, "normal" is suspended. We have to live a wartime life, walking in His Kingdom, not building ours but doing all the discipleship and cross-bearing and hand-to-the-plowing things we must to be His soldiers on this awful battlefield. I believe as we get closer to His returning, the darkness will only increase. That is why we must understand warfare as a way of life, not as a hobby.

8. High combat readiness.

One rule of effective warfare is that troops must maintain high combat readiness. They must be ready to drop everything at a moment and take on all their gear and training and take it to the battle. As believers, we must do the same. "Be ready in season and out of season." (2 Timothy 4:2 NKJV) One old saint said, "Have thy tools ready. God will find thee work." Every day as I look around me, I see the level of demonization increase. Just today, I pulled up to a stoplight and saw a young man, stereo blasting some ungodly and blasphemy filled tune. As I watched him, he was completely taken over, singing, acting out, contorting, throwing gang signs, as if there were no one else in the world. It wasn't imitation – it was demonization. He was taken over by what he had let into his life. It completely took me by surprise, and immediately, all my tools and weapons rose up within me. Not that I was going to get him to pull over and do an extraction on him. But I was ready for whatever. That's high combat readiness. You live, eat and sleep warfare. And if the moment comes, you don't tremble and run, but you are in combat mode because it has been your spiritual training to stay ready. You don't come to this moment just because, no more than you can wield a sword effectively if you carry it and never practice with it. You live a life that includes daily training. You train with prayer and with the Word of God: "But solid food belongs to those who are of full age, that is, those who by reason of use have their senses exercised to discern both good and evil." (Hebrews 5:14) It's training; it's exercise! It's learning to daily walk in holiness: "But reject profane and old wives' fables, and exercise yourself toward godliness." (1 Timothy 4:7)

When you do the daily – and sometimes difficult – work of walking with Jesus, following Him on the easy roads and the hard and letting Him teach you, then when the moment comes – you will be ready.

I used to balk at this as a "grace" person. I remember once when I was being encouraged to have a consistent prayer and study time, I said, "God, I don't want to have to work at this. I don't want to have to discipline myself to read and pray! I want my time with You to be spontaneous!" God said to me, "First learn the discipline, and then I will make it spontaneous." And as prayer and Word time for me became second nature, the "spontaneous" time in which God spoke clearly and deeply to me in His Word was extraordinary. Then when the time came that I was faced with some major trial, difficult event, or confronting some grisly demonic outburst, I was ready. Be ready. Your weapons – Word, worship and prayer - will do you no good if they rust in your "supplies bag." Use them now, and when the time comes, you will be ready for whatever the devil throws your way.

9. Firm and continuous command and control.

This is a must for any military operation. And frankly, we must understand this if we as believers are going to be effective in our warfare and Kingdom advancement. God's Kingdom is set up similar to the military in some ways: You have rank and file, protocol, levels of authority, command and control, soldiers, strategists, planners, and battle orders. Too often in God's house, His people have little or no recognition of the need for following orders and knowing your ranking. It has nothing to do with power or with position; if it does, then the ones who are using it that way are not using it according to scriptures. The last shall be first, the least the greatest, and those that are at the top of the authority chain, in fact, should be doing the most labor and serving and frontline fighting.

In regards to authority, it is crucial that you respond to those around you with respect, with a due understanding of their spiritual place in your life either as a disciple or a teacher, a pastor or a student.

How ridiculous it would be in a war if all the soldiers decided they knew best how to execute the war, came up with their own plan and tried to carry it out. It would be a disaster. A war is won because everyone is willing to respond to the ones placed over them to make sure nothing is lacking and every role is filled. In God's Kingdom, the more there are people running around self-ordained with an "I don't need to listen to anyone but God" attitude, the more chaos and failure will ensue.

In a ministry or in a demon extraction "swat team," knowing protocol is absolutely vital. To not follow protocol and chain of command is dangerous and destructive. It's a primary ministry principle, and in demon extractions, failure to respond accordingly might just get someone seriously hurt.

That leads to the final rule of warfare:

10. Orders are to be followed exactly, without question.

Before you take this out of context, know that there are strict limitations to the use of authority in the church. Authority is to be used to protect and grow and nurture the flock of God. It is not used (1) to control people, (2) to tell them where to live, or who to marry, or what job to take.

Naturally, if a person in the church is committing a sin or error, it is the place of the undershepherds of Jesus to correct the error, confront the sin and lovingly try to restore the person. But that authority is not ever to be used to lord it over the flock. I have seen far too many abuses in the shepherding-type church system, where sheep are expected to do everything they are told without question. That leads to cults.

So what am I saying here? Didn't I just say orders are to be followed exactly, without question?

I am speaking– and I will deal with this more in-depth later – specifically about when you have a ministry team committed to pray for someone who is demonically infested. You need to have a very clear understanding as to who has the authority in the situation. There needs to be *just one person* who is leading the charge, and everyone else needs to obey his or her every word. If not, the devil will try to get everyone to take charge, and that will result in confusion, chaos and a failed extraction. As in a war, you must understand who God places over you, and in a serious situation, you must be willing to follow their lead and do as they say.

I can best illustrate this through an incident that happened at a Bible study in my home one time. It was spring, and we had the front door open. It was nighttime. I live in a not-so-good area. Right in the middle of the study, we began to hear the cry and wail of a child. It was almost blood-curdling. We all stopped. Knowing my neighborhood – and knowing how eager my young people were to stop child abuse – I knew I was in a dangerous situation. I told them, "Everyone stay here, close the door and do not go out until I come back." I took one of our young people outside and said, "Call the police." "No, I'll go with you," he said. "No," I answered. "Just do what I say." He did. I went close enough to the house to be sure nothing happened until the police got there. They did, and they made sure all was well with the child. And it was.

When I went back, I told them, "This was a test run. If this had been a real crisis, a child's life might have depended upon you trusting me and doing exactly what you were told to do. You all passed. I know now that I can trust you if we really do need to do something to rescue a child and it's a life or death situation."

Actually, we *were* dealing with such situations. I know firsthand how important it is to know the person over you, under you, beside you, the person you are responsible for, and the person who has your back. Although I rarely do such dangerous assignments these days, when it comes to demon extractions, it is just as crucial a principle. Be willing to follow the lead and instructions of the person in charge or do not be part of it at all.

There are surely many more rules of war I could share, but for now, I pray these will help you be equipped with a basic understanding of how to conduct a good and effective spiritual battle.

Evil never surrenders its hold without a sore fight. We never pass into any spiritual inheritance through the delightful exercise of a picnic, but always through the grim contentions of a battlefield. We are not 'born again' into soft and protected nurseries, but in the open country where we suck strength from the very terror of the tempest. "We must through much tribulation enter the Kingdom of God."

Dr. J. H. Jowett

22 HOUSECLEANING

"Neither shall you bring an abomination (an idol) into your house, lest you become an accursed thing like it; but you shall utterly detest and abhor it, for it is an accursed thing." (Deuteronomy 7:26)

"…the little foxes, that spoil the vines…" (Song of Solomon 2:15)

I have heard a number of people contest what I am about to say here. They believe that symbols, occult signs, occult jewelry, objects, etc. do not have demons attached to them.

That is a very simplistic and naïve view of the occult world, and of spiritual warfare and reality.

God called occult things accursed. They are cursed, and they carry a curse. Why is that? Because that which is behind them is anti-God, demonically charged and destructive in nature.

In the world of the occult, objects are imbued with "magick" (demonic) power. Most occultists understand that they are using such objects to attach or "send forth" forces, or "spirits" with them. Some call it "divine energy." Others know that they are calling on specific "spirits" (demons) to do a "working." They do so believing they will affect change, alter futures, "bless" a person or curse the person who receives such an object.

And, remember - if you call them, they will come. Anyone who believes they can keep such an object and "sanctify" it is on dangerous ground. **It is an accursed thing.** You cannot sanctify something that has been offered to demons.

Anyone who is skilled in spiritual warfare knows that places and things that are offered to demons or occult practices maintain a certain attachment and power from the enemy. That is why spiritual housecleaning is so important.

I am not referring to the misguided and misleading "ghost busting" antics of some who claim to be "religious" and go to "exorcise" houses and get rid of the "ghosts." As I have stated, there are no "ghosts." There are only familiar spirits and demons. These "experts" are doing nothing but joining in a demonic circus sideshow.

I am speaking about spiritual discernment, which knows by the Spirit of God when a place is given over to the enemy through objects or ritual or other ungodly practices - and prays accordingly. In some ways, this is like spiritual private investigation. It requires sharp discernment, a willingness to dig and uncover the truth, and deal with whatever is found, according to the Word of God, which requires a riddance of all ungodly things.

Those who have battled the forces of hell know that "accursed things" have demonic "tags." A demon doesn't have to be sitting on an object like a gargoyle. The demonic underworld is like a fine-tuned telecommunications network; once a cursed object is used, it is then "activated" and the signal goes out that someone is vulnerable to their influence and attack. Where there are such tags, demons have a legal right to be there in some form, either in person or available at a moment's notice.

Look at it as a huge spider web, with thousands of delicate strands. The spider itself does not have to be seen, and it may be anywhere on that web – but with the slightest motion, it is aware that something has been caught in the web, and no matter where it is, the spider will follow that strand and pounce on the helpless prey to devour it.

That is the demonic webbing that comes with "accursed things."

With these things in mind, let's lay out a little checklist of things that are by no means all-inclusive, but are fairly basic and will help you begin to clean out your house, be it a literal house, or your internal house of body, mind, soul, and spirit. May God guide you as you go before Him and seek to rid yourself of all unclean and accursed things. It will also equip you in helping others to do the necessary housecleaning God requires.

Books

By introduction, let me say that I am amazed and shocked at how naïve many Christians are as to the nature of the occult/new age/new spirituality and how many of them possess books belonging to that world without any idea that they are dangerous and demonic. In my time as a youth pastor, whenever we had a rummage sale, we had a number of occult books, movies, music or jewelry items donated. In one sale, someone even donated an Ouija Board!

Even in our church library, we have had to be very diligent about what came in. I had been for a time the unofficial book-checker for our church library. One of our youth once brought me a book about angels someone had donated. I began to read. It started out rather dull and historical, but halfway through, it began to list angels both from God *and* from Satan. The last portion of the book contained spells and curses you could use to get fallen angels to work for you! It's hard to believe someone who knows Jesus would not know how dangerous it would be to have that book.

On the other hand, there are a number of other books I have seen genuine believers have on their bookshelves, which until they were made aware, had no idea that they were not from God. This is not a criticism – if you don't know, you don't know. But when you *do* know, then you are responsible to act on what you know.

With that in mind, here is a small checklist of books to look for and burn. Remember Acts 19:19:

"Also, many of those who had practiced magic brought their books together and burned them in the sight of all. And they counted up the value of them, and it totaled fifty thousand pieces of silver."

_____ Astrology books

_____ Any occult or supernatural books or stories

_____ Numerology books

_____Yoga, Transcendental Meditation books

_____ Jeanne Dixon, Edgar Cayce, Hanz Holzer books

_____Dream interpretation books

_____ *The Secret* by Rhonda Byrne, *A Course in Miracles*

_____ Harry Potter

"Wait! You want me to get rid of Harry Potter?" Yes. Potter is one of the most intricate occult tomes ever written, including spells and items that are only known to those who are adept occultists. For example, a "hand of glory" is mentioned in an occult bookstore that the children go to. The Hand of Glory is an actual ritual which employs a severed hand from a thief dipped in wax and used as a candelabra. Get rid of the Potter books. It's candy-coated occult literature.

_____ All books related to vampires, werewolves, the undead, supernatural themes, etc.

_____ All pornography, including "adult" soft pornography books.

_____ All books with *any* occult or sexual fantasy content whatsoever.

Music

Music is powerful. Ungodly music can be one of the biggest strongholds in a person's life. It is important to evaluate all of our music and music habits and do a thorough housecleaning of any music that is not pleasing to God.

Evaluating our music must be based on both the message and the messenger. If the message is anti-God, sexually explicit, violent, occultic or encouraging of ungodly things like drugs, drinking, promiscuity or violence, it needs to go.

At the same time, if the artist is living a clearly satanic or antichrist lifestyle, or they use their music as a vehicle to promote a philosophy that is antichrist or ungodly, it needs to go.

We are very quick to criticize rock, rap, and heavy metal as being demonic. But I have heard equally worldly and godless lyrics in country music and in other genres of music as well. It is not about the music genre, but about the music content, message, and lifestyle. A world-famous country music pot smoker is no better example than a devil worshipping heavy metal singer. So let's be brutally honest in our housecleaning.

What about "New Age" music? There was a time when "New Age" music was a distinct category of music that was explicitly tied to new age religion – trance channeling, goddesses, auras, the "divine within," etc. Later, the commercial world broadened the new age music category to include just about any kind of instrumental, space or ambient music out there.

The guideline for "nonverbal" music like this is primarily the theme or the song titles. Examples would be music with titles such as:

Tantra Zone, Healing Vibes, Yoga Healing, Mantras for Life, Yellow Mandala, Mystic Voyage, Chakra Suite, etc.

Sometimes an artist will produce a completely innocent album of instrumental music, and then do a completely new age theme filled album with occult titles.

For those, like me, who love space/ambient type music, we must ask for a strong sense of Holy Spirit discernment. Honestly, there have been some albums that appeared to be new age free, but they unnerved me to the point where I had to get rid of them. Many new age albums are using experimental frequency techniques to produce body/mind effects, some even attempting to produce an altered state of consciousness in the hearer. It can be very dangerous to listen to these. Remember the old adage: If it's doubtful, it's dirty. Get rid of it. Any music that takes you out of yourself or makes you dissociate get rid of it.

I am always hearing people say (especially those who listen to metal/rap) "I don't really listen to the words." (Most often, they really do.) But when they don't, they still get the message. We retain subconsciously everything we see and hear. So regardless of whether you listen to the words, the words are bypassing your conscious mind and being planted into your inner soul and mind. How ideal for Satan to use music and words to bypass our conscious mind to plant his rage and perversion into our subconscious while we're "not listening to it." Don't fool yourself. Evil messages will alter your behavior, thoughts and spiritual life. No one is immune.

Again, be thorough: Message, words, the person's personal agenda. It can be tricky. I remember a few years ago, I had purchased an album that I really liked as a teenager, glad to have it back after so many years. But when I read the liner notes, I read at the end: "As above, so below." That is the central theme of all new age/occult teachings and magick. I had just wasted my money on something for the trash can!

Every one of us needs to do a music housecleaning. Do it prayerfully, brutally, honestly and completely. You will be amazed at how many little demonic songs are hiding in your collection!

Movies

_____ Gratuitous violence

_____ Sexual content

_____ Occult themes

_____ "Slasher" films

Occult themes are movies that have to do with demons, spells, ghosts, vampyres, werewolves, zombies, reincarnation, other religions, etc.

Be honest and brutal with movies concerning their sexual content. I know far too many believers who would never see a movie about witchcraft, but have no problem with R-rated movies with moderate to heavy sex scenes.

The rule of thumb should be, "If Jesus were sitting next to me, would I feel comfortable watching this movie?" (News flash: He always is.)

Art & Jewelry

Be discerning of art or jewelry acquired from other cultures and countries. Some of it is ok, but many objects have been dedicated to occult gods. Be especially diligent with Egyptian artifacts and jewelry. For example, there is a popular piece of jewelry that looks like a beetle. It is in actuality a Scarab, which is the Egyptian symbol for reincarnation. The Ankh symbol, a cross with a loop at the top, is also an Egyptian symbol for reincarnation. Be careful of things with unidentified symbols. Here is a partial list:

_____ Any amulets, talismans or "good luck" pieces

_____ "Stars" to protect farm houses or homes

_____ Any Buddhas, or Hindu gods or goddesses

_____ Any Masonic jewelry, rings, aprons, Eastern Star rings or pins, compass pins, etc.

_____ Egyptian symbols, cartouches, etc.

Be careful with Native American art and possessions as well. While most people think that the Native Americans have a religion where they just worship "The Great White Spirit," they are in reality nature worshippers, and everything becomes a form of a god. There are over 352 specific gods they worship, and they pray to them when creating their art. Even popular items such as "Dream Catchers" have a definite occult purpose, from the belief that it's like a spiritual spider web created to catch negative thoughts and dreams and let only good thoughts and dreams through. It was part of a legend of a "trickster" (hyoka or coyote in some legends) who gave this item in a vision to a Native American spiritual leader. The Kachina dolls of the Pueblo tribes are "spirit beings."

African artwork, artwork from India and other Asian countries such as China, Indonesia, Japan, etc. are very often imbued with spiritual connections to their gods and goddesses. Be careful not to have any item of a doubtful nature in your possession.

I know some will mock this idea. But I remember very clearly one of the most difficult demon extractions I had ever done. We were making no progress despite our prayers and determination. At one point, I looked down and saw an oriental "yin yang" symbol on their wrist – a symbol of the god/goddess, light/dark duality, and equality, etc. I said, "You need to take that off." The person struggled mightily to do so, but the moment they did, the demon screamed and left the person. They were completely and instantly delivered. It will strike many as extreme that such an "innocent" thing could have such a connection. But the proof of its true nature was in what happened when it was removed.

Games

Fantasy role-playing games are usually filled with occult symbols, gods, demigods, and spells. They are not harmless.

I went to the funeral of two young people who were murdered by a satanic cult as a result of their involvement in such a game. It started out as a low-level occult fantasy game called Dungeons and Dragons, which led to more involved occult games, which led to their death. Extreme, yes. But any time you open the door to occult things, "fantasy" or not, there will be a consequence. Video games are especially packed with occult symbols and themes. The violence is an issue all its own. But the fact is, a number of videogames are produced by Satanists and occult practitioners. Playing them is inviting demonic oppression and more. At the very least, it's a sure way to keep your spiritual life at a complete standstill as you spend mind-numbing hours lost in play while your Bible collects dust.

Statues, Candles, and Incense

A statue of a god or a saint has absolutely no place in the house of a believer. Let's not kid ourselves into thinking they are not made, and used, specifically to offer prayers to. According to scripture, praying to a statue is a prayer to the dead, which is useless and forbidden. They cannot help you. They cannot talk to you. They cannot reach you. "Absent from the body, present with the Lord." (2 Corinthians 5:8) There is a reason God forbade this communication and why we are told not to attempt it. Necromancy is very specifically talking to the dead. It does not matter how holy the person was, or how great they were. Dead is dead, and there are only two people who never died as far as we know, and only One rose from the dead to become the first fruits of the Resurrection, Jesus Christ. *He* is the only one we can go to, "For there is one God and one Mediator between God and men, the Man Christ Jesus." (1 Timothy 2:5) But then what is a saint? According to the Bible, (1) It is a "set-apart one," and (2) The Bible says we are all saints if we belong to Him. A saint, scripturally, is not a holy person; it is one who has been set apart for the Kingdom of Jesus Christ by being purchased by His blood. That is the Biblical definition of a saint.

I would not be Biblically honest nor correct if I did not speak the truth on these matters. The reason for its importance is simply that if you pray to *anyone* outside of the Father and His Son Jesus, you are quite simply opening yourself up to, at the least, harmful superstition (a saint for travel, a saint for lost objects, etc.) and at the worst, the opening of doors to familiars that are anxious to enslave people into bondage to a system of idolatry, repetitious prayers and occult-tinged beliefs.

In Jesus, there is no need for departed saints to intercede nor idols to venerate. Be done with them. Honor Mary as she would have wished. "Do whatever my Son tells you to do." (John 2:5)

In the Hispanic community, there is a special danger here with the whole cultural entrenchment of those who practice folk medicine and magick known as "curanderismo," which we have discussed previously. Within that system, there are a number of "specialty" candles you can buy to use for various reasons. The problem is, the church has been very lax on any kind of proscription against such things in Mexico and in the Hispanic community. I know people who practiced both Catholic prayers and Curanderismo/candle prayers for years without even knowing there was a spiritual conflict. I have also prayed for many who have needed deliverance from demons because of such activities.

There is nothing inherently wrong with candles. However, be very careful what kind of candle it is, and where it was obtained. You might have seen some "different" candles being sold in stores like Wal-Mart and other retailers – candles with odd names like "Santa Barbara," "St. Lazarus" or "7 African Powers." These are highly occultic candles that are part of the Santeria religion. Santeria is an African religion that was brought to the Caribbean, where the practitioners were forced to convert to Catholicism. They learned how to hide their religion and its many gods behind Catholic images and made-up saints. It is a potent and extraordinarily demonic religion, and you should avoid these candles at all cost.

Be careful with incense. Some kinds are generic – but many are created for eastern religion worship and have the names of gods and goddesses on them. If it's questionable – toss it out.

Soul Tie Material

In a previous chapter, we spoke of soul ties – those emotional, spiritual and mental ties to someone you have had sexual relationships with. But there are other kinds of soul ties as well – family ones – which may include certain gifts, jewelry, letters, clothes, etc. that may still bind you spiritually to a relationship that was unholy, destructive or demonic. I know many people who, although they acknowledge that a relationship was wrong and out of God's will, or that the person they were tied to was tied to the occult, or was sexually abusive, still have an attachment to a thing that belonged to that person. I've spoken to married people who hold on to a letter, a photo or other object from a former lover and it hinders every aspect of their marriage.

Ask God to help you to identify and get rid of every object that has a "tag" from past relationships.

Television

There has never been an age when more ungodly filth has poured into homes through television. Television can be a huge bondage and open the door to the gutters of demonic clutter and spiritual darkness.

So, is television evil? I will leave that up to the individual to decide. It is an inevitable part of our culture, and yes, we can use it for the glory of God. For many, especially for those who live alone, are lonely or elderly, television can be like a hearth, although an artificial kind of comfort.

But at its worst, television is a cesspool of demons. Just a brief glance at prime-time television will expose you to antichristian ideas, mocking God, sexual perversions, and enticements of every kind. Television has become the great cultural shaper of generations, as have the movie and music industry. The difference is that television has become a family addiction, indeed a family member.

How do you know if you are addicted? Easy. Stop watching it for five days. Monitor your emotions, your reactions. You may feel sad, empty and even experience withdrawals.

We are so numb to the kinds of daily and nightly inputs we get through television that we do not even recognize what it is doing to us. Many people who did a total television fast except for news and weather, came back to watch prime time programming and were horrified at the unrestrained filth, anti-Jesus jokes and outright moral depravity on almost all of the programs.

Children's programming is absolutely permeated with occultism, witchcraft and gender-bending. If there is ever a more crucial responsibility we have in our home, it is that we protect our families from indiscriminate television viewing, which only allows darkness to come into our homes unrestrained. *You* must draw the lines as to what is viewed, and when, and why.

Internet

Very little needs to be said about the way the Internet has been used by

Satan to pour filth into our lives, our homes, and our children. The internet is a beast that is fueled by pornography. It is nearly impossible to completely shield your children from it now. The educational system has made it impossible to *not* use it. With the advent of smart phones, any person is seconds away from pornography. Internet pornography is the biggest problem facing ministers in this hour.

Guard your home. Do *not* let your kids have time on the computer unsupervised. Take it out of the bedroom and put it in a place where everyone sees it. And for yourself, guard your heart and place whatever safeguards you need to not fall into its clutches of demonic filth, whether it is viewing pornography, occult content or violent content. "I will set no wicked thing before my eyes" (Psalm 101:3a) needs to be printed and taped to every computer monitor in every believer's home!

This has just been a brief overview of the things needed to houseclean so as not to allow the enemy to have any foothold or legal right to be in our lives or our homes. Ask the Holy Spirit to take you through your own home and thoroughly examine each possession you have. Ask Him to show you anything that is an open door or a stumbling block to your walk in Him or a nesting place for demonic forces.

Summary

In conclusion, leave no stone unturned in ridding your life and your home from anything that may be a demonic tag or a work of darkness. It is not superstition. It is common sense. If God said not to have accursed things, then any implement of sin, occultic tool or book or literature, any visual corruption or sinful media, any object or jewelry of an unclean or occultic nature, has to go. Be thorough. Many times, I have seen things so carefully hidden that it took a determined "prayer assault" to root it out. Ask the Holy Spirit to show you what needs to go. And then breathe in the freedom of the Holy Spirit of God that will fill your home and your heart!

23 PRAYERS FOR RENUNCIATION AND SEVERING OF BLOODLINE SINS

"The LORD is longsuffering, and of great mercy, forgiving iniquity and transgression, and by no means clearing the guilty, visiting the iniquity of the fathers upon the children unto the third and fourth generation." (Numbers 14:18)

There is a spiritual principle at work regarding sin. It affects everyone and everything around us, in little and big ways, but none so profound as in families. This is especially true concerning families who have a lineage of occult practices, drug and alcohol abuse and/or sexual immorality.

It is important to bring one's entire family history to the Cross of Jesus for cleansing, so that nothing remains of the influences or sins of our ancestors, whether parental or going back many generations.

"But why should I, or anyone, suffer the consequences of my family, my ancestors or my past generations?" I refer you back to an earlier story regarding having a life insurance contract taken out on me when I was born. I knew nothing about it until I was older. But it was a legally binding contract nonetheless. Generational sins and curses are like that. The sins of those who went before us are like legal contracts that give Satan a legal right to bind and hurt us, until we become believers, go to the Cross and break that contract by the forgiveness of Jesus and by His blood.

Some people who have struggled with certain bondages and sins without even knowing why, once they break these ties, find that the power of these sins is broken over them and they experience a complete new freedom in Jesus. Our doing this as parents stop these things from going to our children's generation.

These are some of the "blood tie" issues that may continue to affect us until we break them:

- Occult practices including witchcraft, Curanderismo, séances, Ouija boards, astrology, etc.

- Occult fraternal order membership including Masons, Eastern Star,

>   Shriners, Rainbow Girls and The Order of DeMolay.
>
> -Incest, homosexuality, adultery, pornography, bestiality, rape, and other forms of sexual sins.
>
> -Drug and alcohol addiction
>
> -Violence and crime: murder, brawling, assault, robbery, cartels, Mafia ties, etc.

These are just a few examples. Take some time to sit before God and ask Him to reveal anything in your family lineage that needs to be broken. You may want to make a list and take every individual issue to prayer, and break all the generational effects of these sins.

The following is just a basic prayer to help you; you can pray however the Spirit leads you, but be specific and be thorough. It may help to have a trusted prayer partner pray with you.

It is not necessary but may help, to sign and date the prayer, so that when the enemy tries to come back and place you back into bondage, you can show him this contract and remind him that his contract is broken, and he has no more rights in your life.

Come before the Lord, and ask Him to reveal any ancestral or family sins and curses that need to be broken.

"Father, I come before you in the Name of Jesus Christ, my Lord and Savior. I thank You, Jesus, for dying on the Cross for my sins. I thank you that you came to destroy all the works of the devil.

In the Name of Jesus, I renounce, reject, rebuke and break every curse of sin that has passed on to me or my family because of generational involvement in _____. I ask you to break every contract and sever any spiritual or demonic influence on me or my family as a result of these generational sins.

I rebuke you, Satan, and every demon that has come with these sins. I reject you, and I break your contract over my life. Be gone in Jesus' Name, and do not return! You no longer have any legal right to be here or touch me or my family in these ways ever again!

Jesus, forgive me for any sin I have myself committed of this nature. Cleanse me by Your Blood and the power of the cross, Jesus. Wash me white as snow. Fill me with Your Spirit to overflowing. Fill up every place the enemy has occupied in my heart, my emotions, my body, my thoughts, and my life. I fully belong to You, Lord Jesus.

Thank you for setting me free from every power of darkness, sin, and evil. I worship You and thank You for giving me freedom from all bondage! I give my life to serve You, and You only, all the days of my life.

In Jesus' Name!"

Gregory R Reid

I'm not afraid of the devil. The devil can handle me - he's got judo I never heard of. But he can't handle the One to whom I'm joined; he can't handle the One to whom I'm united; he can't handle the One whose nature dwells in my nature.

- A.W. Tozer

Gregory R Reid

FROM THE FRONTLINES: NOBODY KNEW

She was young, gifted, energetic, and much-loved. Her parents were fine and established members of the church.

She joined us on our annual youth mission trip to the Youth for the Nations conference that June. It was always a life-changing time of worship and preaching and fun for our youth. It was incredible to be in the midst of nearly 1,000 kids worshipping God together with all of their hearts!

Her best friend was with us, as well as his mom, who was the youth coordinator and the second - and in many ways most vital - part of the youth ministry God had entrusted to us.

On the third night, I watched as the young lady made her way through 1,000 kids to the stage during worship. "What is she doing?" I wondered, concerned. They didn't allow people on stage unless they were asked. She made a beeline for the director and was talking animatedly with him. Then he directed her offstage. I saw her friend go to meet her and go into the hallway. I assumed that all was well, so I continued to worship. A few minutes later, her friend grabbed my arm. "You need to come out with me right now. She's manifesting!"

I followed him out to where my young friend was standing. She was in a near panic. "We have to save the children! We have to save the children!" she exclaimed. "Honey," I said quietly, "We need to pray." She went into an immediate manifestation; her body began to twist and contort. "Go get your mom," I told her friend. "Meet us upstairs right away."

I helped her get upstairs, grabbing two interns along the way to be witnesses.

The next hour or two (deliverance erases your time frame, so I am not sure how long it was) was a painful, difficult time. It does no good to give the enemy glory by going into every detail. What I can tell you is that she was "gone" for most of that time. "It" would mock, laugh, speak – and even spoke in fluent Japanese. For that whole exhausting time, we engaged her long enough to discover: (1) she had been placed in a room on campus with two girls who kept trying to talk to her about witchcraft and the occult.

(Their father just registered them and dropped them off. They didn't want anything to do with Jesus. We believed that they might have placed some spiritual binding on her, and she was not protected from it. They even went from room to room looking for her when she was not there.) (2) While she had been in California attending a Hollywood makeup school, she was doing horror movie makeup of an occultic nature and (3) She had been approached by a member of the Nichiren Shoshu Buddhist sect who gave her a prayer in Japanese to pray in order to get her wishes granted. She was not strong in her faith at that time and was very vulnerable. (It may explain the fluent Japanese!)

We prayed and bound and cast out as much as we could. But it was taking a serious toll on her, and on us. We couldn't complete it. One of the interns approached me and pulled me aside. "Sir, we've had a little experience in dealing with this kind of thing." If he only knew…

"I defer to you," I said, and they proceeded for the next long while to try to finish the deliverance, but they reached the same impasse. "We have to get back to the service," they said apologetically. I understood. We did a "patch seal" prayer to seal what God did until we could take her to a safer place to finish the deliverance.

She was traumatized, barely knowing where she was. An extraction is sometimes very difficult like that.

We told the other kids nothing except that she was having a very hard time and needed our prayers. We talked with her parents, and they agreed to send her home on a plane in the morning. Our pastor would take it from there.

The next day I took her and her sister to the airport. I was completely exhausted. We took the kids to a local water park that day. Unexpectedly, two men in an apartment complex right next to the water park fence came out of their second-story apartment complex porch completely naked and exposed themselves to everyone at the park who looked up. Thankfully only one or two of our kids saw them. It felt so wicked, so demonic.

The next day, we packed up to leave and checked into a local hotel for a two day debrief and fun time. As the youth packed up, I felt a horrible presence and anxiety on our third floor. I walked out to see a youth pastor and two of his youth in the hallway in bikini briefs, suggestively gyrating like male strippers. I was stunned.

I took my luggage downstairs. As I was putting things in our van, another youth pastor started to yell, "Get back in that room!" I looked up and watched the youth pastor and one of his youth who had been dancing in the hallway now exposing their naked behinds to all the kids in the parking lot. "I don't have to do anything you tell me to!" the youth pastor shouted down. "I'm coming up there to make you," the man next to me said, and I decided to follow just in case there was a physical altercation. An intern, thankfully, got involved and made the other youth pastor get back in his room, pack and leave with his youth. "I'm never coming back here again!" he screamed angrily. It was so, so demonic. I felt like something, or someone had unleashed a wave of demonic activity in these last two days, and it had affected our young lady and was now manifesting through people around us in grotesque perverted ways. And it wasn't through yet.

"I need you right now!" my counterpart's son said, after knocking loudly on our hotel door after eleven that night. My guys were asleep, so I quietly stepped out and went into the room where he and his kids were. One of the boys was thrashing around violently on the bed in full demonic manifestation. It had happened without any provocation at all! I moved right in to deal with it. My counterpart's son stayed right in back of me, watching my every move and praying silently. Another person quietly read scriptures, and another quietly sang a worship song. I was so proud of them. They lined up like they had been working with me for years.

We finished that deliverance and no sooner was I back in bed than the door was being pounded on again. It was my young friend. "It's happening in another room!" Two more youth were prayed for before it was over. I was exhausted, and I was upset. None of these kids knew what had happened to our young lady, and none of them knew about each other! This was a "jumper" that was trying to disrupt and destroy the entire trip, and young lives with it. Thankfully, Jesus got the victory!

The last night, the kids were now fully aware of what had happened, so we went through the scriptures on fear, explaining very clearly why Jesus was greater than anything the enemy did. We quelled their fears and made sure they knew that Jesus was bigger than all of this. Everyone seemed quite satisfied, even thankful for what God had done. I only told them that they might not want to just bust out of the vans and say, "Hey mom, dad, guess what happened? We got demons cast out of us!" I told them to talk to their parents about it in context with everything else that God did that week.

We returned that Sunday night, not knowing that there was something close to a lynch mob waiting for us from some of the parents. The rumor got out even before I got home that we were casting demons out of everyone and that I had told the kids not to tell anyone about it.

I had not even had a chance to get a good night's sleep before a staff luncheon the next day. Afterward, the pastor told me to meet him back at the office to discuss some issues. Mid-route, the administrator called and told me a parent was on his way to the church, and he was loaded for bear.

I am by nature more Elijah and Peter than John and Joseph, so God really warned me to keep tight reigns on my potentially volatile responses.

The parent confronted us concerning all the events he had heard of, not having any firsthand information about what had actually taken place. (As a parent, I would have been concerned too.) I bit my tongue and sat very still, resisting my natural urge to defend myself. Once he had finished, I explained – in complete detail – what had actually transpired. After about half an hour, he was satisfied with my explanation. But he also informed me that he and other parents had been discussing this, and one set of parents would not be so easily convinced. They were very angry indeed. (Their son was one of those who assisted us by reading scriptures during the hotel incidents.)

It resulted in a meeting between the concerned parents, the pastor, and my counterpart and I. My counterpart's son was there, and he was deeply offended that people were creating a problem over this – and he was not shy in expressing his opinion. I was quite proud of him. And grateful to him. He had seen it all firsthand. He knew it was real.

One of the parents took us to task in one of the most painful barrages of personal attacks I had ever experienced, and again, God told me to keep my mouth shut until he was finished. When he was done, I explained again in minute detail what had actually transpired. I saw God start to work as their reactions softened.

Another set of parents came to support us and explained how the youth trip had touched their daughter and turned her toward a completely committed walk with Jesus.

The parents of our young lady spoke up, explaining that they did not believe in "this stuff," and when we had called them regarding their daughter, they still didn't believe it – until they saw her. But after prayer from the pastor over their daughter – which finished the deliverance – they absolutely knew this was real. They saw it in their own daughter!

With that, and the pastor (God bless him!) standing lovingly and firmly behind what we did, the issue was settled, and peace was made. One of the parents asked for forgiveness. I was thankful for how this turned out.

But we were left pretty raw. I had been doing this for the better part of forty years. I was tired, and I kept telling God I didn't want to do extractions anymore. They cost too much, they were too draining and took too much of a toll. Most of the extractions I was called into were not easy ones. They were usually grueling ones that needed both spiritual acumen and physical endurance, and I had decided long before all of this had happened, that I was done doing it.

But the day before we returned from the missions trip I took one of our other young ladies to the airport to fly home early. Alone on the way back to the hotel, I said, "God, I am not doing deliverances anymore!"

God spoke as clearly to me as He had in years. "This generation is systemically demonized, and I need you to be on the front lines." I immediately broke before God. "I'm sorry Father. You know how tired I am. But if this is your call, then I am willing. Take me and use me any way You want to."

And that, dear reader, is why you hold this book in your hands. This book was that commission.

Lessons:

1. Expect the unexpected, and be prepared to engage if necessary, at all times.
2. Be aware that some extractions can be in stages, as there may be more than one demon present. Don't be discouraged if you can't complete it in one setting.
3. When you do an extraction, be aware that it is like jabbing a hornet's nest with a stick. Pray before, after, all around, for every person, and for all those around you. "Swarms" sometimes can result and it is not unusual, like us, to have several bizarre incidents take place right around you. The enemy is seeking to retaliate, and the swarms will affect anyone who is not covered by the blood of Jesus or not saved.
4. We prepare for attacks before an extraction, but it is also essential we do not put down our armor afterward. Be prepared for a backlash. We had a victory at the conference, not expecting to be attacked when we returned. Never let your guard down!

To put a triumphant end of this story, our young lady has now served on several mission fields and has dedicated herself to mission work. She has walked in liberty and is completely free. She is a blessing to our church, her family, and everyone around her. She shines with the love of Jesus. I am very grateful that God allowed us to be part of her deliverance. Satan was completely defeated, and God has used her over and over to tell people that Jesus Christ is Lord over all the power of the enemy. Thank You, Jesus!

24 BOOTS ON THE GROUND

Now we come to the heart of the matter. Jesus said, "In My Name you will cast out devils." This is not theoretical. This is reality. Everything you have read thus far has been for three reasons:

1. To give you a scriptural foundation for your education on spiritual warfare.
2. For your personal deliverance.
3. To give you practical applications and tools for effective warfare.

Now we have come to the "boots on the ground" chapter, in which all you have learned, walked through and applied in this book will – God willing – have forged mighty weapons and armor in you so that you can do battle with the hater of our God and destroyer of souls and win Jesus' victory over the works of the Wicked One.

Two Kinds of Demonic Engagements

The first kind of demonic engagement is spontaneous. It is unplanned, unexpected and usually quite startling. This is why we must be armored 24/7 because you never know when the enemy is going to manifest.

Biblically, most extractions are of this nature. Paul appears to have made a "sneak attack" on the python spirit in the young lady that was following him. But most of the other times, it was a result of Jesus or His disciples simply walking in the power of God, and demons just came out of the woodwork. Why? They couldn't stand the power of God! That's why they would yell, "What have we to do with You, Jesus, You Son of God? Have You come here to torment us before the time?" (Matthew 8:29)

The majority of extractions I have done have been of this nature. They are rarely convenient, scheduled events!

In fact, I rarely "schedule" an extraction. Some people do. We need to prepare for both.

But if it should be spontaneous, try to find someone you trust to assist. Do *not* involve someone you don't know! Obviously, it is best not to tackle it alone, so if possible, seal and bind it until you've got backup. But if it will not wait, God will give you everything you need.

Basics

1. Whatever you did or learned in the previous battle may not help you at all in this one. Avoid "techniques" at all costs.

2. Most "deliverance manuals" are a bit off base and misleading. How I wish it was as cut and dry as filling out a form, checking off your problems and casting out the corresponding demons!

I'm afraid that method does more harm than good. Demons are far too deceptive and subtle to be "pigeonholed" like that. They rarely are a "demon of fingernail biting" or some such thing.

However, it does make a good decoy to identify themselves by banal or intriguing names so you never really discover who and what they are, so they can remain in place. They also are very good at "faking" leaving.

Well, then, how do you know? You must have razor sharp discernment. Then, you will *know*. And you don't get that from a how-to manual, but from staying very close to Jesus and being full of the Word of God.

3. Demon extractions or "deliverances" are fluid and fast once you have engaged it, so prepare your weaponry and stay spiritually nimble, hyper-vigilant, completely guarded and flexible in the battle.

4. Unless you are Spirit-directed or it is absolutely necessary, do your best to avoid talking to or conversing with the demon except to demand its departure.

This is where many trip up because they don't understand that demons love attention and love to converse. It's a game to them. I will never forget during one extraction where I kept silencing the demon, and it yelled in frustration, "Don't you want to know who I am and why I'm here?" I said, "The only thing I want is your departure!"

There is a certain fascination and curiosity we have with the demonic and supernatural. It is better to admit that, confess it and nail it to the cross before you enter the battle. You are not there to chitchat or get information or an education. You are a demon extraction agent! Be all business, or you will lose ground before the battle begins.

> 5. The authority to demand its departure comes from Jesus, not from you. Without His authority and protection, you are endangered. They do not fear you. They only fear Jesus Christ IN you.
>
> 6. Do not mock.

I know it's amusing when some preachers talk about "that silly old devil" or mock Satan in various ways but read this first:

"Yet even Michael the archangel, when contending with the devil about the body of Moses, dared not bring against him a railing accusation, but said, 'The Lord rebuke thee.'" (Jude 1:9)

Unless you feel you are in a superior station than Michael, you should be very cautious not to step over the parameters God Himself has set. We don't have to like Satan or his demons. But we had better follow the scriptural rules of engagement!

> 7. Do *not* be distracted by a demon's incessant chatter nor be distracted or frightened by any manifestations or supernatural events in the course of an extraction.

I remember well a dear elderly couple who called me to come and pray for their adult son who was manifesting. They let me in and quickly retreated to a back room to pray.

I sat across from the young man, who was sitting in a recliner in a demonic trance.

I began to pray. Suddenly the front screen door slowly opened and then slammed shut with powerful force.

"Are you scared yet?" the demon asked.

"No, not at all," I said, and I proceeded with the extraction, which was, thankfully, successful and short.

Much of what they do is smoke and mirrors and fear tactics. Do not let it catch you off guard or break your focus. Greater is He that is in you! They fear the Name and authority of Jesus and the more strange kind of things they manifest, the closer they are to losing their victim and departing.

8. Go completely cleansed.

Regardless of what you did five minutes before the extraction – get it under the blood of Jesus. To not do so is to risk your sins being exposed before everyone present. The enemy cannot expose what is cleansed and forgiven. Make sure you do this before engaging the enemy.

9. Do not allow a novice to participate unless clearly directed by the Spirit.

There are times when God may allow you to bring in someone you have been discipling in order to help train them in warfare. But this isn't a game. It may sound "fun" on paper, but trust me; it's grueling, nasty and sometimes dangerous work. Although few will tell you this, you never come out completely unscathed. And you will get on a spiritual "hit list" of sorts. Never put someone in that place just because they are available at the time, or someone that is spiritually vulnerable. I have sometimes had to dismiss available people in order to protect them.

10. Leave all arrogance at the door.

This isn't a showdown at the O.K. Corral, and you're not a demon gunslinger. You're going into deadly territory, and Jesus is your only protection. Go in broken and dependent, or you will come out shattered and scarred.

11. Be persistent, focused and determined.

I remember the great apologist and theologian Dr. Walter Martin once talking about an exorcism in which the demon told him, "I know I am going to win." "How?" Dr. Martin asked. "Because I can outlast you," the demon replied. We must take the same stance! I wish all exorcisms were quick and easy. They rarely are. Determine to outlast the demon, stay focused on that goal, and do not relent until the battle is finished.

    12. Don't yell at the demons.

They aren't deaf. Getting loud only shows your uncertainty, not your authority – and, they love the attention.

    13. Don't allow the demons to intrigue you, mesmerize you, or engage you in argument or discussion.

This is a non-negotiable demand for expulsion, not an opportunity to learn or observe their behavior. Remember, they are determined to distract you at all costs. They are very determined, and very good at using every trick there is to keep you off track and off task.

    14. Do not touch or restrain the person unless absolutely necessary for their protection or that of those present.

    15. If it is necessary to restrain the person, do not allow anyone except you and those you have authorized to touch or restrain the person.

When you're in the middle of an extraction, you need to remember that the demon(s) are now cornered. They will do *anything* to avoid being homeless again.

That's where you must guard against "jumpers." If a demon knows it is losing its grip and is about to be cast out, it will reach for any available vessel to transfer to. This is another reason why one must be cleansed because, at this stage of the extraction, the demon is looking for anyone who is uncovered, uncleansed or who has an open door.

I remember once praying for a highly-demonized person. It was "spontaneous," and one of our young ladies in our church was there – one who was still shutting doors on her own sins. She was so filled with compassion for our tormented friend that as we prayed, she reached out to lay hands on him to pray. I gently grabbed her wrist as she did and said, "Don't touch him." She immediately understood the danger she had almost put herself in.

Unless I have missed something, there were few if any incidents of physical contact with demonized people in the New Testament, and that is why the scriptural admonition to "lay hands on no man suddenly" is so crucial here. (1 Timothy 5:22)

    16. Demons can be incredibly deceptive. Make sure they are gone.

One time, we had been engaged in a lengthy and frustrating extraction that had left us exhausted and worn out. We wanted to go home. Finally, after yet one more demand for the demon to leave, it screamed, and the person went limp. Then they began to weep. Then they said, "Thank you, God, I'm free, I'm free!"

However, I got a Holy Spirit caution. "You're still there, aren't you?" I said, and the demon started screaming and tearing the person. The moment had come, the final ruse and hiding had been exposed. "Come out in the Name of Jesus!" I demanded, and it was done.

Be sure it is gone!

    17. It may or may not be necessary to ask questions.

Some teach that it is necessary to get the name of the demon, that once you do that, it loses its power. But frankly, that sounds a bit more like Rumpelstiltskin than scripture to me. It loses its power, not because its name is discovered, but because of the authority of Jesus!

I am not saying on occasion it may not be necessary to ask its name. Jesus did, so we certainly have precedent for it. Paul did not, which tells me we shouldn't make it a rule. Be led by the Spirit.

However, be very careful. They are masters at deception and may give you a false name or identity. Be discerning. An unclean spirit is a category of demons, a job assignment if you will, not a name. I have been able to extract demons without a name, and I have done it with a name. Let the Spirit lead you.

Also, on occasion when the demon has stubbornly dug in, I have found it necessary to ask, "What legal right do you have to be here? What gives you the right to remain?" Often it will be forced to reveal an object a person has, a family sin or secret, or a personal sin. Then if the person is still able to be engaged, bring them forth to renounce it. Many times, this is the breakpoint in the battle.

Again, be measured and on guard with all interaction. Bring down the force of His authority. Lean into it until the demon yields. Make sure any communication is sparse and specific, not curious and probing.

18. They hate worship. Use it.

19. They really hate the Bible. Read it aloud. Psalm 91 and Revelation 18 are especially effective.

I'm always saddened by atheists, skeptics and seminary professors who work so hard at trying to destroy people's faith in the Word of God. Because in real life, if you even bring a Bible close to a person in full demonic manifestation, they scream, blaspheme and even beg to have it kept away from them! Demons know better than all the foolish skeptics about the power of the Word of God, written, spoken or sung.

It's also good to be reminded of a previous observation that whenever a séance is held, the "spirit" (demon) always downplays, mocks and disregards the Bible. They hate it because it is the written Sword that, properly wielded, forces its defeat. Use it!

Your Team

In the event that an extraction is planned out, these are my recommendations:

1. Have one point-person.

The worst thing you can do is "pile-on deliverance." An event such as this requires a complete chain of command structure and protocol. Don't have anyone on the team who is not 100% clear on this. This first rule is crucial: There is one point person leading the extraction, like the point of a spear. He carries the ultimate authority of Jesus. Do not second guess them, do not try to assist them unless asked, and at all costs do *not* overrule or usurp their authority. You are there to do everything they ask of you, nothing more. If they consult you or ask you to move in, only then should you move from your post.

Demons often try to engage secondary team people in order to break the chain of command and break the point person's focus. If you are assisting, do not talk, do not respond, even when a demon becomes antagonizing, insulting, inquisitive, intriguing or abusive. They know how to push your buttons. It's a ruse, a tactic to get you off point. Don't fall into the trap. Keep silent.

2. Have someone quietly reading the scriptures out loud in the background. Have them be available to step forward and read passages up front when needed.

3. Have worship – recorded or live – in the background. It's good to have live worship in case there's a time needed for intense worship to drive the battle line forward. (My personal favorites are "O, The Blood of Jesus" and "At the Cross." They drive demons into a frenzy. But any worship song that speaks of the Cross and Jesus' blood, the power of God, the sacrifice of Jesus or the glory of His Name will work quite well.)

4. Pray with your team before you begin. Fasting is helpful too.

5. Make sure everyone understands the rules: *No one* is to disobey or usurp your authority, *no one* is to attempt to talk to or engage the demon unless you ask them to.

6. Make sure everyone has spent some time in prayer beforehand, putting any and all sins under the blood of Jesus.

7. Forbid any "gang deliverance." Only one voice carries the authority at a time.

8. If any one of these rules are broken, pre-authorize another team member to have the person who broke it removed immediately. Make sure everyone understands beforehand that this will happen if they break the rules.

9. It is good to have a seasoned second-in-command to back you up.

The Process

Although it works differently each time, there seems to be a series of definable moments in an extraction:

The Presence and the Pretense: The point person and his team become aware of another, ungodly, dark presence in the room.

The demon – acting as if it is the person you are praying for - will attempt to convince you that nothing is wrong, and there is no need for concern or prayer. Break through this pretense. Continue to pray, worship and command until the demon is fully exposed and cannot hide itself behind the person as if it were the person.

Breakpoint: This is when the demon is fully exposed. This is usually a moment of complete chaos, and one must be careful not to give in to any fear. Only those who have experienced this understand that when the moment comes, you need to be prepared for the literal tearing down of the spiritual wall of separation between our world and theirs, and it is disorienting beyond description. Everything becomes foggy and surreal, and there is a numbness in the room. At this juncture, be prepared for any number of manifestations including blasphemy, sharp drop or elevation in room temperature, other voices in the room, objects moving, the victim speaking in foreign languages, mocking the point person and the team, hideous laughter. Do not be thrown off guard or give into fear. You are on the frontlines now, and it will do anything possible to avoid the inevitable expulsion.

At this point, the demon often begins speaking of the person it has taken over, in the third person. For example, "They gave me permission to be here!"

As you proceed with authority and unwavering determination, the demon will do everything in its power to distract you, threaten you and keep you from your task. Be especially aware that this may be their best chance to use your own team to get things off track by trying to engage them in conversation, get them curious, attack them or make them afraid. Fully prepare your team in advance to expect that and remain silent and resolute in the face of what is often a vicious assault on their senses, mental facilities and sense of God's presence with them.

The Clash: As the demon loses its ground, you can literally feel the spiritual and even physical pressure in the room, as, in the words of one writer, "the demon has collided with the will of the Kingdom." For the person assigned to lead the extraction, this is the most visceral, intense and teeth-to-teeth moment of the entire deliverance. This is where you must demand and persist and not let up, and where the demon will threaten, manifest, scream, blaspheme and sometimes beg not to be forced from its host human home.

Expulsion: This is the moment in which the will of the demon is broken and all its power to remain has been stripped from it, and it is finally forced to leave. Everyone will know and feel when this happens, and the pressure recedes, the sense of disorientation and darkness is gone, and God's peace fills the room and everyone there. Be sure, as stated before that the demon has not simply pretended to be gone. If you sense at all that it remains or lingers or hides, persist until that 100% sense of completion has been given by the Holy Spirit.

Take time to soothe, pray for and minister to the person. Don't rush the completion, as tempted as you may all be after a strenuous and utterly foreign and ugly event such as this. Stay with them, pray with them, make sure they are hydrated, minister to their fears, and don't leave them alone until they are at peace and all the fear has gone. It is helpful if they can stay with a family member or friend that night.

After Care

There are some basic things that are important to do following an extraction, and it applies to both the team and the person who has been delivered:

1. Drink lots of water for the next few days as well as load up on protein. Extractions do tend to take a heavy physical toll, and our human bodies are weak and not accustomed to raw spiritual clashes.

2. Rest. If possible, take a complete day or two to recover.

3. Soak in the Word of God in that resting time, both in reading/speaking and if possible leaving recorded scriptures on through the night.

4. Expect some after-attack, both for you and the delivered one. Keep your guard up, stay alert, and have others pray intensely for you for a few days.

5. Keep in contact with the person to make sure they are ok and enlist others close to them to keep an eye on them and be available for prayer for them.

I am aware that this short chapter has only given you some very basic – albeit proven – rules of engagement, chain of command protocols and actual event procedures and safeguards.

But my prayer is that it will help you fight well, and successfully, in any battle you engage.

And as for the rest, I am fully confident that the Holy Spirit will give you all you need as you trust Him in this most serious and crucial war.

Gregory R Reid

Soon the battle will be over. It will not be long now before the day will come when Satan will no longer trouble us. There will be no more domination, temptation, accusation, or confrontation. Our warfare will be over and our commander, Jesus Christ, will call us away from the battlefield to receive the victor's crown.

- Thomas Watson

Epilogue

I am now at the end of the longest, most challenging writing commission of my life, the completion of this book.

The battle I have fought to bring this to completion is a testament, to me, of its value and necessity, and the enemy's determination to stop this work.

As I conclude it, I realize how much I have learned in the writing, and how much I still have to learn. I pray God will somehow use these words and experiences and instructions to equip a new generation – perhaps the last one – (come quickly, Lord Jesus!) to take this battle to the very gates of hell and set the captives free.

Gregory R. Reid

October 2014

Be a part of the follow-up book! A question and answer book will be forthcoming. Please send any questions you may have to:

Gregory R. Reid

YouthFire Ministries

Box 370006 El Paso TX 79937

legendaryseeker@gmail.com

www.gregoryreid.com

ABOUT THE AUTHOR

Gregory Reid is an ordained minister with American Evangelistic Association and has an honorary Doctorate of Divinity from Logos Graduate College. He is the author of eleven books, including *Diary of a Devil Hunter, Trojan Church, The Color of Pain* and *Nobody's Angel*. He is the founder of YouthFire Ministries and is actively involved in youth ministry, evangelism, and teaching ministry.

JOIN THE FIGHT!

To receive Dr. Reid's monthly newsletter "Word from the Wall."

Please write to:

YouthFire Ministries

Box 370006

El Paso TX 79937

Or e-mail

legendaryseeker@gmail.com

Newsletter also available as an e-letter

OTHER BOOKS BY THE AUTHOR

TROJAN CHURCH: THE NEW AGE CORRUPTION OF THE EVANGELICAL FAITH

AVAILABLE FROM XULON PRESS

OR AT AMAZON & BARNES & NOBLE

AND AS A KINDLE BOOK

THE COLOR OF PAIN

BOYS THAT ARE SEXUALLY ABUSED AND THE MEN THEY BECOME

LIGHTHOUSE TRAILS PUBLICATIONS

AMAZON

ALSO

HEALING IN HIS WINGS

A CRY IN THE WILDERNESS

TREASURE FROM THE MASTER'S HEART

NOBODY'S ANGEL

AVAILABLE AT AMAZON.COM

Made in the USA
Monee, IL
06 March 2021